Exceptional Experiences

Exceptional Experiences

Engaging with Jolting Events in Art and Fieldwork

Edited by
Petra Rethmann and Helena Wulff

berghahn
NEW YORK • OXFORD
www.berghahnbooks.com

First published in 2023 by
Berghahn Books
www.berghahnbooks.com

© 2023, 2025 Petra Rethmann and Helena Wulff
First paperback edition published in 2025

All rights reserved. Except for the quotation of short passages
for the purposes of criticism and review, no part of this book
may be reproduced in any form or by any means, electronic or
mechanical, including photocopying, recording, or any information
storage and retrieval system now known or to be invented,
without written permission of the publisher.

Library of Congress Cataloging-in-Publication Data
Names: Rethmann, Petra, 1964- editor. | Wulff, Helena, editor.
Title: Exceptional experiences : engaging with jolting events in art and
  fieldwork / edited by Petra Rethmann and Helena Wulff.
Description: New York : Berghahn Books, 2023. | Includes bibliographical
  references and index.
Identifiers: LCCN 2023000761 (print) | LCCN 2023000762 (ebook) | ISBN
  9781805390206 (hardback) | ISBN 9781805390213 (ebook)
Subjects: LCSH: Art and anthropology. | Anthropology--Fieldwork. |
  Experience.
Classification: LCC N72.A56 E94 2023 (print) | LCC N72.A56 (ebook) | DDC
  701/.18--dc23/eng/20230505
LC record available at https://lccn.loc.gov/2023000761
LC ebook record available at https://lccn.loc.gov/2023000762

British Library Cataloguing in Publication Data
A catalogue record for this book is available from the British Library

EU GPSR Authorized Representative
LOGOS EUROPE, 9 rue Nicolas Poussin, 17000, LA ROCHELLE, France
Email: Contact@logoseurope.eu

ISBN 978-1-80539-020-6 hardback
ISBN 978-1-83695-082-0 paperback
ISBN 978-1-83695-222-0 epub
ISBN 978-1-80539-021-3 web pdf

https://doi.org/10.3167/9781805390206

Contents

List of Figures   viii

Acknowledgements   x

Introduction.
Engaging with Jolting Events in Art and Fieldwork   1
Petra Rethmann and Helena Wulff

Part I. Experiencing and Conceptualizing the Exceptional

Chapter 1.
To Be Stunned: Uncanny Experiences and Uncertainty in 'Ordinary' Fieldwork   15
Deborah Reed-Danahay

Chapter 2.
Looking at the African Masks at Musée du Trocadéro – He Understood …   32
Thomas Fillitz

Chapter 3.
Art and Anthropology in Graphic Form: Exceptional Experience and Extraordinary Collaboration in the Making of *Light in Dark Times*   47
Alisse Waterston and Charlotte Corden

Chapter 4.
Exceptional Experiences in Academic Life 69
Moshe Shokeid

Chapter 5.
The Exceptionalism of Art as Disclosure of Deepest Truth: Stanley
Spencer and the Look of Love 89
Nigel Rapport

Part II. Literary Realms of the Exceptional

Chapter 6. Haunted Reading/Haunting Johnson 109
Petra Rethmann

Chapter 7.
Sacred Muses: The Lake Goddess in Flora Nwapa's Literary
Worldmaking 123
Paula Uimonen

Chapter 8.
Experiential Literary Ethnography: How Creative Writing
Techniques Can Capture the Cultural Value of Live Arts-Based
Experiences 138
Ellen Wiles

Part III. Exceptional Visual and Practice Experiences

Chapter 9. Lighting Praxis: Lighting Aesthetics and Creativity
Narratives in Professional Cinematography 155
Cathy Greenhalgh

Chapter 10.
'Hammered by the Image': Exceptional Experiences of Art as
Aesthetic Impact 172
Helena Wulff

Chapter 11.
Shaking up Worlds, Opening up Horizons: Contemporary Dance
Experiences in Ramallah and Beyond 189
Ana Laura Rodríguez Quiñones

Chapter 12.
Participant Growing-Places in and of the World: Rendering the Transformative Atmosphere of a Contemporary Opera in the Making   205
Maxime Le Calvé

Afterword. The Sixth Sense   225
Thomas Hylland Eriksen

Index   231

Figures

3.1.	Thinking. © Charlotte Corden in *Light in Dark Times* (Waterston and Corden 2020).	48
3.2.	The Rich Store of Anthropological World Knowledge. © Charlotte Corden in *Light in Dark Times* (Waterston and Corden 2020).	52
3.3.	Waterston's Presidential Address 2017. © Charlotte Corden.	54
3.4.	The Start. © Charlotte Corden in 'The Making of *Light in Dark Times*' (Waterston and Corden 2021).	56
3.5.	The Magic Begins. © Charlotte Corden in 'The Making of *Light in Dark Times*' (Waterston and Corden 2021).	57
3.6.	The Basement Papers. 2018. © Charlotte Corden.	61
3.7.	'Mutual Understanding on a Gigantic Scale'. © Charlotte Corden in *Light in Dark Times* (Waterston and Corden 2020).	62
3.8.	'Radical Evil'. © Charlotte Corden in *Light in Dark Times* (Waterston and Corden 2020).	64
4.1.	Book cover of *Gay Voluntary Associations in New York*. © Reprinted with permission of the University of Pennsylvania Press. Moshe Shokeid. Front cover. 26 October 2022.	84
5.1.	*The Dustman (or The Lovers)* by Stanley Spencer (1891–1959), 1934 (oil on canvas 115 × 123.5 cm). Source: Laing Art Gallery. © Estate of Stanley Spencer. All rights reserved Bridgeman Images.	96

Figures

10.1.	*Woman Before an Aquarium* by Henri Matisse, 1923. © https:// en.wikipedia.org/wiki/File:Woman_Before_an_Aquarium. jpg. Creative Commons.	173
12.1.	First graphic field note, piano rehearsal. Ink and watercolour, Berlin 2017. © Maxime Le Calvé.	206
12.2.	Jonathan Meese about to enter the stage during a performance of his *Parsifal* project at Berliner Festspielhaus. Ink and watercolour, Berlin 2017. © Maxime Le Calvé.	208
12.3.	'Kundry macht Kung Fu!' Scene from the rehearsal. Ink and watercolour, Vienna 2017. © Maxime Le Calvé.	210
12.4.	Kundry-Barbarella taking over the spear, scene from the rehearsal in Vienna. Ink and watercolours, Vienna 2017. © Maxime Le Calvé.	212
12.5.	Side view of the director's table during the rehearsal at Theater an der Wien, with the choreographer, the two assistants and the artist. Ink and watercolours, Vienna 2017. © Maxime Le Calvé.	214
12.6.	Jonathan Meese posing with his mother during the press tour at the Kunsthistorisches Museum. Ink and watercolour, Vienna 2017. © Maxime Le Calvé.	215
12.7.	Technician vacuuming golden glitter on the stage after the curtain has fallen on the last performance of the show at Berliner Festspielhaus. Ink and watercolour, Berlin 2017. © Maxime Le Calvé.	218

Acknowledgements

Some people can live without art, others cannot. This book is not only for those who depend on making or consuming art, perhaps collecting art and/or researching art, but also for those who might have had a once-in-a-lifetime experience of art. It is an anthropological appreciation of exceptional experiences of art. In addition, it considers how such epiphanies strike during fieldwork, when they can lead to sudden major understandings of social circumstances. So how do such jolting events come about?

We have greatly enjoyed putting this book together, noting with amazement that the chapters align in unexpected ways.

We are most grateful for this opportunity to work with Marion Berghahn and Tom Bonnington at Berghahn. It has been a great privilege and pleasure. Johann Sander Puustusmaa, PhD candidate at York University, prepared the manuscript for delivery with care and speed. Many thanks, Johann!

We also wish to thank the anonymous reader very much for eloquent and inspiring comments.

Finally, this book is dedicated to the memory of Marcus Banks. He was an excellent discussant at the panel which led to this book, at the Lisbon virtual conference of the European Association of Social Anthropologists in July 2020. Marcus was a dear friend and colleague who very sadly died only a few months later, far too early.

Petra Rethmann and Helena Wulff

Introduction

Engaging with Jolting Events in Art and Fieldwork

Petra Rethmann and Helena Wulff

Approaching the Exceptional/Beyond Critique

In anthropology, so far, exceptional experiences are not the kind of experiences to which anthropologists have paid a great deal of attention. Staying close to the ground – with ordinary, common, usual, habitual, and the everyday also being synonyms for ground – the exceptional used to be treated with suspicion. Often situated in the neighbourhood of the extraordinary, serendipitous, wondrous, magical or enchanting (Goulet and Miller 2005), the exceptional seemed just too particular, idiosyncratic, uncritical or eccentric as to engage the social imagination. Yet a number of recent changes in institutional cultures and intellectual thought have opened up new paths to think about the luminous, sublime, artistic, aesthetic and affective.

It goes (almost) without saying that for a long time one purpose of anthropology was to produce critique (Marcus and Fischer 1986), and that one of the best ways to do this was to practise what Eve Sedgwick (2003) has called 'the hermeneutics of suspicion'. The expression captures the attitude of a critical, knowing, self-conscious and tirelessly vigilant attitude. To engage in critique is to expose ideology and the workings of power, encourage resistance, and generally contribute to social and political change. Practitioners of critique must therefore be fundamentally suspicious of anything that presents itself as exceptional, artistic and beautiful. To a suspicious anthropologist, then, art attaches itself to power that seeks to cover its tracks. The conclusion imposes itself: committed and critical anthropologists must analyse 'against the grain'.

Is this really all we can say about the objects and artistic practices of our affection and admiration?

Although the reasoning behind critique seems impeccable, in the last few years it has become clear that critique has lost some of its status as the self-evident goal and method of anthropological and related studies (Latour 2004, 2010). This is so for a number of interlocking reasons. The high hopes identified with a critical moment that literary scholar Eric Hayot (2017) describes as Theory – in the sense of bringing together the diversity of Marxist, structuralist, deconstructionist, psychoanalytical, feminist, queer and postcolonial approaches in a historical and institutional moment – have not entirely worked out. As Wendy Brown (2017) has shown, under neoliberal regimes academic institutions are increasingly gutted, and especially humanist forms of knowledge are under pressure and in danger of being debased. Art historian and critic Hal Foster (2012) has even argued that academics have come to feel so bullied by economically structured and state forms of administration that they turn conservative themselves. All of this is to say that our contemporary moment does not appear to be a very opportune moment to leave critique behind (Ortner 2016). The question that thus forms itself is this: beyond insisting on the increased necessity of critique in bleak times, do there exist other ways to frame the historical and political meanings of current discussions of critique?

In dialogue and concert with others (Stewart 2007; Pandian 2019; Felski 2020; Watson 2020), in this introduction we argue that anthropology's – and this is also true for history, sociology, geography, political theory and other fields – turn to affect constitutes one active and purposeful response to the crises that plague our times. At a time when humanist thinking is under siege, it seems important to articulate compelling accounts of why literature, music, and the visual and performative arts matter. Mired in vocabularies of demystifying and dismantling, critique lacks the vocabulary and ability to support humanistic thought and art. If the exceptional is the affect that hammers, captivates, enchants, smacks, stops you in your tracks, takes away your breath, sets you on a path that you have not walked down before, and makes you look at things anew then it is just about time to do justice to such experiences by attending to the surprising, sensuous, serendipitous, haphazard and unscripted. This is one orientation this book seeks to provide.

Contextualizing Exceptionality through Art

Habitually we think of the exceptional as what stands out from the ordinary, customary and everyday, but those attuned to its stirrings and effects have noted that it is also notoriously hard to categorize and describe (Taussig 2011; Lepselter 2016). This is so because the exceptional does not appear in continuity but in a sudden flash. In a strike of lightning, if you will, that illuminates things just for a second. In and as revelation.

Just look at the photographs by John Cliett of Walter De Maria's 1977 installation *Lightning Field*. Created in a remote area of south-western New Mexico's desert, *Lightning Field* – as Kosky (2013: 16) indicates – is one mile mile by a bit less than a mile long. Four hundred polished and sharpened steel poles, spaced at intervals of 220 feet, emerge from the earth, making a grid of twenty-five poles wide by sixteen poles long. The length of the poles varies with the surface of the earth, so that all rise to the same height above sea level. The grid is an attempt to install order in the desert, but also a powerful attractor of lightning strikes in an area that De Maria chose not only for its isolation, but also for the climatic power and energy manifested there. Extremes of atmospheric moisture, wind and temperature are accompanied by heightened electrical energy. Strong winds blow steadily for days; very little rain falls, and thunderstorms can be seen on the field on an average of one in six days throughout the year. Though not exactly common, lightning strikes are unusually frequent in the area, attracting visitors – 'disenchanted moderns' Jeffrey Kosky (2013) calls them – each year to see the light. What they look for is the 'unique' and 'unusual', the singular, capricious, rare and intermittent event of a lightning flash.

Like Walter De Maria's installation, John Cliett's photographs are magnificent. Commissioned by the DIA Foundation in New York, which also owns and manages *Lightning Field*, they show wild flashes of lightning: swerving, forking and bifurcating zigzags that bring into focus things only momentarily and refuse to be pinned down in one particular place. In the words of astronomer and spiritual seeker Camille Flammarion this jagged flickering is 'capricious. [It] is impossible to assign it any rule. [It] does not give any explanation; it acts, that's all' (quoted in Kosky 2013: 18). Or, to put it another way: we can speak of the effects of the exceptional with more certainty than of itself.

If Michael Taussig (2009: 45) is right, then the lightning is exceptional because it is rare, but also because our understanding of weather – and thus of light – has become so ordinary and banal. Often reduced to idle chatter about 'how it is out there', talk about the weather is a symptom of our boredom, a cliché that we talk about to avoid talking about anything else, and empty chatter. It is only when not-so-boring forms of weather appear that we attune ourselves to the cosmos (although to the media too), and speak about the weather in tones of profound anxiety or hope.

Yet much remains to be seen when the Lightning will not reveal itself in a flash of lightning. Thought the Light itself might remain invisible, the object supposedly absent, light, is everywhere.

The lightning or exceptional can lead us away from the ordinary, but it can also lead us back to it. This is what Erin Hogan (2008: 124–25) has to say when the thunderstorm does not come and lightning fails to strike:

> The sun was thinking, and the relentless heat of the afternoon was starting to abate. ... No longer were the poles static, dully lit rods effaced by the sun high above. They had come alive, reflecting every movement of the setting sun. They blazed with color that stirred, as the sun went down, in a slow wave across the entire field. .... The poles were singing. It was a chorus of soft hues. ... Every single one of those four hundred poles was doing something: together they shimmered and undulated, like a cornfield stirred by a strong wind.

Clouds and shadows, winds and waves, undulations and pulsations: an eventful but not exceptional scene, as the poles begin to happen when the sun falls, its dying light held for a faint moment in the poles, which come alive with its passing and alive in a wave of light that passes through them like a shudder. It surely must be nightmarish to continuously live in a heightened state of awareness, so even the ordinary light of the poles may – at times – come as a relief.

Art

In the last few years, anthropologists have worked hard to show that art is more than a derivative of other expressions of culture. In moving inquiries of art beyond matters of Kantian judgement (agreeable or disagreeable; good or bad), beauty or the sublime, they have moved art in the arena of collaboration (Schneider and Wright 2010; Strohm 2014), healing and the capacity to craft new accounts of the worlds. In leaping between disciplines and genres (Schneider and Wright 2006), *Exceptional Experiences* situates itself within a number of conversations on aesthetics and forms. On the first level, the volume addresses methodological and conceptual issues in anthropology and beyond. On the second level, it seeks to update the urgency of crafting new rationales (and updating new ones) for humanistic scholarship and art. And on the third level, it does not only take exceptionality as its theme, but also seeks to model and explore different tonalities of (re)presenting the exceptional as we see, for example, in the words of Kathleen Stewart (2007), Paul Stoller (2018) and Michael Taussig (2009).

If joy, recognition, everyday experiences of the sublime, fragile experiences of dissent, attachment, and caring for what is not always calculable and measurable are articulations of what is exceptional, then the authors in this book address such experiences and affects. No longer always already suspicious of moods, tones, feelings and emotions, the contributors to this volume push beyond the debilitating effects of suspicion. In what the late Jose Munoz (2009) has dubbed the 'anticipatory illuminations of art', scholars do not wish to break with critical or sceptical modes of analysis, but insist on the inescapable entanglements of power with affective life. In insisting that affect can do serious work, they ask: why are we drawn to a painting or a piece of music in ways we struggle to explain while being left cold by others whose merits we duly acknowledge?

Experiences

One experience tops all other experiences for an anthropologist. It is that of fieldwork. Even in this day and age, when 'fieldwork is not what it used to be' (Hannerz 2003; Marcus and Faubion 2009), with flexible forms ranging from multi-site and mobile to digital and collaborative fieldwork, it is still regarded as a rite-de-passage into the profession. Fieldwork provides experiences of immersive spells that unsettle one's taken for granted sensibilities. This can release not only new anthropological insights, but also revelations that can be formative for the fieldworker as a person. It was not long ago that fieldwork was surrounded by mystique, but with a massive wave of books and articles in anthropological method during the last few decades, the process and phases of fieldwork have been documented in detail, even hitherto untold stories from the field (Okely 2012). Fieldwork experiences, especially some of the exceptional ones, used to be shared among friends only, but now they tend to be included in the anthropological conversation.

Related to the traditional silence around some of the personal fieldwork experiences was the idea that fieldwork should focus on the experiences of interlocutors only. This started to change when Victor Turner took an interest in conveying also the experience of the ethnographer. This he did through narratives, which appear in his work on social drama from the 1950s. With the pivotal volume *The Anthropology of Experience* (1986), which Turner edited together with Edward Bruner, the notion of experience in anthropology was further conceptualized, including considerations of individual versus collective experience. In his introduction (written after Turner's death), Bruner (1986: 3–5) acknowledges that it really was Turner who identified an anthropology of experience, by developing the German philosopher Wilhelm Dilthey's concept of experience, *Erlebnis*, for 'what has been lived through' in a hermeneutical tradition. In line with this, 'the anthropology of experience deals with how individuals actually experience their culture, that is, how events are received by consciousness'. Bruner goes on to note that this does not only concern 'sense data, cognition … but also feelings and expectations'. While experiences had been understood as coming to us through verbalization, *The Anthropology of Experience* provides examples of how they happen through visualization, images and impressions, and that as active selves we can also shape an experience. Importantly, Bruner notes that when we talk about our experiences, we 'include not only actions and feelings but also reflections about those actions and feelings … the communication of experience tends to be self-referential'. This was later developed by Clifford Geertz (1973) in terms of 'thick description', which entailed absorbing accounts of his experiences as an ethnographer, relating human action to a larger level. Building on Turner and Geertz, the 1980s' 'writing culture' debate demanded more precise recollections about the research process, not least the role of the ethnographer, and his or her personal experiences, feelings and relationships. The idea was that such openness would ensure more accuracy, though it also generated critique for making the ethnographer the protagonist of the account at the expense of the people the study was about (Wulff 2021). Inspired by Roger Abrahams' (1986) reflections on the relationships between ordinary and extraordinary experiences, Moshe Shokeid (1972) eventually shared some extraordinary experiences in his own everyday life from childhood to adulthood.[1]

Before moving on to the following twelve chapters, let us recap and note that in accounts of exceptional experiences, whether artistic or ethnographic, or artistic in an ethnographic context, two issues stand out: affect and the senses. It is noteworthy that the affects are strong but not always of a pleasant nature: they can be both repulsive and uncanny, as well as a stroke of beauty. As to the senses, the centrality of the visual in Western thought comes up in understandings of experiences, but so does the aural and even tactility; more rarely taste and smell. With the upsurge in the anthropological attention to the senses, and sensorial experiences, comes the insight that they often appear together in teams, especially sight and sound, not always collaborating but sometimes in conflict. This would apply also to affects or emotions in exceptional experiences: they can take the form of very mixed emotions. Multi-sensorial experiences are probably more common than mono-sensorial experiences in the field and other situations. An investigation into exceptional experiences of interlocutors might even require learning a new indigenous sensorial system

(Howes 2015). Exceptional experiences as scrutinized in this volume are in most cases recent memories. How the memory of an exceptional experience changes over the course of time, perhaps taking different shapes at different stages in a life cycle, is an issue to explore further.

For now, though, we have twelve chapters organized in three parts: they engage with exceptional experiences of a verbal, visual, aural or textual nature which came from listening to a story, looking at a piece of art, taking part in a performance, reading or writing a text, as well as drawing pictures. Many of the chapters combine several senses, such as visual and textual, most of them feature fieldwork experiences, some more explicitly than others. The first part, titled 'Experiencing and Conceptualizing the Exceptional', opens with a chapter by Deborah Reed-Danahay where she explores extraordinary things happening to her in fieldwork that lie beyond our comprehension, beyond our research topics, and even beyond our desire to 'look too far'. The chapter revolves around key moments of experience related to three different fieldwork projects – among farm families in rural France, among former Vietnamese refugees in north-central Texas, and among French migrants to London – that provoked a sense of wonder, and which she prefers to locate in the realm of the uncanny. In Thomas Fillitz's chapter we encounter exceptional experiences in the form of Pablo Picasso's sudden understanding of what it means to be an artist. This happened when he was looking at African masks at the Musée du Trocadéro in Paris. Fillitz points out that exceptional experiences in the art world are not only connected to notions of beauty, however, but may also be reactions of disgust, even vandalism. As Fillitz suggests, by applying Paolo Favero's (2018) concept of 'immersive images', we can capture the process of being attracted into a work of art triggering an exceptional experience beyond categories of the beautiful, the original or the good.

The visual is also in focus in the next chapter, teamed with the textual. Anthropologist Alisse Waterston and artist Charlotte Corden describe their collaboration in the making of *Light in Dark Times: The Human Search for Meaning* (2020), a graphic book rooted in nonfiction and comprised of fictionalized encounters with writers, philosophers, activists and anthropologists. Prompted by certain exceptional experiences in academic life evoking issues of collegiality, ethics and methodology, Moshe Shokeid's chapter moves on to an ethnographic episode where the interpretation of how to view a painting was at stake. This echoes Nigel Rapport's argument in his chapter that the otherness of art as an aesthetic form enables the individual viewer to use it as an entrance into an exceptional and critical perspective on everyday life as traditional cultural construction. Rapport's case is the work of the British artist Stanley Spencer and his own explanations of it, as well as how it was received by a general audience. This is exceptionalism of art as disclosure of deepest truth. Following the Kantian tradition, Rapport identifies art as truth, compensation and ethical guide.

In the next part 'Literary Realms of the Exceptional', Petra Rethmann considers the German writer Uwe Johnson's biography and writings, as well as his experiments with narrative form, through the lens of attunement. Johnson's escape from East Germany, which was a recurrent topic in his work, tied in with stories Rethmann had heard about her family members, also escaping from East Germany. Her take is that it was the aesthetic aspects of Johnson's writings that were so exceptional to her that they began to function as a kind of *Ersatz* or ancillary memory: a memory that acts *as if* it could have been true. In a similar vein, Paula Uimonen in her chapter takes us to exceptional encounters with water deities during fieldwork in Nigeria. Focusing on the Lake Goddess in the Nigerian writer Flora Nwapa's aesthetic worlds, she suggests that spirituality constitutes an exceptional source of creativity, a sacred power that can be released through literature. Starting by acknowledging the importance of art-based experiences, Ellen Wiles remarks in her chapter on live literature events in England that they are elusive, difficult to define and analyse. It was her background as a novelist that opened up her understanding of exceptional experiences at literary salons and festivals and how these could be applied to a wider audience outside academia.

In the volume's final section 'Exceptional Visual and Practice Experiences', Cathy Greenhalgh draws on long-term ethnographic fieldwork with feature film cinematographers. Her focus is on accounts of lighting faces and locations for specific scripts. At the *Camerimage* festival, which is an unusual environment, cinematographers share stories about creative collaboration, aesthetics and technique. These sometimes involve declarations of epiphany and revelation, and how specific conditions might have led to their occurrence. Such stories may impact their careers. Helena Wulff in her chapter analyses transformative exceptional experiences of art, drawing on the memories by Patricia Hampl's (2006) recollection of how she unexpectedly was 'hammered by an image', a painting by Matisse, despite not being a museum goer with any particular interest in the arts. Transformation through exceptional experiences also drives Ana Laura Rodríguez Quiñones' chapter on Palestinian contemporary dancers. She shows how certain experiences, whether physical, aesthetic or even social, can act as turning points in individual lives. In a context where the existence of the nation itself is denied by the occupant, and in which some actors are administratively and geographically excluded from the national project, diverse dance events – such as creation processes, performances or the singing of the national anthem in a festival opening – appear to be life-changing moments that release a sense of communality. The idea of exceptional experiences as transformative, as life changing, which stays with us forever, continues in Maxime le Calvé's chapter on a series of key creative moments during the rehearsal of the contemporary opera *Mondparsifal*, staged by the visual artist and performer Jonathan Meese in Vienna in 2017. In a short series of ethnographic stories, Le Calvé presents here some decisive aspects of the work within the team of this artist. The pervasive qualities which Meese instils in collaborative situations, positive and individually empowering, have been reported by the singers and by many collaborators as strongly impacting the way they perform their tasks – building an ephemeral environment into which personal growth is made possible within the frame of this music theatre production. Coincidentally, Le Calvé's documentation methods also underwent a significant metamorphosis during this period of fieldwork, as he switched to the use of watercolour drawings to put the observed situations to paper on the spot. If ethnographic drawings can picture atmospheres, they do not only convey a report of what happened in the field; they also bear witness to a transformation of the ethnographers in both their perceptive and expressive capacities. As Le Calvé notes, some ethnographic topics teach us so much that the memories of these moments stay with the aura of the exceptional forever. Some of these moments actually have a lasting effect on the way we do anthropology, as we are caught by an atmosphere and transformed by it.

To conclude, exceptional experiences, so it appears, are not the kind of experience to which anthropologists have heretofore paid a great deal of attention. While anthropologists tend to engage that which is extraordinary, serendipitous or enchanting, that which is beyond the fray of the customary, common and usual has received lesser attention. The chapters in *Exceptional Experiences* address experiences and encounters with what punctures, jolts and is unusual. In taking art, aesthetics and ethnography as its lens through which to register and understand exceptional experiences and encounters, this volume examines, firstly, the knowledge and affect of exceptional experiences; secondly, it stages, narrates and performs conceptual concerns with agency, ethics, creativity, enchantment and wonder; and thirdly, it makes art an integral part of anthropological inquiries. The volume also addresses the fieldworker's experience of unexpected events that can lead to key understandings, as well as revelatory moments that can happen during artistic creation *and* while looking at art, watching a performance: not only to specialists such as critics, art collectors and art dealers, but to members of a general audience, even a first-time visitor to an art event. By exploring exceptional experiences through art, we ask probing questions for anthropology, but does not do so in a narrow or confining way. In recognizing that art is capacious – including narrative, performance, dance, images and a host of other objects – and often has analysts spanning genres and disciplines, *Exceptional Experiences* situates itself among a number of conversations on aesthetics and forms. While the chapters address methodological and conceptual issues in anthropology and beyond, they are also meant for interested readers, students and former students: anyone wondering about the world and the objects and persons who inhabit it.

Petra Rethmann is Professor of Anthropology at McMaster University and Director of the Institute on Globalization and the Human Condition. She is the author or editor of three books, and the author of numerous articles that have appeared – among others – in *American Ethnologist, American Anthropologist, Anthropologica, Anthropologie et Sociétés* and *Sinij Divan*. She has held guest professorships at the University of St Petersburg, University of Cape Town and Aleksanteri Institute/Helsinki. She is currently working on an ethnographic memoir entitled *Less Than/A Dream*, a book on ethnography and form, and one preliminary entitled *Liberal Wounds*.

Helena Wulff is Professor Emerita of Social Anthropology at Stockholm University. Her research interests are in expressive cultural form – dance, art, images, text. Key engagements are now in the anthropologies of literature and writing, with a focus on migrant writing in Sweden. Among her publications are three monographs: *Ballet across Borders: Career and Culture in the World of Dancers* (1998), *Dancing at the Crossroads: Memory and Mobility in Ireland* (2007), and *Rhythms of Writing: An Anthropology of Irish Literature* (2017). Her edited volumes include *The Anthropologist as Writer: Genres and Contexts in the Twenty-First Century* (2016). There is also the entry 'Writing Anthropology' in the *Cambridge Encyclopedia of Anthropology* (2021) http://doi.org/10.29164/21writing. Drawing on her research, she occasionally writes autofiction and creative nonfiction.

Note

1. It was this article, 'Exceptional Experiences in Everyday Life', by Moshe Shokeid (1972) that sparked the idea for the panel at the European Association of Social Anthropologists in 2020.

References

Abrahams, Roger D. 1986. 'Ordinary and Extraordinary Experiences', in *The Anthropology of Experience*, Victor W. Turner and Edward M. Bruner (eds). Urbana: University of Illinois Press, pp. 45–72.

Brown, Wendy. 2017. *Undoing the Demos: Neoliberalism's Stealth Revolution*. Brooklyn: Zone Books.

Bruner, Edward M. 1986. 'Experience and Its Expressions', in *The Anthropology of Experience*, Victor W. Turner and Edward M. Bruner (eds). Urbana: University of Illinois Press, pp. 3–30.

Favero, Paolo S.H. 2018. *The Present Image: Visual Stories in a Digital Habitat*. New York: Palgrave Macmillan.

Felski, Rita. 2020. *Hooked: Art and Attachment*. Chicago: University of Chicago Press.

Foster, Hal. 2012. 'Post-Critical', *October* 139: 3–8.

Geertz, Clifford. 1973. *The Interpretation of Cultures: Selected Essays*. New York: Basic Books.

Goulet, Jean-Guy and Bruce G. Miller (eds). 2005. *Extraordinary Anthropology: Transformations in the Field*. Lincoln: University of Nebraska Press.

Hampl, Patricia. 2006. *Blue Arabesque: A Search for the Sublime*. Orlando: Harcourt, Inc.

Hannerz, Ulf. 2003. 'Being There … and There … and There! Reflections on Multisite Ethnography'. *Ethnography* 4(2): 201–16.

Hayot, Eric. 2017. 'Then and Now', in *Critique and Postcritique*, Elizabeth S. Anker and Rita Felski (eds). Durham, NC: Duke University Press, pp. 279–95.

Hogan, Erin. 2008. *Spiral Jetta: A Road Trip through the Land Art of the American West*. Chicago: University of Chicago Press.

Howes, David. 2015. 'Senses, Anthropology of the', in *International Encyclopedia of Social and Cultural Anthropology*. 2nd edition, Vol. 21. Oxford: Elsevier, pp. 615–20.

Kosky, Jeffrey L. 2013. *Arts of Wonder: Enchanting Secularity – Walter De Maria, Diller + Scofidio, James Turrell, and Andy Goldsworthy*. Chicago: University of Chicago Press.

Latour, Bruno. 2004. 'Why Has Critique Run Out of Steam? From Matters of Fact to Matters of Concern', *Critical Inquiry* 30(2): 225–48.

Latour, Bruno. 2010. 'The Compositionist Manifesto', *New Literary History* 41(3): 471–90.

Lepselter, Susan. 2016. *The Resonance of Unseen Things: Poetics, Power, Captivity, and UFOs in the American Uncanny*. Minneapolis: University of Michigan Press.

Marcus, George E. and James D. Faubion (eds). 2009. *Fieldwork is Not What it Used To Be: Learning Anthropology's Method in a Time of Transition*. Ithaca: Cornell University Press.

Marcus, George E. and Michael G. Fischer. 1986. *Anthropology as Cultural Critique: An Experimental Moment in the Human Sciences*. Chicago: University of Chicago Press.

Munoz, Jose Esteban. 2009. *Cruising Utopia: The Then and There of Queer Futurity*. New York: New York University Press.

Okely, Judith. 2012. *Anthropological Practice: Fieldwork and Ethnographic Method*. London: Routledge.

Ortner, Sherry B. 2016. 'Dark Anthropology and Its Others: Theory since the Eighties', *Hau: Journal of Ethnographic Theory* 6(1): 47–73.

Pandian, Anand. 2019. *A Possible Anthropology: Methods for Uneasy Times*. Durham, NC: Duke University Press.

Schneider, Arnd and Christopher Wright (eds). 2006. *Contemporary Art and Anthropology*. Oxford: Berg.

Schneider, Arnd and Christopher Wright. 2010. *Between Art and Anthropology: Contemporary Ethnographic Practice*. Oxford. Berg.

Sedgwick, Eve Kosofsky. (2003). 'Paranoid Reading and Reparative Reading, or You're So Paranoid, You Probably Think This Essay is about You', in *Touching Feeling: Affect, Pedagogy, Performativity*. Durham, NC: Duke University Press, pp. 123–51.

Shokeid, Moshe. 1992. 'Exceptional Experiences in Everyday Life', *Cultural Anthropology* 7(2): 232–43.

Stewart, Kathleen. 2007. *Ordinary Affects*. Durham, NC: Duke University Press.

Stoller, Paul. 2018. *Adventures in Blogging: Public Anthropology and Popular Media*. Toronto: University of Toronto Press.

Strohm, Kiven. 2014. When Anthropology Meets Contemporary Art: Notes for a Politics of Collaboration. Collaborative Ethnographies 5. Retrieved 2 November 2014 from https://imaginative-ethnography.com/2014/11/02/when-anthropology-meets-contemporary-art-notes-for-a-politics-of-collaboration.

Taussig, Michael. 2009. *My Cocaine Museum*. Chicago: University of Chicago Press.

Taussig, Michael. 2011. *I Swear I Saw This: Drawings in Fieldwork Notebooks, Namely My Own*. Chicago: University of Chicago Press.

Turner W. Victor and Edward M. Bruner (eds). 1986. *The Anthropology of Experience*. Urbana: University of Illinois Press.

Waterston, Alisse. 2020. *Light in Dark Times: The Human Search for Meaning*. Toronto: University of Toronto Press. Illustrations by Charlotte Corden.

Watson, Matthew C. 2020. *Afterlives of Affect: Science, Religion and an Edgewalker's Spirit*. Durham, NC: Duke University Press.

Wulff, Helena. 2021. 'Writing Anthropology', in *Cambridge Encyclopedia of Anthropology*, Felix Stein, Sian Lazar, Matt Candea, Hildegard Diemberger, Joel Robbins, Andrew Sanchez and Rupert Stasch (eds). Retrieved 6 March 2021 from http://doi.org/10.29164/21writing.

Part I

Experiencing and Conceptualizing the Exceptional

Chapter 1

To Be Stunned

Uncanny Experiences and Uncertainty in 'Ordinary' Fieldwork

Deborah Reed-Danahay

During my first fieldwork in rural France as a young woman, I became friendly with a young male farmer from a nearby village. Once, when we were having a discussion, the specifics of which I no longer remember, he said to me *'C'est comme ça. Il ne faut pas chercher plus loin'* – meaning, you don't have to look further or get creative to understand this. That was the first time I had heard this French dictum about not looking further, and I found it perplexing because he left the rest of his response ambiguous and suggested that the answer was obvious. But it was not obvious to me, and he did not explain further. *'C'est comme ça'* was a common saying in this mountainous region of the Auvergne – similar to the contemporary American English expression 'it is what it is'. My anthropological training had instilled in me the desire to look further, and dig deeper in order to fully comprehend what I was observing and experiencing during my fieldwork. This conversation from forty years ago continues to resonate with me because my friend's statement really stopped me in my tracks.

This chapter[1] explores extraordinary things that happen in fieldwork, which lie beyond our comprehension, beyond our research topics, and even beyond our desire to 'look too far'. They disrupt the temporal flow of fieldwork – stunning us and stopping us 'in our tracks'. They entail sensations and emotional responses to occurrences and objects that are unexpected and out of the ordinary. This chapter revolves around key moments of exceptional experience related to three of my fieldwork projects – among farm families in rural France, among former Vietnamese refugees in north-central Texas, and among French migrants to

London – that provoked unsettling feelings and a sense of unmooring, and which I locate in the realm of the uncanny. They go beyond the more mundane aspects of tropes of the familiar and the strange in ethnography.

I refer to my experiences as 'uncanny' because they were startling. Although this term is often associated with fearful emotions, my use of uncanny is a broader one. The Miriam-Webster online dictionary captures its essential meaning as something 'strange or unusual in a way that is surprising or difficult to understand'.[2] How best to capture these feelings in words? I think of the French term *insolite*, which means something strange or bizarre. As part of a long passage in which he attempts to describe the uncanny, Nicholas Royle (influenced by Freud's classic essay on the topic), writes: 'It is concerned with the strange, weird and mysterious, with a flickering sense (but not conviction) of something supernatural. The uncanny involves feelings of uncertainty, in particular regarding the reality of who one is and what is being experienced' (2003: 1). In his essay *The Uncanny*, Sigmund Freud (2003 [1919]) notes that fear and unease are frequently associated with not feeling or being 'at home' in an emotional sense, and the term uncanny is translated from his original use of the German words for things associated with home and things that are 'unhomely'.[3] Without fully adopting Freud's psychoanalytic perspective, I can see that these events of fieldwork evoked feelings of uneasiness and unmooring. I was not 'at home', in an emotional as well as a geographical sense.[4] I narrate these events below by way of a collage of experience,[5] accompanied by depictions of each fieldwork context, upon which I will reflect in a final section.

The Ghostly Bedroom

My first fieldwork was in a remote mountainous region of central France – the Auvergne. The inhabitants at that time, early autumn of 1980 to December 1981, were primarily dairy farmers and people in occupations that supported the local farm families. The seventeen hamlets in Lavialle, the pseudonym with which I refer to this township (*commune*), had a population of about 420 back then, and although this dipped a bit after my fieldwork, it is now approaching 450. My fieldwork topic[6] was centred on schooling and on educational policy (the ways in which policies of the centralized educational system of France were or were not implemented as planned at the local level). I considered myself to be a political anthropologist using education as a lens to study the French nation-state and issues of identity among a local rural population. As I have written elsewhere regarding wedding ritual (Reed-Danahay 1996b), with a touch of self-irony, I was very focused on not being the kind of anthropologist who looked for 'traditional' things in rural Europe. I wanted to study the nation-state! And yet, as I became more embedded in local life, I encountered and experienced many aspects of everyday life that were associated with local practices and traditions.

When I began living in this township, as I wrote in my fieldwork diary, I felt like Alice having fallen down the rabbit hole. It was a very unfamiliar environment for me, and it took me a while to get my bearings. I already spoke French fairly fluently but had to adjust to the local accent and pick up some of the dialect of Auvergnat. There was a two-classroom primary school that served the children of the township. I had my first lodging at the school itself. The two teachers, a married couple, lived in the school building on the floor above the classrooms, a traditional arrangement in rural France. I was permitted to live in a room on the opposite side of the building, where I had a bed and a desk. This was during a time when no internet, email or mobile phones existed. I corresponded with family, my professors and friends primarily via aerogrammes sent through the postal service.

I gradually got to know many people, and in addition to my fieldwork at the school itself, expanded my purview to spend time with the families whose children attended the school, younger unmarried adults, and elderly people. One family I got to know well, and who befriended me early on, was that of the local café-grocery store owners. I will call them here Jean and Francine.[7] They were of an older generation, and Francine was the same age as my mother. They eventually helped me settle outside of the school into an apartment nearby, in the same block of connected buildings in the main village that housed their home and café.

Francine and Jean had a daughter, Laure, who I also came to know. Laure was a few years older than I was, and married with a small daughter. She lived in another township about an hour away, but frequently came to visit. Jean and Francine had also had a son, Pierre, who had tragically died in a motorcycle accident not many years before my arrival, and who would have been my age. Francine became quite fond of me and spoke to me often of her son. I began to get the impression she fantasized that, had he lived, he and I may have dated or at least become friends. It was not uncommon for people in the township to imagine I would stay and settle there, since I seemed so happy and fitted in so well.

One day, when I was still living at the school, I had to vacate my room for the night because of some work being carried out in the building. Francine offered to let me stay at their two-storey house. Downstairs were the café, a small grocery store and their kitchen; and upstairs were their lodgings – three bedrooms, a sitting room and a bathroom. Laure was visiting the day I was to stay over. When her mother announced that she would have me sleep in her deceased brother's room, Laure became quite cross with her mother. 'Why have Deborah sleep there?', she said, 'She should sleep in my old room.' I began then to experience some unease about the situation, given the tension about this between the two women, and to wonder why it was indeed that I would be sleeping in the room of the dead son.

I had already heard gossip among local people that Francine had 'special powers', and that she could stop fires and perhaps had visions. She never shared any of this with me. During my earliest fieldwork there, this local region was a Catholic stronghold, and most people attended Sunday mass and other services on a regular basis. After Jean, Francine's husband, passed away, many years after my first fieldwork, Francine wore black mourning clothes for a long period of time – and was criticized by others for being too 'traditional'. Francine was devoutly religious (*pieuse*), but I had not experienced anything in her presence to cause me to believe the rumours of her spiritual powers. I once asked Laure about this, gingerly probing when I visited her at her own house, and she adamantly denied it and said these were vicious rumours and I should ignore them.[8]

I frequently encountered references to uncanny occurrences in the course of my research in Lavialle, and was aware that spiritual beliefs and practices were part of everyday life in the township. One local friend, close in age to me, told me that her father used to see lights (small globes of light) when he was younger and would walk or ride his bike long distances over fields and trails. Other people also spoke of this, and there was a mystery surrounding these occurrences. Once, I visited a spiritual healer I had heard about because another friend went to her for a medical condition, and others also talked of her. She worked with people and animals, and since it was illegal to treat animals in this way and also technically illegal to treat humans,[9] most people were quite circumspect in mentioning this to me. While visiting a young mother and her toddler son at their farm one day, I hurt my back while reaching over to do something, and she suggested we go to see 'la Maria'. I did not believe that la Maria would really heal me, but wanted to experience going to see a local healer as part of my fieldwork. We travelled by car, as she lived in another township, and waited our turn to see her. She was in a dark room lit with candles. My mid-twenties self considered her to be very old, although I am not sure now of her age. Her humble ancient lodgings suggested that she was poor, and I suspect that she was Romani (*une gitane* in the local parlance), although no one mentioned that to me when referring to her (perhaps because it was so evident to them). I remember la Maria praying in words I did not understand and touching my back. I think she knew I was not hurt that badly and probably was quite uncomfortable herself with the situation because I was a stranger (and not local or even French) and might expose her to legal sanctions should I reveal her practices.

I remember that I did try to talk to some other people about la Maria, but most did not want to discuss it. Going to a spiritual healer was a form of 'cultural intimacy' (Herzfeld 2016) that many local people did not want to divulge. In retrospect, I did not ask enough questions about all of this at the time. My visit to la Maria was a more casual research experience in that I did not view it as relevant to my main project of studying education, families and children. Had my research focused on such practices, I surely would have spent more time establishing relationships with those who would talk to me about it.

All of this is background to my uncanny experience, which was creepy and unsettling, sleeping that night in Pierre's room. The village was very dark at night, and quiet except for the occasional mooing of cows from the nearby farms or the screeching of an owl, barking of a dog, or a rare passing car. Generations of people had lived and died in the same old stone buildings where people now lived. The cemetery was situated near the centre of the village, next to the church, and I could see it if I looked out the window from Pierre's bedroom. The room was left very much as it had been when Pierre was alive, and there was a framed photo of him on the dresser. I worried that I might see or feel his ghost or spirit, some manifestation of the dead young man whose mother had somehow decided to have this young woman (me) sleep in his bed. It never occurred to me to refuse to sleep there, or to leave the room during the night. I was doing fieldwork in an unfamiliar and remote place and was dependent on the goodwill and acceptance of the local inhabitants. I did not want to offend Francine, who had been so kind to me.

The end of this story may seem anti-climactic because I did not, in the end, see a ghost.[10] I do not think that I had a spiritual experience. I slept badly if at all, however, on hyper-alert! But this uncanny experience is one that has stayed with me on a very visceral level ever since. I still, so many years later, have a bodily memory of the fear, bordering on panic, and unease I felt as I worried that I might indeed have an encounter with a ghostly presence in that dark room. This was an exceptional experience in my life – connected to the fact that I was unmoored from familiar surroundings during fieldwork and affected by the atmosphere of a place where life, death and the afterlife were more present in everyday life than in the suburban North American settings of my childhood and youth. Here, in this remote Auvergnat township, I had an uncanny experience that stunned me but about which I have never written. I am reluctant to apply theoretical and analytical analysis because I remain uncertain about, as Edith Turner (1994: 86) has written regarding her own encounters with the unusual, 'what actually' happened.

The Blessing of the Statue

My next story comes from fieldwork closer to 'home' in the geographical sense if not the cultural one. Between 2005 and 2008, I undertook ethnographic research among former Vietnamese refugees. The aim of this research was to examine the citizenship practices and forms of civic engagement among Vietnamese and Asian Indian immigrants in north-central Texas.[11] When the research began, I was living and working in this region. Although I later relocated out of state, I returned frequently for subsequent periods of research. This was not, therefore, the same type of immersive fieldwork that I undertook in rural France. I worked as a professor while doing the research, and employed undergraduate and graduate student research assistants – some of whom were Vietnamese American students majoring in other subjects, and some of whom were graduate students in my department.[12] This project involved people who had come to the US after the Vietnam War as refugees and their adult children (some of whom had been born in Vietnam and some in the US). My research topic lay in the realm of political anthropology (citizenship and civic engagement) and migration studies (with a focus on refugees and diaspora). And yet, as in the case of rural France, I found religious practice to be a significant part of everyday life among the population I studied.

Religious institutions played a large role in the settlement practices of Vietnamese Americans when they arrived after the war. I conducted participant-observation research at a large Vietnamese American Catholic Church and at a local Vietnamese Buddhist Temple. I also spoke to ordained and lay religious leaders. Although I was not studying religious practice and belief specifically, I was interested in the role that churches and temples played in teaching and learning 'civic skills' among this population.[13] I was also interested in how the religious practices of these former refugees and their children had helped them adjust to life – to emplace themselves – in this large metropolitan area of the US.[14]

I spent many Sundays at the local Buddhist temple, which followed the Theravada tradition of Buddhism. One of my main Vietnamese American research assistants was Buddhist and had been involved in youth leadership positions at that temple, through which she helped introduce me to the temple and guided me as I began to attend events there. I learned a lot about Buddhism, but primarily from my interlocutors at this particular site, rather than through any additional reading or study. I attended preparations of the temple's 'Lion Dancers' for the New Year's Tet celebrations that took place each year; I attended Sunday services that included chanting and a dharma talk by the monk; and I attended the 'Sunday school' classes for Vietnamese American youth. I also helped and shared in the meal that was prepared most Sundays for children and youth.

This temple was in the sparsely populated outskirts of a city in the region, and was surrounded by imposing ornate gates, as was the Catholic Church where I also did some research. There were large white Buddha statues on the grounds. My, admittedly casual, understanding of life at the temple was that the two monks, who lived in a modest one-storey house in the compound, meditated for most of each day and only ate once a day. Vietnamese American women who volunteered at the temple prepared and served their daily vegetarian meal. There was also a Buddhist nun in residence for most of the period of my fieldwork, and she lived in a building at the back of the temple. I got to know one of the monks more than the other religious leaders. He was a young man, perhaps in his late thirties or early forties, and himself a refugee from Vietnam (as were the other monk and the nun). He wore simple robes, had a shaved head, and was fluent in English.

My conversations with this monk, who had been very kind and welcoming to me during my visits, had been brief and 'in passing' on the grounds of the temple. I had arranged an interview with the priest at the local Vietnamese American Catholic Church and also hoped to have a one-on-one interview with the monk. Having been raised Catholic and having got to know both the local priest in rural Auvergne and priests who were relatives of families my family knew when I was growing up, I was relatively comfortable approaching a priest and meeting with one. There was, however, more of an aura of mystery for me surrounding a Buddhist monk – especially one who spent long hours meditating and seemed very 'unworldly' to me.

The temple had a small shop where people could purchase carved wooden statues of the Buddha and other religious items. The statues were made in Sri Lanka, a stronghold for Theravada Buddhism. I had decided to purchase a particularly nice wooden carving of the Buddha, seated in a lotus position, as a memento from my fieldwork and as a goodwill gesture by contributing a donation to the temple. After I purchased my carved statue of the Buddha, a research contact suggested that I ask the monk to 'bless it', and I saw this as a perfect opportunity to meet with him inside his living quarters and discuss my research with him. I approached this as an entrée to his inner sanctum via the 'guise' of having the statue blessed, because I did not truly consider at first that

I could attribute much meaning and significance on a spiritual level to having that statue blessed. As I write these words in my home office, looking down at me from a shelf (along with two other Buddhist figures I later acquired at the temple), is that statue – a relic from my fieldwork that recalls my experience when the monk blessed it.

The monk and I were seated at a table in his quarters, an oblong table, and I was sitting diagonally opposite to him. At first, we discussed my research and he told me about the ways he helped serve these former refugees, many of whom had experienced immense trauma during and after the war. He briefly explained the tradition of Buddhism at this temple, and how its practices had adapted to accommodate life in this Bible Belt region, where religious observance took place primarily on Sundays. He also spoke to me about his own life trajectory. I found him to be very open and gentle as a person – surprisingly trusting of me as we spoke.

He told me about the concepts of 'karma' and loving-kindness, and of how learning to control your mind can lead to enlightenment. I remember one story he told me that has stuck with me throughout the intervening years. He said that many of the former refugees who came to his temple experienced frustrations and prejudice in their lives – especially in their encounters with 'American' employers and others. He counsels them, he told me, to fight fire with water. That is, if you are suffering and upset about something, and someone is evoking 'fire' into your emotions, respond internally with calming water to douse the flames.

After we had chatted for a while, and our time together was coming to an end, the monk said that now he would honour my request and bless the statue. I had an exceptional experience as he undertook to do so. He took the statue into his hands and held it in front of him. Then he closed his eyes and seemed to silently concentrate for several minutes. What I felt in this silence was an intensity in the room that I had not noticed before. My eyes were open and, while I was watching the monk, I had the uncanny feeling that there was a strong energy 'in the air' that was emanating from his meditative concentration. I had never encountered anything like this before, and have trouble explaining exactly what it felt like in a physical sense. It was as though the air had become denser, charged somehow, but also very calm and quiet. I recall that I felt momentarily calm on both an emotional and physical level. In contrast to my night in the ghostly bedroom, the blessing of the statue did not provoke fear or unease – quite the opposite. The sensations were fleeting, however, and short-lived. After the monk finished the blessing and returned the statue to me a few moments later, I thanked him and we said our goodbyes. I did not discuss this phenomenon with him because at the time, I was not really sure what had happened, or even how to articulate it. I was certainly not expecting anything like that and was very unprepared. It 'stunned' me. I remember mostly thinking 'wow, what was that?' As with my experience in the 'ghostly bedroom' of the dead son in rural France, this memory for me is now dreamlike, and remains mysterious and in the realm of the uncanny. In both cases, my memory is both murky and vivid. It is very vivid as an emotional and bodily memory – a sensorial memory – but murky in terms of all of the details of setting, place and time that surrounded it and which I have reconstructed from my notes and previous writings about the circumstances.

The Body on the Floor

My third story of an uncanny experience comes from more recent fieldwork among French people living in London. I conducted over twelve months of fieldwork in London off and on from spring 2015 to summer 2022, during periods ranging from two weeks to three months – although typically I spent about a month at a time there.[15] It took me a while to get my bearings living in such a large city as London, with which I was only fleetingly familiar from short visits in the past. From the beginning, however, this research has involved people who were more familiar to me than those of my previous fieldwork among farm families in rural France and among former Vietnamese refugees and their children in Texas. Given my long engagement with France and the French, over many years of travel back to the Auvergne, contacts with academic colleagues in France, and time spent in Paris and other French cities, working among French citizens in London was not an unfamiliar experience. I am fluent in French and, although there have been occasional hiccups in my interactions with my research participants, and I must work to establish 'rapport' with them, this is all quite ordinary for me. In addition to that, my husband is British-born, and so I have spent a great deal of time (albeit not in London) visiting with his family and travelling around the UK over the many years of our marriage.

Therefore, the example of the uncanny that I will soon relate below comes out of quite ordinary rather than extraordinary field research in which I am in a familiar setting, doing the more or less 'sideways' type of fieldwork identified by Ulf Hannerz (2006), and speak the languages (French and English) fluently. My research has focused primarily on French women's experiences of migration to London. Although I started the project with an interest in the French as 'mobile Europeans' before Brexit occurred, after the 2016 Referendum I began to see the disruptions, uncertainties and emotional toll that the UK's departure from the EU brought to the lives of my interlocutors. Given the longitudinal nature of my research, I have been able to get to know a few women very well – who range in age from around thirty to their nineties – as I have returned for visits.

One elderly woman, in particular, has been someone with whom I have established close ties over the course of my visits. I have met with Juliette both at her small apartment and at events in London (where we either arranged to meet or just ran into each other), and have spent numerous long sessions discussing her life and taking notes as we talked in her apartment. I am in the process of assembling and writing about her life story, which involved a childhood in the German occupied region of north-eastern France during the Second World War, and later a move to London when she was around thirty. She has never married and came alone to London as a young woman. Our discussions are always in French, although we may occasionally intersperse this with English. She retains a fairly strong French accent, although over the years she became fluent in English.

Juliette retains a small apartment in Paris, to which she returned frequently in the pre-Brexit and pre-pandemic years. She worked as a teacher at a private school in London, and lives on a small state pension in subsidized housing for the elderly. I was introduced to her by another French woman, who I met through a French association and who had volunteered at a non-profit in London that serves lower-income French and Francophone residents in need of social and medical services. This association also provides social support to a group of elderly French residents in London via a club that holds monthly events and organizes outings. Juliette is a member of that group. The contact who suggested that I meet Juliette told me that she would be a good subject for my research, and indicated that she was a bit lonely and isolated in her old age and welcomed company. She also indicated that Juliette had lived a very interesting life and would have many stories to tell me. I found this all to be true. Juliette received her undergraduate and graduate degrees in France in philosophy and history, and is very interested in intellectual ideas and culture. She was intrigued by my study and willing to meet with me. Significantly, she knew immediately what anthropology was (not always the case for anthropologists in the field!) and had kept up with recent intellectual figures in France due to her devotion to the French radio station France Culture, to which she listens via her internet radio.

The first time that I visited Juliette's small apartment, I was 'stunned' by a sculpture in the middle of the floor at the far end of the main room. Her lodgings are small, with one room that includes a small kitchen area, table and living area, plus a bedroom and a bathroom. After greeting me at her door, and showing me around her modest apartment, Juliette invited me to sit at a table jutting out from a wall and dividing the kitchen area from the rest of the room that had a rug on the floor and bookshelves. Juliette put out a plate of biscuits and offered me some fruit juice. This was so familiar to me from visits to older women in the rural villages I frequented in the Auvergne – the same type of food. In subsequent visits, I would bring her some nice biscuits that I had picked up in shops (even once a tin from the Victoria and Albert Museum store).

This uncanny carved wooden sculpture is of a prostrate naked woman, with dimensions of about two feet long and about eight inches wide. It is a suffering figure, of someone in agony. It disturbed me greatly at first to have it in our midst – in some ways disrupting this fairly mundane domestic scene of an ethnographic conversation. Because the figure is on her side, when I first noticed it, I was not sure if it was a male or female figure, as I noted in a brief mention of the sculpture in some fieldnotes I took, but I later came to see it was a woman. I was curious, not knowing Juliette well, as to why she would have such a thing so prominently placed in her small lodgings. I did not ask her right away, or even mention the statue during my first visit, as I did not want to intrude on something that might be quite personal during our first encounters. There was something about it lying on the floor, rather than being a sculpture displayed on a table or other surface, that seemed particularly strange to me. You would have to walk around it to get to the window at the far side of the room, or the bookcases lining the wall. It is very life-like, although in miniature. This sculpted woman has been present at all of my subsequent visits to Juliette, up to my most recent one in June 2022.

I learned over time that Juliette suffers from fibromyalgia and has periods of time when she is in immense physical pain, requiring physical therapy treatments from home health workers. I also learned that she suffers from anxiety and has done so since her youth, which was one reason she decided to flee from her life in France and start over in London. I came to eventually suspect that this figure symbolized for Juliette her own emotional and physical pain. But at the same time, there was a sort of existential aspect to the suffering figure – something that could speak more broadly to the human condition. Over time and with some gentle probing questions, I came to learn that Juliette knew the female sculptor who had created this figure and who had, as Juliette explained, 'lent' it to her. This artist had herself suffered from some physical and emotional pain, which Juliette has explained to me affected her choice of subject.

I have never probed Juliette too much about her own emotional tie to the sculpture, feeling that this is a delicate and personal matter. When I have asked, she has answered in somewhat matter of fact answers about the artistic qualities of the sculpture and the artist who carved it. She does not seem to want to engage with what I experience as the uncanny and unsettling nature of the figure. I have hesitated, as with my other uncanny experiences, to *'cherche plus loin'* – to go further in my queries. I have not been able to easily articulate what I feel or want to know. I only know that having that body lying on the floor during my visits to Juliette has been disturbing when my gaze wanders in that direction. Over time, I have become more used to it and less affected by it. But it is indeed a disconcerting presence during my visits to Juliette's flat, particularly because it is so lifelike.

Reflections: The Familiar and the Strange

There is not a great deal of writing in anthropology about having such uncanny encounters with objects, people and places during fieldwork. Most who write of the uncanny or unusual are anthropologists who work on religious and/or ritual themes and focus on the 'sense of the uncanny' (Throop 2005) among the people they study. Some write of trying (but not always succeeding) to find rational explanations for uncanny feelings they experienced during fieldwork that were not easily understood. Jon P. Mitchell (1997) has, for example, written about a moment during his fieldwork in rural Malta when he was working alongside of a group of men to clean a niche in the local Roman Catholic Church housing a wooden statue of Christ that was believed to have miraculous powers. He offered to go up on a ladder in the niche to clean the windows near the statue and, while up there, experienced unusual bodily sensations – excitement, light-headedness, and a pounding heart (ibid: 82). A confessed 'non-believer', Mitchell uses this example to discuss belief, social memory and emotion as a way to understand the indeterminacy of belief and the aspect of choice regarding what to believe.

In another example, Peter Gardner (2007) notes several bizarre things he observed and experienced while doing fieldwork among the Dene of Northwest Canada. Rather than having an uncanny emotional experience himself, he is confronted by seemingly uncanny experiences among the Dene. He writes about two of these, that although he sought rational explanations, they left him 'absolutely stumped' (ibid: 35). Tanya Luhrmann, an anthropologist who specializes in the study of witchcraft and religion, has written about her own 'anomalous experiences' (2020: 63), beginning with one during her early twenties when she was on a train to London reading a book on spiritualism and felt as she describes it 'power in my veins' (ibid: 61). She concludes that some people have a proclivity for spiritual experiences, but that training can enhance them. Drawing upon Edith Turner's concept of 'an anthropology through experience', Jill Dubisch, an anthropologist and trained Reiki practitioner, writes (2008: 333) about her own unexpected 'vivid encounter' when she experienced a vision of an archangel during a Reiki session she was performing. As in the case of Turner's point about her own experiences that I mentioned above, there is a sense of uncertainty about what happened that resists explanation.

Even though my fieldwork topics have not been focused on issues of the supernatural or uncanny, I have had stunning and startling experiences (in Dubisch's words 'vivid encounters') primarily because my work as an ethnographer has permitted me some access to the intimate spaces of other people's lives. It is precisely because of the value of 'messy' and unpredictable ethnographic encounters that I was confronted with these uncanny discernments and objects (two sculptures and a dead son's room). They all took place in people's homes, into which I had been invited. In each case, the unsettling emotions I felt were associated with the suffering of my research participants – a grieving mother, war refugees and an elderly woman with physical and emotional pain. I was drawn into their worlds in unanticipated ways through the relationships I had formed with them.

The uncanny, notes Mark Windsor (2019: 62) in a discussion of this feeling in relationship to art and aesthetics, is associated with a perceived 'threat to one's grasp of reality'. It provokes uncertainty. He poses the question of what circumstances or conditions lead us to attribute the uncanny to an object, story, or experience. In an essay in the classic volume *The Anthropology of Experience*, Roy Abrahams argued that what might be encountered as extraordinary (or significant) during fieldwork is largely a product of one's own expectations about what is ordinary or extraordinary. We distinguish between events and experiences (Abrahams 1986: 55) and, Abrahams argued, are compelled to write down what we experienced in the field largely due to the fact that 'ethnographers will carry into participant observation a recognition of their own culture's notions of significant actions and their related emotions and sentiments' (ibid: 70). The trope of the familiar and the strange in anthropological research and writing about it is persistent and long-standing, so that there is frequently an aura of the unfamiliar (and often this is indeed sought by ethnographic practitioners) during fieldwork as an experience that takes place outside of our 'ordinary' lives.

And as I reflect upon all of this, I see that those in whose presence these things happened to me did not view what I found uncanny in the same way. Neither Francine, the monk, nor Juliette were perturbed or unsettled by the things that moved me. For them, these reside in the realm of the ordinary – their taken-for-granted acceptance of such phenomenon as ghostly presences, the effects of meditation, and an art object depicting a suffering woman. My experiences in many ways brought me closer to an emotional as well as an intellectual understanding of their worlds. Each unsettling moment reminded me of the unknowable, and the limits of ethnographic understanding, but also of the ways that 'being stunned' in unexpected ways does not need to find a clear explanation. Being open to such experiences is the key. *'C'est comme ca'* – it is like that; and perhaps we don't always need to look further.

Deborah Reed-Danahay is Professor of Anthropology at the University at Buffalo. Her most recent book is *Bourdieu and Social Space: Mobilities, Trajectories, Emplacements* (Berghahn, 2020). She is also the author of *Education and Identity in Rural France* (Cambridge University Press, 1996) and *Locating Bourdieu* (Indiana University Press, 2005); and co-author (with Caroline Brettell) of *Civic Engagements: The Citizenship Practices of Asian Indian and Vietnamese Immigrants* (Stanford University Press, 2012). Her edited volumes include Auto/Ethnography: Rewriting the Self and the Social (Berg, 1997); and (with Caroline Brettell) *Citizenship, Political Engagement, and Belonging: Immigrants in Europe and the United States* (Rutgers, 2008). She has conducted fieldwork in France, the US and the UK . Her current research interests include the intersections of ethnography, fiction and memoir; the ethnographic applications of Pierre Bourdieu's thought; and migration. Her most recent ethnographic project, about which she is writing a book, is on French migration to London in the twenty-first century.

Notes

1. I want to thank Ellen Badone, Luc Foisneau, Kimberly Hart and Linda Kahn for their help in reading and commenting with suggestions for revision on an earlier version of this essay.
2. 'uncanny', Merriam-Webster, uncanny: https://www.merriam-webster.com/dictionary/uncanny.
3. For an anthropological use of the Freudian 'uncanny' connected to 'unhomeliness', see Srinivas (2018).
4. See Cannon (2010) for a discussion of the French concept of *chez soi* as related to feelings of 'homeliness' in contemporary French fiction. The idea of what it means to be

chez moi (at home), about which I have interrogated my French interlocutors in London (see Reed-Danahay 2020), can connote the geographical location of home as a place (dwelling, locality or nation) and/or the embodied and emotional aspects of feeling at ease, secure and at home.

5. Clifford (1988: 146–47) identifies the use of ethnographic collage as a form of writing that accepts the fragmented and unknowable. See the use of this method in Danforth (1989). A related and emerging term in contemporary anthropology is that of the 'montage'. See McLean (2013: 59) on its use in producing a 'generative instability that inheres in juxtaposed elements and the spatiotemporal intervals that both conjoin and differentiate them'.
6. This dissertation research was generously funded by NSF and by a Bourse Chateaubriand (from the cultural services of the French government). See Reed-Danahay (1996a).
7. I use pseudonyms for all of my fieldwork contacts mentioned in this chapter.
8. For a study of witchcraft accusations and reactions to them in the Bocage region of western France, see Favret-Saada (1980 [1977]). See also her later, more reflexive book (2015 [2009]) about anthropological practices in the study of witchcraft.
9. See Cloatre (2019) on legal issues regarding alternative healing practices in France.
10. For a discussion of the emerging interest in anthropology in theorizing ghostly appearances through the concept of hauntology, influenced by the work of Jacques Derrida, see Good (2019). See also Fernandez (2017) for a reflection on a haunting by her cat.
11. This was a collaborative and comparative project, funded by a grant from the Russell Sage Foundation. My co-PI, Caroline B. Brettell, studied Asian Indian immigrants. See Brettell and Reed-Danahay (2012).
12. I would like to acknowledge here, in particular, the help of Marilyn Koble and Quynh Anh Ton, although I had several other research assistants during this research to whom I am grateful.
13. Because of this, my research on religious institutions was limited, not being my main area of interest. I did not, for example, investigate beyond the major religions of Buddhism and Catholicism, although I had long conversations with people about what they referred to as 'ancestor worship'.
14. See, for example, Reed-Danahay (2012).
15. This research has been supported by a Jean Monnet Chair funded by the Erasmus+ Programme of the European Commission, as well as The Humanities Institute, the Office of the VP for Research, the Gender Institute, and The Baldy Center for Law and Social Policy at the University at Buffalo.

References

Abrahams, Roy D. 1986. 'Ordinary and Extraordinary Experience', in *The Anthropology of Experience*, Victor W. Turner and Edward M. Bruner (eds). Urbana and Chicago: University of Illinois Press, pp. 45–72.

Brettell, Caroline B. and Deborah Reed-Danahay. 2012. *Civic Engagements: The Citizenship Practices of Asian Indian and Vietnamese Immigrants*. Stanford: Stanford University Press.

Cannon, Daisy. 2010. *Subjects Not-at-Home: Forms of the Uncanny in the Contemporary French Novel*. Amsterdam and New York: Editions Rodopi.

Clifford, James. 1988. *The Predicament of Culture: Twentieth-Century Ethnography, Literature, and Art*. Cambridge: Cambridge University Press.

Cloatre, Emilie. 2019. 'Regulating Alternative Healing in France, and the Problem of 'Non-Medicine', *Medical Law Review* 27(2): 189–214.
Danforth, Loring. 1989. *Firewalking and Religious Healing*. Princeton: Princeton University Press.
Dubisch, Jill. 2008. 'Challenging the Boundaries of Experience, Performance, and Consciousness: Edith Turner's Contributions to the Turnerian Project', in *Victor Turner and Contemporary Cultural Performance*, Graham St. John (ed.). Oxford and New York: Berghahn Books, pp. 324–37.
Favret-Saada, Jeanne. 1980 [1977]. *Deadly Words: Witchcraft in the Bocage*. Trans. C. Cullen. Cambridge: Cambridge University Press.
———. 2015 [2009]. *The Anti-Witch*. Trans. M. Carey. Chicago: HAU Books.
Fernandez, Mayanthi. 2017. 'Supernatureculture'. Retrieved 1 January 2022 from https://tif.ssrc.org/2017/12/11/supernatureculture/.
Freud, Sigmund. 2003 [1919]. *The Uncanny*. Trans. D. McClintock. London: Penguin Books.
Gardner, Peter M. 2007. 'On Puzzling Wavelengths', in *Extraordinary Anthropology: Transformations in the Field*, Jean-Guy A. Goulet and Bruce Granville Miller (eds). Lincoln: University of Nebraska Press, pp. 17–35.
Good, Byron. 2019. 'Hauntology: Theorizing the Spectral in Psychological Anthropology', *Ethos* 47(4): 411–26.
Hannerz, Ulf. 2006. 'Studying Down, Up, Sideways, Through, Backwards, Forwards, Away and at Home: Reflections on the Field Worries of an Expansive Discipline', in *Locating the Field: Space, Place and Context in Anthropology*, Simon Coleman and Peter Collins (eds). Oxford and New York: Berg, pp. 23–41.
Herzfeld, Michael. 2016. *Cultural Intimacy: Social Poetics and the Real Life of States, Societies, and Institutions*. 3rd edition. New York: Routledge.
Luhrmann, Tanya. 2020. *How God Becomes Real: Kindling the Presence of Invisible Others*. Princeton: Princeton University Press.
McLean, Stuart. 2013. 'All the Difference in the World: Liminality, Montage, and the Reinvention of Comparative Anthropology', in *Transcultural Montage*, Christian Suhr and Rane Willerslev (eds). Oxford and New York: Berghahn Books, pp. 58–75.
Mitchell, Jon P. 1997. 'A Moment with Christ: The Importance of Feelings in the Analysis of Belief', *Journal of the Royal Anthropological Institute* 3(1): 79–94.
Reed-Danahay, Deborah. 1996a. *Education and Identity in Rural France: The Politics of Schooling*. Cambridge Studies in Social and Cultural Anthropology. Cambridge: Cambridge University Press.
———. 1996b. 'Champagne and Chocolate: "Taste" and Inversion in a French Wedding Ritual', *American Anthropologist* 98(4): 750–61.
———. 2012. 'The Vietnamese American Buddhist Youth Association: A Community of Practice for Learning Civic Skills', *TSANTSA* [Journal of the Swiss Ethnological Society] 7: 76–85.
———. 2020. 'Leave/Remain: Brexit, Emotions, and the Pacing of Mobility among the French in London', in *Pacing Mobilities*, Vered Amit and Noel Salazar (eds). New York and Oxford: Berghahn Book, pp. 142–62.
Royle, Nicholas. 2003. *The Uncanny*. Manchester: Manchester University Press.

Srinivas, Tulasi. 2018. *The Cow in the Elevator: An Anthropology of Wonder*. Durham, NC: Duke University Press.

Throop, C. Jason. 2005. 'Hypocognition, a "Sense of the Uncanny," and the Anthropology of Ambiguity: Reflections on Robert I. Levy's Contribution to Theories of Experience in Anthropology', *Ethos* 33(4): 499–511.

Turner, Edith. 1994. 'A Visible Spirit Form in Zambia', in *Being Changed by Cross-Cultural Encounters*, David E. Young and Jean-Guy Goulet (eds). Toronto: University of Toronto Press, pp. 71–95.

Windsor, Mark. 2019. 'What is the Uncanny?' *British Journal of Aesthetics* 59(1): 51–65.

Chapter 2

Looking at the African Masks at Musée du Trocadéro – He Understood ...

Thomas Fillitz

Introduction

Some time ago, I talked about art and exceptional experience with my artist friend Sylvia Kummer, and she replied without hesitation: 'Thomas, art is always an exceptional experience, isn't it?' Sylvia continued to argue that a visit to a museum of fine art, an art biennial, an art fair or even an artist's studio, implies the intention of looking at art – in the case of the museum, art that has been validated as masterpiece, in the case of the other institutions or locations, art that still may be subject to debate about its status.

We went on discussing whether there are differences when looking at a picture, for example a painting, in a museum, and seeing the same picture in a TV-documentary, on a website ... or reproduced in a public space. There are, obviously, spaces which stimulate a spectator to experience art, locations dedicated to art, where art is intentionally removed from spaces of everyday life – such as shopping malls, wine bars or airports. Jacques Rancière emphasizes this distributive aspect of art, asserting that entering such a space implies a looking and thinking to identify art, and this is a complex process of differentiation (Rancière 2004: 15). The perception of art thus entails an experience that is generally separated from everyday processes, and from the individual's interaction with images in quotidian life. My driving question here thus concerns the spectator's exceptional experience within the overall interaction with art.

John Dewey's theory of *Art as Experience* (2005 [1934]) constitutes the core of the first part of this chapter, 'The Beautiful, Pleasing and

Enjoying'. As Richard Shusterman highlights, Dewey's central notion is 'aesthetic experience' which 'holds the key to understanding all experience' (2010: 31). From Dewey's considerations of the experience of art, this section turns to Alfred Gell's anthropological conceptualization of art as element of an overall system of techniques, whereby the art technologies stand out for their 'technically achieved level of excellence' (ibid.: 43). Gell speaks of a 'technology of enchantment' (ibid.), and highlights that the quality of a work of art is the technically 'made beautifully' (ibid.). In attempting to understand this excellence of technology, Gell moreover argues for the need of an abduction of the artist's agency (1998).

The second section, 'Hostile Experiences' widens the framework of exceptional experiences of art. On the one hand, the correlation between art and beauty, fundamental elements of Dewey's and Gell's theories, cannot be upheld. Since the early twentieth century, the field of art and the realm of social life may not be conceived as manifestly separated – neither is regarding art as material thing, nor regarding art as skilled technology. On the other hand, Paul Silva argues for a more complex differentiation between various 'unusual aesthetic emotions', such as hostile ones (2009: 48). This section combines the reflection of hostile emotions with Jonas Tinius's concept of 'awkward art' (2018). Determining a particular art as awkward turns the analytical attention towards the activity of demarcation, which allows to anthropologically grasp a hostile exceptional experience.

The third section, 'Exceptional Experiences 1 and 2', pulls together the various lines of insights. It argues for a differentiation of exceptional experiences in the interaction with art. Exceptional experience-1 is linked to a momentaneous gaze, that is, the possible activation of the beholder's senses when a specific art gets into one's eye. At this very instant, this gaze would neither involve specific visual skills of how to look at art, nor analytical capacities and/or knowledge to elaborate about the meaning of this art. Nonetheless, such a momentaneous gaze contributes to either sensuously attract or repulse the beholder from this very art. Whereas I connect repulsion to Tinius's awkward art, the process of being attracted into the work of art will be considered in relation to Paulo Favero's concept of 'immersive images' (2018, 2019). For Favero, this corresponds to a picture's quality and is created by specific artistic practices. In the context of exceptional experience-1, I argue that immersion is a potential of the spectator's perception, and its activation is paramount for the transition into exceptional experience-2. This is moreover an intensified visual interaction with the work of art. But while Dewey considers aesthetic experience as a complex process to understand the work of art, I view exceptional experience-2 as mainly determined by the visitor's imaginative work and intentionality.

The Beautiful, Pleasing and Enjoying

My first example deals with Pablo Picasso's visit to the Musée du Trocadéro in Paris, which he undertook together with his colleague Éric de Vlaminck in early 2007.[1] Looking at the masks, he describes his exceptional experience as follows:

> They were against everything – against unknown threatening spirits. ... I, too, I am against everything, ... I understood what the Negroes used their sculptures for ... I understood why I was a painter. All alone in that awful museum with the masks ... the dusty mannikins. *Les Demoiselles d'Avignon* must have been born that day, but not at all because of the forms; because it was my first exorcism painting – yes absolutely! (Foster 1985: 45–46)

John Berger reminds us about the confrontative dimension of *Les Demoiselles* (1907) at the time, and comments that it 'was a raging, frontal attack, not against "sexual immorality," but against life as Picasso found it – the waste, the disease, the ugliness, and the ruthlessness of it' (1989: 72). Patricia Leigthen provides another contextual information for Picasso's emotive agitation and painting as revolt. In 1905–6, the first revelations of French and Belgian colonialist violence had reached these colonial centres, and were hotly debated both in the Chamber of Deputies and in the media. She argues that the affinity of some modernist artists to African masks, such as Picasso, was as much a search for new art as an expression of social criticism (1990: 609).

My second example concerns Chéri Samba's encounter with African art at the museum of ethnography, University of Zurich, which Miklós Szalay, curator of the African Department reported to me. He had invited the famous Congolese artist to see several artworks while he was preparing an exhibition of African art. When Chéri Samba and Szalay had entered into the hall where the artworks were loosely scattered on tables, the artist asked whether he could stay alone for some hours with these artworks. After a long time, Szalay met again a deeply moved artist. Chéri Samba assured the curator that he had felt the spiritual powers, which were still embodied within the sculptures. Later, the artist painted a picture of this experience, *Hommage aux anciens créateurs* (1994).[2] In the central part the artist is sitting in front of some old master carvings, and on the right and left columns he provides evidence about his emotions and spiritual interaction.

> I felt as if some of these objects triggered thrills all over my body. Hence, I got persuaded that these objects emanated still their supernatural powers, and these were true ones, as at the time there was no competed market, and there would not be any fakes.[3] (Samba 1996: 51; my translation)

Léopold Sédar Senghor's perception of paintings of Pierre Soulages is my third example. Pierre Soulages's painting *Peinture 81×60 cm, 3 décembre 1956* was to be sold at an auction on 23 January 2021. Media reported that besides the prominence of the artist, the painting was particular as it belonged to the collection of Senghor. He had acquired it in Soulages's studio in December 1956, a few years before being elected first President of Senegal. The painting's background is in light ochre, while broad black, vertical and horizontal brush strokes dominate the picture. At this occasion, several journalists were reminded of Senghor's own words about his emotions when looking at Soulages's paintings:

> The first time I saw a painting of Pierre Soulages was a shock. I received a punch in the hollow of the stomach, which made me vacillate, like the stricken boxer who suddenly breaks down. This is exactly the thrill I felt at the first sight of a 'Dan' mask. This is not fortuitous, the paintings of Soulages always remind me of the paintings, the negro-African sculptures. It is the same contempt of any vain elegance, the same evidence that imposes itself, the same capture of the spectator at the root of life.[4] (Senghor in Huctin 2021; my translation)

A comparison of these three statements of exceptional experiences unravels some aspects of these uncommon experiences. First, all three personalities are trained in looking at art, and have acquired specific knowledge: Picasso about occidental art history, but none about African art; Chéri Samba about the ritual embeddedness of African figurines; and Senghor both about African art and European modernism. Second, all these encounters occurred in spaces that were separated from everyday life: Picasso and Chéri Samba visited ethnographic museums, Senghor the studio of Soulages. Regarding the ethnographic museums, I would further differentiate between the display at Trocadéro, where the masks were shown as artefacts, while Szalay clearly dealt with the African objects as art. Third, regarding the time of interaction, Chéri Samba's statement is clearest. The sensuous feeling of the arts' supernatural powers required time and an undisturbed, single contemplation. Picasso, too, emphasizes the single interaction, while the attraction of the African masks corresponds to a momentaneous gaze, which instigates him to further immerse into these works. Senghor highlights the effect of the rapid gaze both in relation to Soulages's paintings and the Dan masks – they produce the feeling of the punch in his stomach.

Further, one needs to ask to which goals these exceptional experiences are oriented towards, to the understanding of the work of art, or to an intention of the spectator? Picasso, as his peers of the time, was not interested in further knowledge about meanings and functions of these

African objects in their respective local cultures. For them, they were not artefacts but works of art. Nonetheless, his imagination about African masks led the artist to the self-awareness of why he is a painter and what his painting is about. Chéri Samba expresses his deep understanding of the artworks' fundamental connections to ancestral powers of the societies they come from, although they had long been in a European collection. Senghor elaborates a comparison between a work of European abstract modernism and masks of the Dan, a population living in the border area between Côte d'Ivoire and Liberia. Independently of the formal correlations he sees in the two abstractions – black as dominant colour for Soulages and the black brilliance of the masks, or the splendid rigor of the paint brush and the one of the ornament-free, smooth carvings – Senghor's comparison is, rather, owed to his ideas of Négritude[5] in art, more specifically to his concept of a culture's rooting–uprooting and opening [*enracinement et ouverture* (see Mbaye 2021: 39)].

The relationship between art and experience is fundamentally connected to John Dewey's *Art as Experience* (2005). As Richard Shusterman emphasizes, Dewey's notion of experience is polysemic (2010: 32). Experience concerns, by and large, the interaction of any individual with the physical and social environment. At this level, experience is nothing specific to the field of art. For my purpose, I shall further consider Dewey's differentiations between *an* experience, aesthetic experience, instantaneous experience and instantaneous impression. *An* experience is a distinct one, complete in itself, different from what happened before and what would come afterwards (ibid.: 37). Yet, according to Shusterman, the notion 'aesthetic experience' is key in Dewey's theory of art:

> aesthetic experience is especially and distinctively unified so that it 'stands out' as vital, noteworthy, or memorable, thus constituting what Dewey famously called '*an* experience', though also sometimes described as 'a vital experience' or an 'integral experience'. (ibid.: 37)

I see, however, a certain difference between *an* experience and aesthetic experience. For the latter, Dewey considers 'cumulative series of interaction' (2005: 228), various acts of seeing that supplement each other with 'another increment of meaning and value ... in a continuous building up of the esthetic object' (ibid.: 228). This process requires a temporal quality of seeing by the beholder. Hence, Dewey discards any 'instantaneous experience' (ibid.: 229), as it would interrupt the experiencing of the work of art. Rather, an instantaneous experience would apply to a person who passes quickly by an aesthetic object, and who would not take the time for a continuous interaction with the artwork. Nonetheless, he conceptualizes an 'instantaneous impression' which may radiate from the artwork to the spectator the moment when the latter sees it (ibid.: 229). This may be the point of entry for the aesthetic experience, the process of repeated looking at the work of art from all viewpoints, but one should not confuse both notions. Appreciation, pleasing and enjoyment characterize the aesthetic experience (ibid.: 49), not the instantaneous impression.

This rejection of any momentaneous, uncommon experience, and the insistence on the act of seeing as plural and additive, highlight the major aspect of Dewey's theory. The goal of aesthetic experience is the unravelling of the various levels of meaning of the artwork. Nonetheless, my three examples provide another image. Only Chéri Samba's exceptional experience connects to a fundamental quality of the African pieces he could interact with: their radiating spiritual powers. Picasso and Senghor make account of their personal visions, which have hardly anything to do with the art they were looking at. Instead of claiming aesthetic experience as the exhaustive vision of art, the examples of Picasso and Senghor, rather, orient themselves towards asserting that individuals perceive and experience the pictures they interact with by means of their personal imagination (cf. Belting 2001: 82).

Gell, too, deals with the appraisal of the work of art as a particularity of the beholder, insofar as she or he needs to understand (in their imagination) the process of artistic practices through which the work of art took visual form:

> that the attitude of the spectator towards the work of art is fundamentally conditioned by his notion of the technical processes which gave rise to it, and the fact that it was created by the agency of another person, the artist. (1992: 51)

In Gell's concept, the personal imagination of the beholder is, first, conceived as 'internal awareness of his own powers as an agent' (ibid.), and second, the target of his, or her, experience is not the work of art as such, but the technical process of its making – art belongs to a wide technological system, and its characteristic is the excellence of the artist's skills. He therefore speaks of art as a 'technology of enchantment'. Gell further emphasizes the viewer's imaginative activity on the work of art, insofar as she or he needs to imagine the 'technical mastery' of the artist (ibid.: 52). For Gell, the difficulty resides in the imagination, how the artistic masterpiece was or is technically created, 'since it transcends my understanding, I am forced to construe as magical' (ibid.: 49), thus artistic practices as enchanting technologies, and the work of art as *'made beautiful'* (ibid.: 43, italics by the author).

In the context of the experiences of Picasso, Chéri Samba and Senghor, Gell's approach allows better understanding of the individual's imaginative process of an exceptional experience, what he defines as 'abduction of agency' (1998). This power as agent is apparent with Picasso's view, which consists largely in a total misconception of the African artist, but leads him to a new self-awareness as painter. Senghor, in turn, applies elements of Négritude upon artistic creations from totally different cultural environments. Furthermore, although Gell incorporates art within a vast field of technologies, he nonetheless considers it as a well demarcated one – on the grounds of its technically achieved level of excellence. As a matter of fact, Picasso, Chéri Samba and Senghor had their experiences in non-everyday spaces, in museums and in an artist's studio.

Hostile Experiences

So far, I have dealt with exceptional experiences in the realm of the beauty of art, creating emotions of enchantment, delightedness, pleasure … Truly, Dewey's and Gell's theories connect the aesthetic experience, or the artistic practice to the beautiful.

Nonetheless, many examples of art in Modernity cannot be appraised on the basis of beauty, neither regarding the appearance of the picture, nor regarding the applied artistic skills. Marcel Duchamp's *Ready Made*(s) are such an example; Picasso's *Les Demoiselles d'Avignon* 1907) was, for a long time, not perceived as beautiful and could not be exhibited until 1937 (Berger 1989 [1965]: 72); Arte Povera (late 1960s) … In a general way, one can say that the more objects of everyday life would be included into works of art, and the more artists are pushing out of art's autonomous field into socio-cultural spaces, or with the rise of global art and the end of the monopoly of a universal art canon, the more ideas of beauty in relation to art are outmoded, yet no more consistent.

This also impacts on the interconnection of exceptional experience with enchantment, pleasure or enjoyment. Collective iconoclasms (see Gamboni 1997) – for example, during the French Revolution, the Nazi regime and the production of 'degenerate art' (*entartete Kunst*), the end of the Socialist regimes in Europe, and the ravage of communist monuments – are examples where experience turned into violence against works of art. Possible artistic qualities of the things to be destroyed were totally neglected. They were discomforting, they would not conform to ideologies, or to new, collectively validated knowledge and experiences. Iconoclasm, whether collective or individual, is a vast phenomenon, and as Gamboni (ibid.) demonstrates, these acts of violence require various explanations. My following reflections, however, relate to individual uncommon hostile experiences as refusals to intensively interact with a specific work of art.

For the fifth edition of the Biennale of Dakar in 2002, curator Bruno Cora was invited to compose an exhibition within the frame of 'Individual Exhibitions'.[6] He selected three prominent artists of the Euro-North American art world, Jannis Kounellis, Jaume Plensa and Franz West. In particular, Kounellis's installation *Untitled* (2002) was highly disputed in Dakar. Around several pillars of the building, 'a circle of bags' was arranged, 'containing seeds or grains, as we can often see them in the city foodstuff markets or those in cave-like spice stores' (Cora 2002: 103). As the site of the show, Cora chose the Ancient Palace of Justice (*Ancien Palais de Justice*), at the far end of Dakar's central area close to Cap Manuel.

Iba Ndiaye Diadji, an art historian who had, for many years, organized the Biennale's discussion forum 'Encounter and Exchanges', was revolted. In a review of this Biennale's edition he writes:

> Of course, not all the main and fringe events met with the same success. ... the show Bruno Cora put on in the Law Courts' 'Salle des pas perdus' justified some people's rejection of all that is art. 'What a nerve!', 'It's just plain lazy', commented several visitors. (Diadji 2002)

A year later, Iba Ndiaye Diadji's anger had not vanished. In a commissioned evaluation of the Biennale in 2003, he angrily comments that this was a true denial of art, both from the curator and the artist, to display the large bags of cereals 'meant to tell them ['Negroes of 2002', the author's formulation] the cultural contempt into which one locks them up and to prove one's ignorance worse than all that the racist, colonial ideology had developed'.[7]

Even during my fieldwork on the Biennale, some interlocutors referred to this exhibition and confirmed the art historian's indignation. The hostile extraordinary emotions were obviously triggered both by Kounellis's installation and the site, the Ancient Palace of Justice. Regarding the art, Iba Ndiaye Diadji was aware about Arte Povera, of which Kounellis was a founder in the late 1960s in Italy. Nonetheless, he connected the large bags full of cereals to the multitude of similar ones at Dakar's colourful markets, and not to the artist's conceptual approach, 'exit from the painting', and the ensuing implications on his artistic practice (Cora 2002: 103). The building, moreover, was not considered as being worthy of exhibiting contemporary art. Actually, it was the centre for the exhibition of modern art during Senghor's *Premier Festival Mondial des Arts Nègres* 1966. But since then, it had been abandoned to weather and heavy environmental degradations.

My other example stems from a visit I undertook some years ago with my seminar group on contemporary art. As we were walking through a show in a distinguished Viennese space for contemporary art, and as we were entering into another hall, a student suddenly turned to me, said she would join us again in the next hall, and hurried away. This room was dominated by a huge painting, one of the famous 'splatter' paintings of Hermann Nitsch. A priest's white surplice was applicated on the canvas, and out of plastic buckets the artist had spilled pig's blood all over it. It was a work that was realized during one of his characteristic performances with religious ritual elements (his *Orgien Mysterien Theater*), for which Nitsch is famous in the Euro-North American art world.

I remember that later, in the gallery's café, the student explained that the sole sight of this artwork rose disgust in her, and if she had stayed, her body would have been shaken by nausea. Even at the next meeting of the seminar at the department, she refused to further reflect on the work of art, about which element was determinant – the pig's blood and the animal's slaughter, the reference to religious rituals, the violence of performances. She rejected it altogether, and thus explicitly demarcated herself from this piece, and obviously put up a sensual and intellectual barrier.

In a study on unusual aesthetic emotions, Silva highlights that hostile emotions towards art are quite common, though understudied (2009: 49). Specifically, he distinguishes within hostile aesthetic emotions between anger, disgust and contempt, the so-called *hostility triad* (ibid.). Anger, for instance, involves an appraisal 'as contrary to one's goals and values', while 'unlike anger, disgust involves appraising something as unpleasant, dirty, or harmful' (ibid.: 49–50).

For art that raises hostile emotions, Tinius proposes the concept of 'awkward art': 'that is, first, practices, institutions, objects and discourses whose status as art is contested, and which, second, are considered uncomfortable' (Tinius 2018: 132). Tinius emphasizes that the contestation of such art is not grounded in its formal qualities, that is, its embeddedness within art world discourses, but, rather, 'because the social relations they retrospectively embody are seen as troublesome' (ibid.).

Tinius elaborates his concept of 'awkward art' within his analysis of the collection the art trader Gurlitt acquired while these works of art were de-validated as degenerate art (*entartete Kunst*) by the Nazi regime, a collective ideological dictate.[8] Precisely individual hostile experiences highlight that awkwardness constitutes not a quality inherent to an artwork, but a spectator's judgement, as Tinius asserts collective de-validations (ibid.: 133–34). Both the presented cases show an exceptional experience as manifest distanciation from the specific artworks. The Senegalese art historian transfers the work into the field of Dakar's everyday life, and disregards the artistic conceptualization of his practice – which is well grounded in the occidental art historical discourse. This shift from the art field into the local social-cultural environment is, moreover, reinforced with the space of presentation, a dilapidated non-art building. The student, however, is confronted with Nitsch's work within a space specifically dedicated to the presentation of contemporary art. She moreover does not question the art discourse itself. But with her instantaneous rejection, she refuses a perception and an experience to this piece which she is granting the other works of art in the exhibition. Hence, in an overall perspective, individual, hostile uncommon experiences in art are connected to a visitor's specific construction of an artwork as awkward art, and this occurs independently of art world discourses.

Exceptional Experiences 1 and 2

Having considered both pleasing, knowledge enriching, and hostile exceptional experiences of art, several notions become visible in these interactions between art and beholder: authenticity, site specificity, and non-habituation. First, the importance of art's authenticity is most revealing in the case of Picasso, Chéri Samba and Iba Ndiaye Diadji: Picasso is particularly attracted by the African masks though he perceives the museum as awful and the masks' supports (the mannikins) as dusty; for Chéri Samba the authenticity of the African pieces is paramount to experience the radiation of their supernatural powers; and Iba Ndiaye Diadji explains his hostile exceptional experience precisely in transferring the various parts of the installation (the large bags with cereals) into the field of quotidian life.

Site specificity refers to areas which are defined as particular spaces by an art world. Among the five cases, Soulages's studio is unequivocally a space for modern art; the same is true for the institution where Nitsch's splatter painting was on display. Dakar's Ancient Palace of Justice was only temporarily occupied as an art space, though obviously a contested one. The examples of the two museums of ethnography are of special interest, as both are primarily society museums and not galleries of fine art. Nonetheless, Szalay, the curator of the African collection, was conceiving the figurines as art, while in the early twentieth century, the masks at Trocadéro were still exhibited as material culture amidst other cultural documents. Hence, while Chéri Samba's experience reinforced the artness of these master carvings, Picasso transfers the masks from artefacts to African art to create his own self-awareness as artist of early Modernity.

Both the authentic art and its site specificity contribute to the system which produces a distinction between the field of art-pictures and the one of quotidian activities (cf. Belting 2001: 81). Both fuse in the notion of non-habituation, that is, any exceptional experience of art needs to be separated in one way or another from the flow of ordinary, common daily experiences. One may object that Kounellis was precisely connecting his installation with food markets, and that curator Bruno Cora attempts to stretch beyond the field of art with the selection of the exhibition space. The discrepancy, however, becomes apparent when relating Iba Ndiaye Diadji's rejection of the artwork and the site with Kounellis's 'exit from painting', as discussed above. The Senegalese art historian emphasizes the socio-economic environment and cuts off any connection to spaces of artistic research, whereas the artist's problematization of artistic practice stretches out from the field of art into socio-cultural spaces.

These three categories – authenticity, site specificity, non-habituation – are fundamentally connected to the experience of art. I subdivide an exceptional experience of art into two concepts: exceptional experience-1 and exceptional experience-2. In contrast to Dewey's 'instantaneous impression' (2005: 229), exceptional experience-1 corresponds to the rapid gaze, which produces a certain reaction of the beholder's senses. Senghor's description of his 'punch into the stomach's hollow' when looking at a painting of Soulages or at a mask of the Dan is such a case. Another may be seen in Picasso's fascination of the African masks, as this group of objects manifestly stands out for him amidst all the other things in this 'awful' museum. The student's reaction in front of Nitsch's splatter painting belongs, too, in this realm. Thus, exceptional experience-1 may either create delightedness and interest, but also hostile emotions such as anger or disgust. This momentaneous vision therefore creates within the spectator's body two opposed movements: attraction or repulsion.

If exceptional experience-1 entails repulsion, I view it as supplemented with the individual's appraisal of awkward art. In contrast, I connect attraction to Favero's concept of 'immersive images' (2018). Favero conceives this approach primarily in relationship to new software technologies for virtual reality, augmented reality and mixed reality, which

> seek to wrap viewers in the image and hence to blur the distance between viewer and viewed, self and world ... Immersion is an important modality through which human beings, in different times and places, have engaged with the visual world. (ibid.: 12)

However, Favero expands his study of immersive images to other, explicit artistic techniques in past epochs and regions of the world (2018, 2019).

Hindu popular representations of Gods are, for instance, 'considered to be direct emanations of Gods' (2019). Or, in Roman Antiquity, Favero mentions the rich paintings on the walls of *Villa dei Misteri* (House of Mysteries) in Pompei, 'scenes blending mythology and everyday life' in such a way that spectators immerse into the whole scenery (2019).

Favero makes the important remark that 'the space of immersive images is … a space of contemplation rather than of narration and representation' (2018: 61). This is also substantial for seeing as a process of attracting into the work of art under exceptional experience-1. Nonetheless, while Favero considers immersion as a quality created by the artistic practice, thus inherent to the artwork, in the cases I presented, the dragging into a work of art depends on the beholder's perception. Chéri Samba mentions the thrills he felt when he entered the hall with the figurines, and Soulages's rigor of the brush stroke and the colour black are attracting Senghor's vision. It is a brief contemplative process that requires neither specific skills of looking at art, nor the interference of any knowledge of related art discourses.

Exceptional experience-2 depends on the quality of exceptional experience-1. If this latter turns into repulsion and awkward art, the process ends there. If the viewer is attracted towards the work of art, then exceptional experience-2 may unfold. This process then requires another quality of the act of seeing, and to supplement the visual perception by a knowledge that is acquired through other experiences. Here, contemplation shifts into Dewey's continuous cumulative seeing, a 'continuity of the total act of perception' (2005: 228), a process that requires, above all, skills in visual perception.

Regarding the knowledge that complements the visual enriching, Dewey links it to the 'the nature of the problem: that of recovering the continuity of esthetic experience with normal processes of living' (ibid.: 9), in order to understand the work of art. But in the first part I argue that this interfering knowledge is diverse, and dependent on the beholder's imaginative work: Chéri Samba appeals to his knowledge of African religious rituals, Picasso applies his artistic skills of vision, and Senghor subordinates his insights in African arts and European modern art under the framework of Négritude. Accordingly, exceptional experience-2 may lead towards a deepening in the understanding of various levels of meanings of the work of art; for Dewey this 'inexhaustibility … is a function of this continuity of the total act of perception' (ibid.: 228). However, as an experience which stands out from among the aesthetic experiences of other art, exceptional experience-2 may, as well, unravel as a product of the spectator's imaginative intentionality.

Conclusion

The acknowledgement 'this is art' corresponds to the activation of a distinctive set of experiences, as Rancière emphasizes (2004). Art world discourses generate this process of contemporary art, as do specific art institutions such as museums as harbourage of older pictures, of biennale sites or temporary art fair buildings. Discourses, institutions or buildings provide implicit references to skills of looking, or of art-related knowledge.

With artists' thriving out of explicitly circumscribed art spaces into areas of everyday social life – public places, neighbourhoods and so on – circumstances change for the spectator. The thing (e.g. painting, sculpture, installation) or the process (e.g. performance, relational art) is defined as art whereas the environment is manifestly no more art dedicated. Does the spectator realize the unusual experience? Following Rancière's argument, mainly the site of presentation or interaction changes, but the art in question calls for a distinct experience (2004).

I therefore propose in this chapter that any exceptional experience requires, on the side of the art, its authenticity (or the original process), the place specificity, and from the spectator the disposition for a distinct experience – one that is not routinized, nonetheless not necessarily art related. Both exceptional experience-1 and exceptional experience-2 are depending on this readiness to interact with art. Yet none requires some knowledge of art world discourses, or of regional art histories. Precisely the individual dimension of any exceptional experience becomes apparent with the attraction (Favero's immersive images) or repulsion (Tinius's awkward art). Neither of them is an individual re-positioning of the art in question. This is a fundamental difference to an overall aesthetic experience of art. A focused, intensive appraisal of art within art worlds demands specialized knowledge, whereas even an exceptional experience-2 stands out because it arises out of the spectator's intentionality.

Thomas Fillitz is Professor Emeritus of Social and Cultural Anthropology, University of Vienna. He was visiting professor, amongst others, at Université Lumière Lyon-2 (2008) and Université Paris Descartes (2011), and was External Examiner at NIU-Maynooth (2003–9). Between 2007 and 2013, he was secretary of the European Association of Social Anthropologists. His main research interest is contemporary African art, with field research in francophone West Africa, and with a specific focus on the Biennale of Dakar. Publications include, together with Ugochukwu Smooth Nzewi (eds), *Dak'Art. The Biennale of Dakar and the Making of Contemporary African Art* (Routledge, 2021), and 'Persistent Universals in

Biennial Research: A Perspective from the Biennale of Dakar', in Andre Gingrich (ed.), *Anthropology in Motion: Encounters with Current Trajectories of Scholarship from Austria* (Sean Kingston Publishing, 2021).

Notes

1. The title of this chapter alludes to Picasso's description of his feelings and thoughts.
2. 'Tribute to the ancient creators' (see Samba 1996: 50–51).
3. 'Je sentais comme si quelques uns de ces objects me faisaient des frissons au corps. J'étais donc pesuidé que ces objets avaient toujours leur pouvoirs surnaturels et c'étaient des vrais puisqu'à cette époque le marché n'était pas concurrencé et il ne devait donc pas avoir de fausse pièce.'
4. 'La première fois que je vis un tableau de Pierre Soulages ce fut un choc. Je reçus au creux de l'estomac un coup qui me fit vaciller, comme le boxeur touché qui soudain s'abîme. C'est exactement la sensation que j'ai éprouvé à la première vue d'un masque 'Dan'. Ce n'est pas un hasard, les peintures de Soulages me rappellent toujours les peintures, voire les sculptures négro-africaines. C'est le même mépris de toute vaine élégance, la même évidence qui s'impose, la même saisie du spectateur à la racine de la vie.' Senghor wrote this in the text 'Pierre Soulages', *Les Lettres Nouvelles*, March 1958, no 58.
5. Senghor omits the fundamental differences of the abstractions at stake: Soulages's is a purely formal solution, whereas the abstraction of the mask correlates with cultural meanings.
6. It consisted of invited exhibitions, where artists not originating from Africa could be displayed within the Biennale's official spaces.
7. In an unpublished commissioned paper (June 2003), I could consult, he writes: 'c'est leur dire le mépris culturel dans lequel on les enferme et prouver son ignorance pire que tout ce qu'a développé l'idéologie coloniale raciste'.
8. The other body of pieces is the Colonial Neighbours Archive at SAVVY Contemporary (Berlin-Wedding).

References

Belting, Hans. 2001. *Bild–Anthropologie*. Munich: Wilhelm Fink.
Berger, John. 1989 [1965]. *The Success and Failure of Picasso*. New York: Pantheon Books.
Cora, Bruno. 2002. 'Seeds of the 21st Century: From One to Several', in *Dak'Art 2002*, Ousseynou Wade (ed.). Dakar: La Biennale des Arts de Dakar (exhibition catalogue), pp. 102–5.
Dewey, John. 2005 [1934]. *Art as Experience*. New York: Perigee Books.
Diadji, Iba Ndiaye. 2002. 'Dak'art on the Threshold of Maturity'. *Africultures. Les Mondes en relation* (31 August). Retrieved 1 February 2023 from http://africultures.com/dakart-on-the-threshold-of-maturity-5620/.

Favero, Paolo S.H. 2018. *The Present Image: Visible Stories in a Digital Habitat*. Cham: Palgrave Macmillan.

Favero, Paolo S.H. 2019. 'A Journey from Virtual and Mixed Reality to Byzantine Icons via Buddhist Philosophy: Possible (Decolonizing) Dialogues in Visuality across Time and Space', in *Aesthetic Encounters: The Politics of Moving and (Un)Settling Visual Arts, Design and Literature*, Thomas Fillitz (ed.). *Anthrovision* 7(1). https://doi.org/10.4000/anthrovision.4921.

Foster, Hal. 1985. 'The "Primitive" Unconscious of Modern Art', *October* 34 (Autumn): 45–70. Retrieved 20 March 2021 from: https://www.jstor.org/stable/778488.

Gamboni, Dario. 1997. *The Destruction of Art: Iconoclasm and Vandalism since the French Revolution*. London: Reaktion Books.

Gell, Alfred. 1992. 'The Technology of Enchantment and the Enchantment of Technology', in *Anthropology, Art, and Aesthetics*, Jeremy Coote and Anthony Shelton (eds). Oxford: Clarendon Press, pp. 40–63.

———. 1998. *Art and Agency: An Anthropological Theory*. Oxford: Clarendon Press.

Huctin, Alexandra. 2021. 'Pierre Soulages et Léopold Senghor: deux hommes et une amitié dans un tableau vendu aux enchères à Caen'. *3 Normandie*. Retrieved 25 January 2021 from: https://france3-regions.francetvinfo.fr/normandie/calvados/caen/pierre-soulages-et-leopold-senghor-deux-hommes-et-une-amitie-dans-un-tableau-vendu-aux-encheres-a-caen-1905810.html.

Leigthen, Patricia. 1990. 'The White Peril and *l'art nègre*: Picasso, Primitivism, and Anticolonialism', *The Art Bulletin* 72(4): 609–30.

Mbaye, Massamba. 2021. 'A Politico-Economic History of Modern and Contemporary Art in Senegal: From *Négritude* to the Logics of the Open Society', in *Dak'Art: The Biennale of Dakar and the Making of Contemporary African Art*, Ugochukwu-Smooth C. Nzewi and Thomas Fillitz (eds). London and New York: Routledge, pp. 37–51.

Rancière, Jacques. 2004. *Malaise dans l'esthétique*. Paris: Galilée.

Samba, Chéri. 1996. 'Hommage aux anciens créateurs'. In Miklós Szalay (ed.), *Afrikanische Kunst aus der Sammlung Han Coray 1916–1928*. Munich and New York: Prestel, pp. 50–51.

Shusterman, Richard. 2010. 'Dewey's Art as Experience: The Psychological Background', *The Journal of Aesthetic Education* 44(1): 26–43. DOI: 10.1353/jae.0.0069.

Silva, Paul J. 2009. 'Looking Past Pleasure: Anger, Confusion, Disgust, Pride, Surprise, and Other Unusual Aesthetic Emotions', *Psychology of Aesthetic Creativity and the Arts* 3(1): 48–1. DOI: 10.1037/a0014632.

Tinius, Jonas. 2018. 'Awkward Art and Difficult Heritage: Nazi Collectors and Postcolonial Archives', in *An Anthropology of Contemporary Art: Practices, Markets, and Collectors*, Thomas Fillitz and Paul van der Grijp (eds). London: Bloomsbury Academic, pp. 130–45.

Chapter 3

Art and Anthropology in Graphic Form
Exceptional Experience and Extraordinary Collaboration in the Making of *Light in Dark Times*

Alisse Waterston and Charlotte Corden

Introduction

On a chilly day in late 2020, a science journalist in an interview about Waterston's work including the graphic novel, *Light in Dark Times*, posed this question to the anthropologist: 'I wonder', she asked, 'how do we know that we live in dark times? How do we recognize the darkness?' (von der Lehr 2020).

'We don't need to look very far to see that we live in dark times', Waterston noted, offering a sampling of deeply disturbing statistics, updated here: an estimated 768 million people worldwide go to bed hungry each day; 924 million are exposed to severe levels of food insecurity and 2.3 billion people in the world did not have regular access to safe, nutritious and sufficient food (Food and Agriculture Organization of the United Nations 2022); an estimated 89.3 million people worldwide have been forcibly displaced, a number that keeps rising – this figure is 19.3 million more than is documented in *Light in Dark Times* (UNHCR, the UN Refugee Agency 2022); an estimated four million people have died as a result of US wars in Afghanistan, Iraq, Syria, Pakistan and Yemen since 9/11 at a financial cost to US taxpayers of $6.4 trillion (Vine 2020a, 2020b). Then there is the pandemic. At the time of the interview, there were an estimated 1.3 million deaths worldwide and 220,000 deaths in the US from COVID 19. At the time of writing in August 2022, that number has risen to almost 6.5 million deaths worldwide and over one million deaths in the US from the coronavirus (Johns Hopkins University & Medicine 2022).

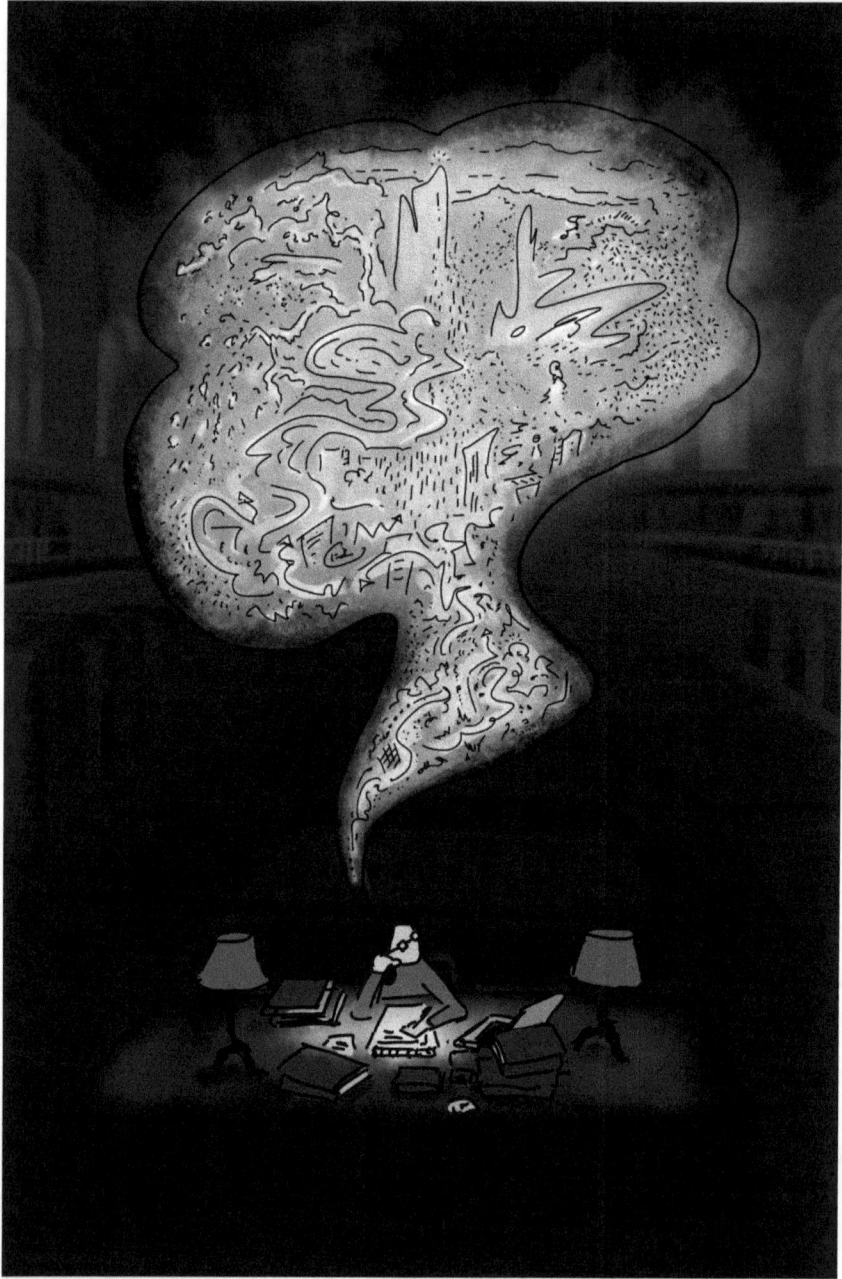

Figure 3.1. Thinking. © Charlotte Corden in *Light in Dark Times* (Waterston and Corden 2020).

The statistics, alarming as they are, signal that the conditions that sustain human life are deeply off kilter. There are the numbers, and then there are the contexts of devastating economic collapses, ever-expanding militarism and worship of weapons, racism and nationalist fervour, environmental crisis and irreversible climate damage, rampant power abuses and everyday structural violence. Social, political and economic inequities are expanding; people are suffering 'stupid deaths' as anthropologist Paul Farmer (2011) observed. Meanwhile, private, concentrated wealth continues to expand under global, neoliberal capitalism, a system that maintains conditions of scarcity and insecurity through a politics of fear and fragmentation, and draconian policies and practices that too often do more harm than good.

'Some may not want to confront the darknesses', Waterston asserted, 'but it is there, nevertheless'.

In an extraordinary collaboration with illustrator Charlotte Corden, Waterston co-produced *Light in Dark Times* to disrupt denial about the darknesses of the past and the present, to affirm what many people sense, feel, know or seek to know, and to inspire taking action on behalf of a liveable future. The author (Waterston) and the artist (Corden) invite readers/viewers to experience a visually stunning journey to explore those political catastrophes and moral disasters that bring outrage and sometimes despair, and that beg to be identified, studied, revealed, understood, confronted and resisted. The exploration takes the form of encounters with writers, philosophers, activists and anthropologists, some recognizable, others unfamous: Virginia Woolf and Vivian Gornick, Hannah Arendt and Bertolt Brecht, Sherry Ortner, Roger Berkowitz, Peg Birmingham, Roger Lancaster, Eben Kirksey, Carolyn Nordstrom, Paul Farmer, Bryan Stevenson and Eduardo Galeano. Waterston and Corden are avatars that animate the book's storyline and its two central questions: What of us in these times? How will we pass the time that is given us on earth?

This chapter focuses on the making of *Light in Dark Times*, offering reflections by the writer and the artist on various aspects of their experience and collaboration. It situates the work in the larger context of movements in anthropology towards public engagement and experimental writing and invokes the book's public afterlife. It considers the roles of serendipity, privilege, negotiation, strain, satisfaction and practicalities that resulted in a work that is aesthetically pleasing, identifies deadly serious issues facing humankind and asks of the reader/viewer: how do I want to be human?

With implications for meaningful engagement and for the sustainability of anthropology as a discipline, the process of examining the production of this graphic novel of art and anthropology brings into focus opportunities and obstacles as scholars increasingly seek to stretch disciplinary boundaries in representing what they have come to learn. It also enables the co-producers of the work to find compassion and sometimes humour in their missteps and to intensify their appreciation of one another's strengths. To address the stylistic challenge in writing a co-authored chapter centred on our individual observations, the chapter uses the first person narrative for each reflection, and the third person narrative written by Waterston in this introduction and the sections subtitled 'Context' and 'Conclusion'. Corden's illustrations are featured throughout.

Context

For decades, anthropologists have been participating in a series of interconnected debates about the discipline's disengagement from the public sphere that marked post-Second World War anthropology, at least in the US (Kirsch 2018). They have called one another to task for failing to venture beyond the narrowest confines of the ivory tower to engage with the world. In academic circles, these debates have been centred on the politics of representation, writing culture, how to decolonize the discipline, and how to put knowledge to use in the interest of a more just, ethical world.

This calling to task has generated lively discussion among anthropologists who recognize the dangers of a schism, not least the split identified by anthropologist Gina Ulysse (2013, 2017) between the scholar and the responsible global citizen, between the artist in us and the anthropologist, and between the artistic and the scholarly in representing what we have come to learn. Anthropologists know a great deal about the social, cultural, political-economic, intellectual, emotive, experiential and affective aspects of human experience. Yet there has long been another schism – the one between what scholars produce in academic settings and what gets read, interpreted and understood. For example, anthropologists know a lot about how social categories are produced and how difference is constructed and can be turned into ideological infection. They know a lot about the macro dynamics of power, past and present, how it works to infiltrate, shape and manage human lives and how violence gets normalized. These analyses too often get lost in translation when scholars try to share them with students, with one another and with audiences beyond academia.

Anthropologist Didier Fassin's (2008) plea for a 'moral anthropology' reflects an intensification of the dilemmas anthropologists confront in the face of the world as it exists marked by expanding globalization, militarization, inequalities, ecological disasters and human suffering. Fassin's is not a new call but a reminder that the question of the scholar's own values, assumptions, prejudices and judgements needs to be made explicit, at least in the mind of the scholar, considering that 'telling right from wrong and the necessity of acting in favour of the good and against the evil' (Fassin 2008: 334) shapes the who, what, where, how and why of any anthropological endeavour – perhaps this is also true for other disciplines.

Considering the state of the world, there is no turning back from an explicitly engaged anthropology. We are left with the 'perils and promises', noted by anthropologist Kay Warren (2006: 213), which means engaged anthropology may expand or limit knowledge, may facilitate analysis or inhibit it, may uncover or occlude information and may advance or hinder understanding. Amid the moral longing in anthropology to do good, there is also no way of avoiding critical reflexivity – no turning away from reflecting on the limitations, possibilities and contradictions of the engaged observer. Feminist anthropologists and those looking to decolonize the discipline have long issued the call for critical reflexivity, recognizing that anthropologists are always 'at risk of participating in ideologies blind to [their] own', a caution Fran Mascia-Lees and colleagues (1989) offered the discipline over three decades ago.

The point is that all modes of thought have social origins, the specifics of which must be brought out of the shadows. This implores anthropologists – and scholars in any discipline – to be consistently mindful of their own centrisms and privileges. Likewise, Fassin posits that 'The more we are conscious and critical of our own moral presuppositions or certainties – instead of keeping them in the black box of self-contentment – the more we are capable of respecting the epistemological grounds and of preserving the political engagements of our scientific work' (2008: 338).

These discussions have led to the current, wonderful moment where anthropologists are participating in praxis and the public sphere. Many more are paying careful attention to writing and engaging multimodal practices and possibilities, developing new and exciting ways to make knowledge accessible, which facilitates interaction with diverse audiences. *Light in Dark Times*, rooted in these intellectual concerns and conversations, sociocultural formations and political circumstances and events, enters into this moment and in good company with new efforts among scholars to engage the graphic form (Sousanis 2015; Hamdy and Nye 2017; Jain 2019; Magee 2019). It is designed for students of the world looking to understand the darkness and what they, and we might do to transform it.

Figure 3.2. The Rich Store of Anthropological World Knowledge. © Charlotte Corden in *Light in Dark Times* (Waterston and Corden 2020).

Origins

Alisse

Even as our graphic novel emerged in this context, it has an origin story that is exceptional, unique to itself and to serendipity. It begins deep in the secluded world of academe.

In 2013, I was elected to top leadership positions of the American Anthropological Association (AAA) when anthropologists, anthropology and the association were standing at a historic moment with difficult issues and conversations before them. As I anticipated taking on the AAA presidency in late 2015, I fully expected to focus my energies on ensuring productive discussion on those subjects and to help bring anthropology more fully into the public conversation about critical local and global social issues and policy debates. Top of my agenda was *World on the Move*, the AAA's public education initiative on migration, a timely, enduring and difficult to discuss topic that matters to anthropologists and to the larger public. As it turned out, the toughest issue in the first year of my presidency was Israel-Palestine, and the courses of action the association would take to address the very real and painful human suffering brought on by the Israeli occupation of the West Bank and Gaza. In the second and last year of my presidency, the toughest issues resulted directly from the policies, practices, statements and actions of the then US president, not least those that threatened human rights, human dignity and academic freedom and that attacked the value of critical thinking and scientific knowledge and information.

In the months preceding the close of my term, I began preparing the presidential address, a lonely endeavour to craft and a task I consider an honour and a responsibility. What would I say to this audience of anthropologists who would gather in a ballroom to hear my remarks? Considering the material, environmental and political state of the world, I felt a sense of urgency to cut through mass confusion resulting from purposeful, political obfuscation to identify sources of global human suffering and to convey what I thought was important for us, as anthropologists, to think about and to do.

The result was 'Four Stories, A Lament, and an Affirmation', in which I explored some meanings and implications of being introspective, of thinking in dark times, of truth, lies and the danger of the trivial, and of envisioning and acting to create an alternative world from that within which we now dwell (Waterston 2018). I had arranged that the lighting in the room shift to capture the mood over the course of the talk – sometimes dark with purple hues, sometimes standard, and sometimes a light and bright amber.

Figure 3.3. Waterston's Presidential Address 2017. © Charlotte Corden.

I knew I wanted to share my thoughts and concerns with this congregation of anthropologists about the world and the role of anthropology in it. I had no idea how it would be received.

Charlotte and I had not met when I stepped onto that ballroom stage in early December 2017. The next morning, I received a beautiful gift from the artist. She had drawn a most spectacular rendition of the address, capturing the spirit and the details of my words – the light as golden and the darkness in all its fury and dangerousness, the specks of red, the cotton wool that obscures and the rich store of world knowledge in a rushing movement outwards.

Charlotte

I had come for the first time to the AAA's annual meeting as an artist/anthropologist to be part of a panel on 'The Arts Matter'. I spoke about the value of using drawing as a research tool, and shared examples of how the act of drawing enables examining and developing complex ideas that support and sometimes surpass thinking with words. As a freelance artist I offered to create some sketch-notes for the AAA, including the keynote speech and the presidential address. On that Saturday evening of Alisse's talk, I was present, iPad and iPencil poised.

Alisse began to speak, and I was amazed by her words, their rich imagery, and the honest human experience of our world that she described. She spoke about ideas that I immediately wanted to know more about, such as 'darkness hidden in plain sight', the ways 'trivia obscures' and 'the will to resist'. She spoke about the hopelessness that we feel in our own insignificant abilities. She highlighted the importance of lament and offered words to use when conflicted by the inequalities of our blatant privileges when held up against the suffering of so many in these times. And amidst all the darkness she spoke of the powerful hope we have in our collective ability to work towards a process of mutual understanding on a gigantic scale. It became evident from the first few sentences that I ought not to attempt to sketch her speech live, but instead take down as many notes as possible and create something more intricate and profound after she had finished.

In the years leading up to this, I had begun to use drawing as a means of unravelling complex philosophical ideas. Drawing had become my tool for thinking and describing beyond words. Here I had been given a visually rich, complex and meaningful message that I couldn't wait to decipher pictorially.

I went back to my hotel and spent hours sifting through the notes and sketching out Alisse's lecture as best I could. I pulled it apart visually and put the pieces back together to create an image underneath her message. I wanted to find the visual thread that knitted her words together. I needed to 'see' what she had said. Where was the darkness in relation to the light? How did that fit with the store of anthropological knowledge and of envisioning an alternative world? To me, what I produced was a rough sketch – a first attempt to think through her ideas with drawing. I set down the pen once it seemed complete, even though I was not entirely satisfied. My desire was to go deeper and visualize more intricately than I had done with the one illustration. Little did I know that would be for another day.

Conceptions

Alisse

Charlotte's incredibly gorgeous and powerful rendition of my talk is a most special gift because, as I thought then and still do, her very effort to interpret my words in such an aesthetically pleasing way suggests that she appreciated my effort and what I had come to say. I received

Figure 3.4. The Start. © Charlotte Corden in 'The Making of *Light in Dark Times*' (Waterston and Corden 2021).

Charlotte's illustration via email from a member of the AAA staff and showed it to my husband as I prepared for my last duty as president that Sunday morning. Charlotte illustrates what happened next in figure 3.4.

By January of the new year, Charlotte and I began the collaboration, meeting weekly by Skype. Neither of us had ever done a project like this before, working in the dark to imagine, create and craft a graphic novel. To begin with, we analysed other graphic books to assess their infrastructures and their elements: how many pages altogether? How many images on a page? How long each chapter? What shape the narrative arc? How are characters presented? We each deconstructed my written document, pulling out what seemed the key points of each line, paragraph and section. We came together to compare notes and discuss, trying to take the project to the next level. Eventually, the story we developed unfolded as a journey through knowledge and we transformed the scholars, activists, anthropologists and poets I had cited into characters we meet along the way.

We were getting to know one another and our individual working styles, two temperaments enjoined in an ever growing and enthusiastic commitment to the project.

Charlotte

Back in England, I produced a few initial sketches of the introduction, attempting to decide on a style. Did Alisse like small comic strip boxes, a series of illustrations flowing down the page or full-page illustrations? We soon realized that communicating via Skype for a project such as

Figure 3.5. The Magic Begins. © Charlotte Corden in 'The Making of *Light in Dark Times*' (Waterston and Corden 2021).

this was too cumbersome. I needed to be in the same room as Alisse. I wanted to ask her questions as I sketched. We needed to go deep into the meaning of her words together so I could interpret them into images that helped make sense of them, and do so without the interruption of a jittering video or waiting for the audio to catch up.

In June 2018 I arrived in New York – Alisse had invited me stay in her home. We transformed her basement children's play-area into our workshop, clearing the toys aside and taping a long roll of child's art paper on the wall.

These became 'The Basement Papers', our space of focus and an integral part of the process. I outlined blank, double-page spreads in rows on which the illustrations and words would unfold. We could look up-close at the spreads or from afar see the unity of the piece, the balance and relationships of meaning we were trying to convey. I was also able to use the space to stand and walk around with my thoughts. To approach the work, and then go further away from it physically, so that my mind, too, could expand and contract, like breathing.

We laboured every day for months-long periods at a time. Working together became fluid and magical. Sometimes it felt as if the book was creating itself.

Foundations

Alisse

The material conditions of our lives as well as our personal and professional circumstances enabled the magic to happen. I have a home large enough to host Charlotte comfortably, to provide space for the storyboard that was expanding across the basement walls and to do our work, whether solo or together.

The privileges of my professional status were also a factor. Over the course of my life as an anthropologist, my commitment to public anthropology sharpened and my experiments in stretching methodological boundaries and 'writing otherwise' (Hannerz 2016) continued to grow. With each of my books, I had grown more confident in experimenting with non-traditional writing formats, having, as Carolyn Nordstrom (2011: 35) writes, 'knocked a host of academic critics off my shoulder who tell me I *can't, shouldn't, wouldn't* write what I believe in; that I *must* follow their guidelines for "truth", academic style, and that (by the way) I'm not good enough, never will be'. Recognizing that junior faculty are more vulnerable to being denied tenure and promotion should they engage in public scholarship and experimental, multimodal forms of expressing and communicating knowledge, I have long felt it is a responsibility of senior scholars to take chances and thus help pave the way for a less repressive and more inclusive and vibrant academy (American Anthropological Association 2017). Here, with this graphic book, was a chance for me to do what gives me intellectual satisfaction and creative pleasure that might also be a contribution to junior scholars and, ultimately, to the discipline.

I also came to this project with a set of organizational skills, experience in publishing, and a professional network. Early on, I explored the possibility of securing a grant as Hamdy and Nye had done for *Lissa* (2017: 275), the first graphic novel published in the ethnographic series of the University of Toronto Press, which is also our publisher. I found no grant to support a project such as ours, realizing that the only way we could pull this off would be to create a partnership sealed with a handshake. I proposed to Charlotte that we share equally in the risks and gains of this project. She agreed.

Whether by disposition or learning from life experience, I organize my work according to a schedule, listing out tasks to accomplish (and check off) and delivering results sooner rather than later. It is a rigid way of operating but a way to get things done. For this project, the schedules I created facilitated our day-to-day work activities even as I learned to back off when Charlotte needed to proceed in her own time to create art.

Charlotte

The privileges of my circumstances also enabled me to take the time and risks needed for creating *Light in Dark Times* with Alisse. Just prior to this project and with a Master's degree in anthropology in hand, I worked at an innovation consultancy helping various organizations develop products or services. I also helped run workshops with the UK's National Health Service with the aim of improving services for people with psychosis. My role, in part, was to illustrate service solutions that depicted the innovative ideas suggested by care providers and service users. They felt immense joy at seeing their work visually. This was the first time I had experienced what it was like to work closely alongside others, to listen to their thoughts, and quickly turn their ideas into pictures – a magical experience. I knew that I had so much more of this work in me and wanted to do it again and again. After some introspection, I made the big decision to take up the title of artist and illustrator. I left the consultancy world and began landing freelance work that enabled me to keep going. I had to leave London and find ways to live more frugally, but it gave me enormous freedom of time and the flexibility to move about the world wherever I chose. This was a great privilege. The moment we proposed I come to New York, I began looking at flights.

I have one other great privilege: parents who support me no matter what. It was a risk to give up a salary, but when you have people with resources who love you, take you in and pay for a flight to New York so that you can follow your dreams, you have everything you need.

For as long as I can remember, I have been drawing and painting. I was taught to use drawing as a memory tool for revision, how to use it as enjoyment in my spare time, and later, it became a kind of therapy for survival. As an undergraduate, I studied architecture, which helped my drawing skills. I was taught to think with my pencil, to always carry a sketchbook with me and to scribble and sketch roughly and quickly, not worrying too much about what it looked like but using it as a tool for understanding one's thoughts. On discovering anthropology, I went straight to the anthropology of art, materials and architecture. I had found what I was looking for – people trying to understand what art is, why humans make art and other objects, and what it is all for. I began drawing during lectures, listening to what was being said, and developing patterns and mark making that most clearly described what I heard. This practice helped me to re-work my thinking from a different perspective and so form a greater understanding of the whole context of observation. Sketching daily improved my skills in drawing figures, abstract shapes and marks to depict concepts. This was the foundation to the drawing processes that enabled the illustrations in *Light in Dark Times* to be what they are.

I came to this project with a love of using drawing to describe complex truths and a tenacity that wouldn't let go of a drawing until I knew I had the truth of the meaning conveyed with as much honesty as possible. Alisse's rigorous method and schedule of working helped push the work forward; when I didn't make the deadlines, we made new ones. The tension between structure and spontaneity was the fire behind the making of the work. As an artist I work best within such a structure. In Alisse's world, I lived, worked, breathed and created within her home, her thoughts, her work and her method, which gave me a kind of freedom to listen, sketch and scribble down whatever came to me in the moment.

Dynamics

Alisse

With our working infrastructure in place and our mutual commitment to the project established, Charlotte and I began the nitty-gritty, step-by-step process of making what would become *Light in Dark Times: The Human Search for Meaning*, published in November 2020. In addition to place and space, the process comprised relationship, dialogue, words, writing, sketching and illustrating. We experienced challenges and joys, and enchantments and epiphanies. Our enthusiasm for the project remained consistently high. I felt we shared an almost spiritual belief in the value of the project even as we were not exactly sure how the book would turn out, if it would land a publishing home, find satisfied readers or have a public afterlife.

When Charlotte first arrived in New York, she stayed with friends and came to my home for a weekend. How smart, I thought; after all, I was on home turf while Charlotte did not know where and how I live and knew me only from our video calls, emails and texts. It didn't take long for us to relax in one another's company and set to work. Charlotte moved in.

In our magic space, most often I would sit on a couch, computer on lap, open to the script. Charlotte would generally be moving – standing, sitting, pacing, circling, pencil in hand ready to draw. She would ask me a question ('What does … mean?'). I'd answer, explain and give examples while trying to read her furrowed brow, eyes focused in the distance, looking away from me, and her mouth no longer in the warm, cheery smile I saw at breakfast. I thought she was angry – at me.

She wasn't. She was listening. She was thinking. And then she'd go to the wall and scribble-scrabble, inviting me to come over and see.

Exceptional Experience and Extraordinary Collaboration 61

Figure 3.6. The Basement Papers. 2018. © Charlotte Corden.

Charlotte dazzled me with her ideas and visions for the pages. Sometimes, I couldn't quite understand an image, and once in a while, I'd reject an element that I thought missed the mark. We discussed again, using words to describe the concept or condition I was looking to convey. We negotiated – sometimes putting a contested issue to the side to resolve later or coming to a place that worked for both us.

The times we were deep into the darknesses of the world were some of the most difficult. I have long been going to the dark places, working to understand and confront them. I am not shocked by their existence but appalled by rationalizations and justifications for what ought to be unacceptable. For Charlotte, I observed, it was unbearable to dwell in so much darkness. In those instances, she would exit the space, get away from me and out of the house, go for a run.

We thought we should take participant-observation notes of our process, which was at once wonderful and gruelling. By the end of the workday, I was generally too tired to write fieldnotes, although I did find this typed entry in my electronic files, dated 19 July 2018:

> We've been working intently and intensely. It's an incredible experience, which I can't explain in a short note. Some snippets might give a taste: deep

diving into and discussing/deliberating/explaining each word, sentence, paragraph, figuring out meanings, imagining visual representations/the just-right image; it's a dance; there's disagreement and epiphany, tension and talking it all out sometimes gently, sometimes not so; there's frustration, and great joy, an incredible intimacy/bond, a joining of the minds and hearts; a creative process like no other I've ever experienced. Age differences, generation differences, experience differences, cultural differences, belief differences; likemindednesses, personality similarities, ability to be utterly honest and utterly direct with one another; overcoming obstacles; ability to come out the other end all the better personally, intellectually, creatively; deeper appreciation of one's self as a result – for me, about my writing, and also even about my ability to get incredibly focused and staying with it despite distractions; and more that I can't think of right now. As of this morning, we have the storyboard laid out and some drawings partially rendered.

I never tire of looking at Charlotte's illustrations. There is beauty and intelligence on each page. The words come alive with drawings that are composed with fine detail and extraordinary artistry: the violence of lying the truth (pp. 52–54); pretence, affectation and exaggeration (pp. 56–57); radical evil (p. 65); a lament (p. 82); mutual understanding on a gigantic scale (pp. 110–11).

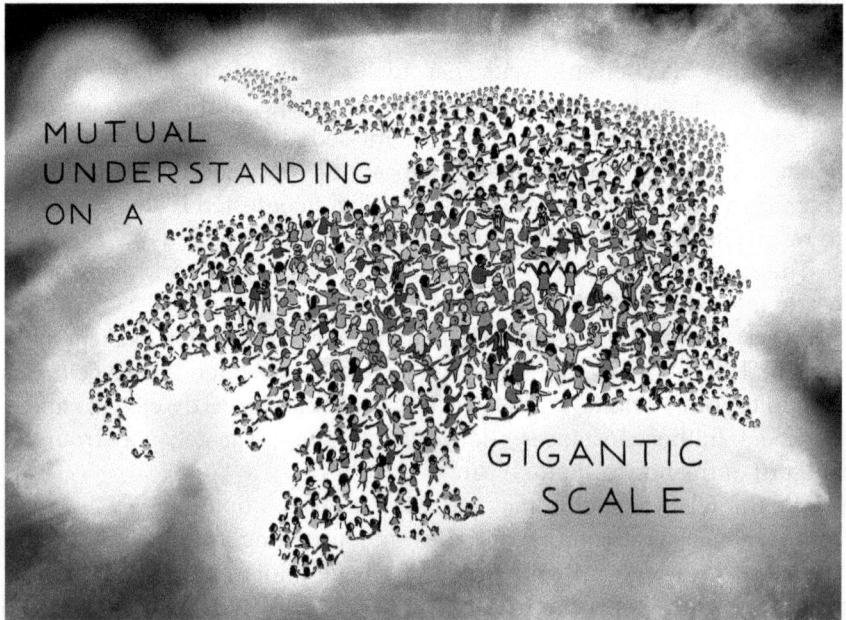

Figure 3.7. 'Mutual Understanding on a Gigantic Scale'. © Charlotte Corden in *Light in Dark Times* (Waterston and Corden 2020).

Charlotte

Working with Alisse was extraordinary. From the start, there was a trust between us, an unspoken understanding that we were to get this book out into the world, despite not knowing the challenges, time or force of will that it might require. We were united in it as equal partners, and both adoring of the other's skill.

Alisse would read out a few sentences, and I would sit on the floor, eyes closed, imagining, giving free reign to the visuals in my mind, holding gently to the greater meaning of what she was saying. I would often walk around with the images and words, literally pace the room in circles. Once, whilst finding it difficult to come up with a visual depiction for 'seeing ... perceiving ... understanding', I began watching my feet take the same position pacing around and around. I let myself imagine the ground as sand and saw what shape my footprint would make in it. Suddenly, I had a revelation. I was enacting the very thing I was looking to illustrate (see page 17 of the published book). The whole world at once seemed united as if everything were moving towards a greater force, with myself happily caught up in its stream, like Woolf's description of 'a shock, a sledgehammer blow' (Woolf 1985).

While Alisse kept an up-to-date master copy of the manuscript as a Word document, I drew the manuscript on the basement papers and, later, on an iPad using the Procreate app. Communication between us was always held with great importance. We were able to speak our minds with confidence that disagreement, even if heated, would bring us to common ground, an unusual joy. How could we not exercise mutual understanding when it was the finale to everything we were creating?

My intention, and the greatest challenge, was to create the truest possible reflection of the meaning behind Alisse's words and the words of others quoted in the book. How does one begin to draw concepts like 'radical evil', 'trivia', 'the will to resist'? There were moments of great frustration as I sought to illustrate what the consequences of detachment versus engagement looked like or 'the power that makes human beings superfluous'. I asked myself, 'How much of a realistic portrayal of events should I attempt, and how much should I keep the visuals abstracted and generalized?'

For example, I originally sketched 'radical evil' as a character with a gruesome, face-like grin, which in the context of Alisse's point, was too cartoon-like. The seriousness and reality of radical evil, and Hannah Arendt's conception of it, needed to be honoured. The final illustration depicts people being made less than human by forces without a face, which better captures Arendt's notion.

Figure 3.8. 'Radical Evil'. © Charlotte Corden in *Light in Dark Times* (Waterston and Corden 2020).

At every stage, it was the writing that inspired the drawing, and it is no exaggeration to say Alisse's words have changed my life. She has taught me how to think with a new perspective. Through investigating how to draw prejudice, I have had to face my own prejudices. Often, when I see events taking place on the news, in my mind I turn to the relevant page of *Light in Dark Times*, lamenting that 'even anger against injustice makes the voice grow harsh', thinking that to make a difference I must 'get proximate to human suffering'. When I see people acting in ways I can barely comprehend, I come back to Alisse's words: 'They are afraid of annihilation and desire protection.' In these moments, I know I must turn to myself and ask the central question, 'How do I want to be human?'

Conclusion

The descriptions that Waterston and Corden provide in this chapter demonstrate how serious scholarship and contemporary aesthetics combine to present complex philosophical and political themes in a mixed media format, elevating the graphic genre. Their experience shows the potential of collaboration to enhance creative endeavour. The relationship between the author and the artist grew alongside the thriving project. The book is a mix of words and images informed by anthropology, the singular discipline that involves critical inquiry, speculation, being attentive and responsive, incorporating the whole world, engaging multiple perspectives, acknowledging conflicting statements, being broad, comparative and holistic, moving toward understanding and attending to the conditions and possibilities of human social life.

Their graphic novel emerged in the context of new and exciting ways to communicate anthropology to larger audiences, which has inspired more anthropologists to pay careful attention to writing and engage multimodal practices and possibilities (Wulff 2021). Looking back, it is remarkable that Waterston and Corden managed to conceive the book in early 2018 and see it officially enter the world less than three years later. Just as their book is situated in the history and context of the discipline, so too was Anne Brackenbury's vision for producing, supporting and publishing public scholarship in graphic form and the emergence of the game-changing book series *ethnoGRAPHIC* under her editorship. Without this series and the support of editor Carli Hansen and the team at University of Toronto Press, the book – in the professional quality of its published form – may not have seen the light of day.

The greatest challenge to conveying and communicating the ideas and issues with which *Light in Dark Times* grapples had to do with the very complexity of the concepts and the painfulness of the real life, human consequences of the issues and conditions the book depicts. The graphic form helps address these challenges because it does not privilege writing over other forms of constructing and representing knowledge, enabling the reader/viewer to grasp meaning from the different, multilayered ways the writer and the artist evoke it.

This chapter has focused on the path of the project's first life – the exceptional experience and extraordinary collaboration in the making of *Light in Dark Times*. The work has now entered its public afterlife – its reception by readers and viewers (Fassin 2015: 594, 596; see also Waterston 2019: 16–17). There are strong indicators that the book resonates with audiences. In less than two years since its publication, Waterston and Corden have given over thirty invited talks, podcasts and webinars in Europe and the US, and the book has been adopted in fifty-three undergraduate and graduate courses, reaching nearly 2,500 students. Beyond the numbers are the thoughtful comments and incisive questions posed to the author and the artist and the discussions that have ensued, suggesting that *Light in Dark Times* might, indeed, prove useful to the future of anthropology and to help heal a deeply troubled world.

Alisse Waterston is Presidential Scholar and Professor, City University of New York, John Jay College of Criminal Justice and author or editor of seven books including, most recently, the graphic novel, *Light in Dark Times: The Human Search for Meaning* (University of Toronto Press, 2020), illustrated by Charlotte Corden. A Fellow of the Swedish Collegium for Advanced Studies (SCAS) in the Programmes in Transnational Processes, Structural Violence, and Inequality, Professor Waterston served as President of the American Anthropological Association in 2015–17. She is author of the award-winning *My Father's Wars: Migration, Memory, and the Violence of a Century* (Routledge, 2014), of 'Intimate Ethnography and the Anthropological Imagination' (*American Ethnologist*, 2019) and is editor of the Berghahn Books series on Intimate Ethnography. Recent publications include 'Imagining World Solidarities for a Livable Future' (*kritisk etnografi – Swedish Journal of Anthropology*, 2020), the short story, 'Interiors' (*Anthropology Now*, 2020) and 'Just Imagine' in *philoSOPHIA: A Journal of transcontinental Feminism* (2022).

Charlotte Corden is an illustrator and fine artist whose work centres around what it is to be human. She is fascinated with the power of hand-drawn images and how they can be used to reveal and describe complex truths. As anthropologist and illustrator, she regularly illustrates for

Anthropology News, and has worked as a consultant and live sketch-noter for Stripe Partners, the British Cabinet Office, and the National Health Service, UK. As a fine artist, she has studied drawing and painting at the London Fine Art Studios and the Arts Students League, NY. Her main publication, *Light in Dark Times*, was published by University of Toronto Press in November 2020.

References

American Anthropological Association (AAA). 2017. Guidelines for Tenure and Promotion Review: Communicating Public Scholarship in Anthropology. Retrieved 23 June 2021. http://s3.amazonaws.com/rdcms-aaa/files/production/public/AAApercent20Guidelinespercent20TPpercent20 Communicatingpercent20Formspercent20ofpercent20Publicpercent20Anthropology.pdf.

Farmer, Paul. 2011. 'How We Can Save Millions of Lives', *Washington Post*, 17 November 2011. Retrieved 12 August 2018 from: https://www.washingtonpost.com/opinions/how-we-can-save-millions-of-lives/2011/11/11/gIQAf1rBWN_story.html.

Fassin, Didier. 2008. 'Beyond Good and Evil? Questioning the Anthropological Discomfort with Morals', *Anthropological Theory* 8(4): 333–44.

——. 2015. 'The Public Afterlife of Ethnography', *American Ethnologist* 42(4): 592–609.

Food and Agriculture Organization of the United Nations (FAO), IFAD, UNICEF, WFP and WHO. 2022. 'The State of Food Security and Nutrition in the World 2022. Repurposing Food and Agricultural Policies to Make Healthy Diets More Affordable'. Rome: FAO. Retrieved 22 August 2022. https://doi.org/10.4060/cc0639en.

Hamdy, Sherine and Coleman Nye. 2017. *Lissa: A Story about Medical Promise, Friendship, and Revolution*. Toronto: University of Toronto Press.

Hannerz, Ulf. 2016. 'Writing Otherwise', in *The Anthropologist as Writer: Genres and Contexts in the Twenty-First Century*, Helena Wulff (ed.). New York: Berghahn Books, pp. 254–70.

Jain, Lochlann. 2019. *Things that Art: A Graphic Menagerie of Enchanting Curiosity*. Toronto: University of Toronto Press.

Johns Hopkins University & Medicine. 2022. Coronavirus Resource Center. Retrieved 22 August 2022 from: https://coronavirus.jhu.edu/.

Kirsch, Stuart. 2018. *Engaged Anthropology: Politics Beyond the Text*. Berkeley: University of California Press.

Magee, Siobhan. 2019. 'Drawing the Adult Child: US Graphic Memoir and the Anthropologies of Kinship and Personhood', *Anthropology and Humanism* 44(1): 88–111.

Mascia-Lees, Frances E., Patricia Sharpe and Colleen Ballerino Cohen. 1989. 'The Postmodernist Turn in Anthropology: Cautions from a Feminist Perspective', *Signs* 15(1) (Autumn): 7–33.

Nordstrom, Carolyn. 2011. 'The Bard', in *Anthropology off the Shelf: Anthropologists on Writing*, Alisse Waterston and Maria D. Vesperi (eds). Malden, MA: Wiley-Blackwell, 35–45.

Sousanis, Nick. 2015. *Unflattening*. Cambridge, MA: Harvard University Press.

Ulysse, Gina Athena. 2013. 'Untapped Fierceness: My Giant Leaps'. TEDx University of Michigan. Retrieved 8 December 2019 from https://www.youtube.com/watch?v=xHhngXU8Zw4.

———. 2017. *Because When God is Too Busy: Haiti, me & THE WORLD*. Middletown, CT: Wesleyan University Press.

UNHCR, the UN Refugee Agency. 2022. 'Global Trends: Forced Displacement in 2021'. Copenhagen: United Nations High Commissioner for Refugees. Retrieved 22 August 2022. https://www.unhcr.org/62a9d1494/global-trends-report-2021.

Vine, David. 2020a. 'The Costs of War'. Investigative Reporting Workshop. 8 September. Retrieved 23 June 2021. https://investigativereportingworkshop.org/investigation/the-costs-of-war/.

———. 2020b. *The United States of War: A Global History of America's Endless Conflicts, from Columbus to the Islamic State*. Berkeley: University of California Press.

von der Lehr, Natalie. 2020. 'In Search of Light in Dark Times'. SCAS Talks, Episode 5 (22 October). Retrieved from https://scastalks.podbean.com/e/scas-talks-episode-5-percente2 percent80 percent93-alisse-waterston-in-search-of-light-in-dark-times-recorded-22-oct-2020/.

Warren, Kay B. 2006. 'Perils and Promises of Engaged Anthropology: Historical Transitions and Ethnographic Dilemmas', in *Engaged Observer: Anthropology, Advocacy, and Activism*, Victoria Sanford and Asale Angel-Ajani (eds). New Brunswick: Rutgers University Press, pp. 213–27.

Waterston, Alisse. 2018. 'Four Stories, a Lament, and an Affirmation', *American Anthropologist* 120(2): 258–65.

———. 2019. 'Intimate Ethnography and the Anthropological Imagination: Dialectical Aspects of the Personal and Political in *My Father's Wars*', *American Ethnologist* 46(1): 7–19.

Waterston, Alisse and Charlotte Corden. 2020. *Light in Dark Times: The Human Search for Meaning*. Toronto: University of Toronto Press.

———. 2021. 'Making *Light in Dark Times*', *Anthropology News* July/August 62(3).

Woolf, Virginia. 1985. *Moments of Being*. Edited by Jeanne Schulkind. New York: A Harvest Book, Harcourt, Inc.

Wulff, Helena. 2021. 'Writing Anthropology', in *The Cambridge Encyclopedia of Anthropology*, Felix Stein, Sian Lazar, Matt Candea, Hildegard Diemberger, Joel Robbins, Andrew Sanchez and Rupert Stasch (eds). Retrieved 17 June 2021. https://doi.org/10.29164/21writing.

Chapter 4

Exceptional Experiences in Academic Life

Moshe Shokeid

The promoters of the Lisbon panel and editors of this volume have cited my 1992 article – 'Exceptional Experiences in Everyday Life' – as trigger for their project. Naturally, I consider that auspicious fortuity as presenting an exceptional experience in my professional record. I admit, I do not remember the circumstances that triggered the 1992 article. I was at that time deeply engaged in the New York gay synagogue research (1995/2003). That impromptu paper was composed in contrariety to my early and more recent type of ethnographic assignments, which were conducted during a long period in a bounded field-site – a village, an urban neighbourhood, an institution. The introduction explained, 'I wish to comprehend a type of ethnographic experience – though a personal and apparently unstructured phenomenon – which I believe has not yet been considered as a field for anthropological research' (1992a: 232). That unusual 'shapeless' field-site related to my encounter with some unanticipated and 'extraordinary' incidents recorded in my life history. I defined these incidents as 'typically having an arbitrary beginning and ending out of the stream of chronological temporality. Although these events usually lack any relationship to major passages in our life cycle, they leave strong marks on the map of our life experiences' (ibid.: 234).

Searching for an analytical framework to integrate those arbitrary events, I explored the anthropological and sociological literature dealing with different types of personal and collective experiences. Dewey (1934), Freud (1958), Simmel (1959), Jaeger and Selznick (1964), Abrahams (1986), Turner and Bruner (1986) and others have dealt with the persistence and meaning of 'experience' in human life. The individual's engagement as an active or passive, culturally oriented participant in either a personally initiated behaviour or in a collectively organized action carries important social-cultural significance. The sort of events I chronicled in that paper, in spite of their apparent triviality, nevertheless (I claimed) remain stuck in memory as symbolic insignia of our individual destinies.

The list of these extraordinary experiences included a category of 'uncanny reunions and incidents', such as: on a tourist visit to the Portuguese Synagogue in Amsterdam on The Day of Atonement, I met Professor Eisenstadt, the authoritative leader of Israeli sociology. Or, on a first visit to a gay bar in New York, I was approached by a stranger who turned out to be an anthropologist familiar with my work. These unrelated events shattered the anonymity of one's existence in the world: 'The big wide world had shrunk to the size of another street in the Israeli "village" I thought I left behind' (ibid.: 237).

Another category, 'on the threshold of chaos', included youthful traumatic events, such as being accused by an aging, pompous high-school literature teacher of 'corrupting' his favourite fourteen-year-old female student. Or, discovering I was being enrolled by a clever missionary into a Buddhist religious cult, lacking any information about its true mission and activities. My personal integrity, both as a boy and as an adult, has been occasionally in serious jeopardy.

In my conclusion of the 'indeterminate' element in social life, I returned to Turner's focus on the processes of mid-transition and the liminal period in the rites of passage. Turner was looking for the grand, staged dramas of social life: 'These paradoxically expose the basic building blocks of culture just when we pass out and before we re-enter the structural realm' (1967: 110). However, I suggested that the battle for life in culture eventuates no less in the mini-dramas of everyday life, as we repeatedly stumble and climb back on the path ordained by society.

The Ethnographic Present

No doubt, the anthropological arena of methods, field-sites and theories, have changed dramatically since my 1992 article has entered the anthropological archives. That transformed reality is clearly demonstrated in many of the contributions to the present collection of exceptional 'anthropological' experiences. Not only anthropology has changed, but no less the world of academic institutions has been altered, and the humanist forms of knowledge in particular. I avoid expanding on the fluctuating world socio-political-economic-ideological circumstances, as well as introducing the leading academic figures who affected these prime conversions, and those who commented on them. These have been thoroughly deliberated in the editors' introductory chapter in particular.

The following testimonies of exceptional experiences narrow the arena of sites and subjects to one major domain of social/professional life – the 'academy' – and include confronting professional interlocutors, the ethnographer's comportment conducting research, responding to fieldwork, and chronicling actualities. I focus the presentation with a list of incidents of unexpected encounters with colleagues (mostly anthropologists), as well as other impromptu circumstances engaging the anthropologist in the public forum, revealing sensitive episodes conducting fieldwork research or generating ethnographic publications. However, current modes of anthropological theory and research offer us supporting tools of analysis and exposition of our unusual ethnographic evidence; 'public ethnography' and the 'ethnographic present' in particular.

As suggested by Fassin (2018: 7–8), public ethnography produces unique effects compared with other modes of apprehending social worlds; the presence of the ethnographers in the field attests to the veracity of their account of facts and events; the researcher and author's personal involvement with the work and people who inhabit it calls for a critical take on the deceptive transparency of what is related and offers an effect of realism – a descriptive narration that generates more concrete and lively knowledge than other rhetorical forms do. In conclusion, Fassin claims, 'What is at stake in the project of public ethnography is the sort of truth that is produced, established, and, in the end, told' (ibid.: 8). The present exposition might suit the textual construction and the advocated agenda of public ethnography. And last, the experiences presented in this text are not bounded by a time space of major events that triggered its recording. It includes long and short occurrences I engaged in during an academic career, as a researcher, writer and commentator. That mode of presentation reflects the terms of the 'ethnographic present' (Sanjek 2013); expanding the provisions of the 'normative' fieldwork endeavour.

Essentially, the academic role represents a major facet of one's sense of performance and achievement in the world, often also the source of existential anxieties. Our discourse will try to comprehend the impact of these mini-dramas on the processes of cultural creativity and self-assurance of both the young 'novice' and the mature professional.

Uncanny Encounters with Professional Colleagues

The Van Teeffelen/Diamond–Shokeid Encounter

During my first sabbatical leave in Amsterdam (1975–76) I was approached by T. Van Teeffelen, an MA student at the University of Amsterdam, wanting to interview me about Israeli anthropology. I spent a few hours introducing him to the history and the list of ethnographers who conducted research in Israel, among them some Manchester graduates, studying both Jewish and Israeli Arab communities. He was considerate enough to send me his MA dissertation about Israeli anthropology (1977), and later I came across an article he published in *Dialectical Anthropology* (1978, reprinted in 1980), based apparently on that interview and other information I provided as well as a short visit to Israel. I was stunned to read, among the conclusions in the first manuscript, that Israeli anthropologists, mostly Jews, have been committed to Zionist goals and values, an orientation manifested in their conformity to the 'romantic' anthropological tradition. Thus, for example, their books presenting Jewish communities carried romantic titles, while in contrast, Jewish anthropologists' studies of Israeli Arabs have been remarkably different: with them, 'there is no dramatic description of people struggling on their path to a more satisfactory world' (1978: 11). But most disturbing was his omission of major ethnographies conducted by Israeli anthropologists in Arab communities (published in Hebrew and English). Moreover, they all studied similar societal issues (inter-communal conflicts, adjustment to new social-economic-political circumstances, etc.) and revealed a similar 'romantic' anthropological tradition in their narratives and titles.

In his *Dialectical Anthropology* article, Van Teeffelen expanded his thesis. He described Israeli anthropologists' work as representing the Manchester School 'colonialist' tradition of research in Africa, a wider ethnographic context that imagined an evil academic gang within the arena of British anthropology. No doubt, a few among the founders of Israeli anthropology were indeed associated with the Manchester School, and its leader Max Gluckman had an important role in their professional careers. But the Manchester School's work and ethnographies conducted in Africa and elsewhere had no different agenda, in theory or practice, than other British schools of anthropology. The Manchester School's claim to fame was mostly related to its fieldwork methods, the 'extended case' or 'situational analysis' (e.g. Van Velsen 1967). It seemed to me beyond doubt that Van Teeffelen had adapted his 'findings' to a theoretical-political agenda that expressed his own convictions about the ongoing conflict in the Holy Land. This position represented a prevalent mood encountered during my stay in Amsterdam: Dutch university students revolted against the hierarchical structure of university life and lent their support to the disadvantaged and oppressed in Vietnam, the Middle East and elsewhere.

I felt I had to respond to Van Teeffelen's indictment of Israeli and Manchester anthropology. I approached Stanley Diamond, the editor of *Dialectical Anthropology*, offering to write a comment on Van Teeffelen's article. I was pleased to receive from his editorial assistant the following invitation: 'Rather than merely writing a "critique", we would like to encourage you to address yourself to the issue of whether or not Van Teeffelen's interpretations and goals relate to anthropology and anthropologists in Israel'. In May 1982, the manuscript I had prepared (titled 'Modern Armchair Anthropology') was formally accepted for publication. Two years later, in June 1984, I wrote to the editor inquiring about the delay in its publication but got no reply. I wrote again a few months later, and at last, in February 1985, I received a letter from Diamond informing me that, on reading the manuscript more carefully, it was decided not to publish it on two grounds: 1) 'We do not publish debates', 2) 'Disagreement with your position was sufficient for us not to publish your paper'.

In a short reply, I told the honourable editor that his belated realization the paper was unsuitable for his journal – three years after having accepted it for publication – was uncivil, unethical and in contradiction to the alleged spirit of critical anthropology. This time, for a change, I received a quick response, though not an apology. An angry letter included this final sentence: 'I consider it a minor slip, and heavily unbalanced by the success of our more or less acephalous operation'. I was also lectured about the nature of the journal, which is dedicated to 'radical and critical thought with reference to the human condition'. I was advised to submit another paper about Israeli anthropology, addressing 'its function with reference to Zionism, its position to the Arabs within and outside of Israel, its attitude towards cultural evolution, and hopefully in the level of the article by Van Teeffelen'. I never contacted the journal inquiring whether the promotion of 'radical and critical thought' had any reference to the reality of facts on the ground and truthful reporting.

No doubt, both the Dutch student and the renowned American don have bluntly revealed their ideological-political inclinations. To this day I am astounded by Diamond's arrogant and pompous comportment. I am grateful to Eric Wolf, a member of the *Dialectical Anthropology* editorial board, who on discovering the story apologized to me in a personal letter, referring to Diamond's erratic behaviour: 'You are probably aware that Stanley runs the journal very much as his personal preserve and mouthpiece … and seems to be in an unusually autocratic and uncooperative phase'. He offered to support publishing my article (with minor changes in the initial page) at the *American Ethnologist* or with *Theory and Society*. I was too dismayed and upset to take up his kind offer at that time. The full account of the Van Teeffelen/Diamond–Shokeid confrontation, representing a 'situational analysis' in terms of the Manchester School's methodology, was reported a few years later in *Israel Social Science Research* (1988/89).

The Swedenburg–Shokeid Encounter

About ten years later I was involved in another conflict of ethics in ethnographic work. It started when I came across an article in *Cultural Anthropology* by Ted Swedenburg: 'Occupational Hazards: Palestinian Ethnography' (1989). Swedenburg's project concerned the memories of elderly Palestinian villagers about an insurgency that took place under British rule between 1936 and 1939. The revolt became a watershed in the relationship between Arabs and Jews in Palestine. Although the revolt was directed against British Imperial rule, Jews and their property were a major target of attack.

As reported in the article, Swedenburg experienced a major problem during fieldwork: the reluctance of those interviewed to reveal details of their participation during the revolt. However, there was no secret about their involvement in actions of violence against their Jewish neighbours, as clearly stated by the anthropologist:

> My study of these memories of revolt, related to an unstable present [under Israeli occupation of the West Bank], has required an effort on my part to unlearn academic training in anthropology and history that compels one to unveil objective truth ... This truth lies in an unequal relation of power, between occupier and occupied, between researcher and subject ... I feel compelled to participate in these veilings ... Such a narrative will necessarily be based on partial truths and strategic exclusions. (1989: 270)

Swedenburg also served as an advocate of the lower classes of Palestinian society, arguing against the myth of the revolt as established by the educated Palestinian urban strata.

Swedenburg's thesis, though based on 'traditional' fieldwork engagement, nevertheless reminded me of Van Teeffelen's report, oriented as it was by the researcher's personal and ideological commitment to his subjects. Moreover, Swedenburg admitted he resisted feeling compelled to 'unveil objective truth'! I felt 'compelled' to respond to his far more complex product of ethnographic reporting on a field close to my home. Fred Myers, editor of *Cultural Anthropology*, was pleased to publish my critique, which raised the question (also relating to Van Teffeelen's case): 'Are personal convictions of the committed and often egocentric anthropologist sufficient for his colleagues or advisors to condone "facts", in the anthropological corpus as well as in the field, whose "truth" is ideologically tailored? Are anthropologists entitled to rewrite the myths or correct the rituals of the societies they study?' (1992b: 473).

In any case, I was careful in my critique to avoid any slighting remarks about Swedenburg's personal comportment, framing my argument and comparisons in terms of the sociology of knowledge. However, some time before publication, the editor asked if I would mind sharing my response with Swedenburg for his comments. Naturally, I gave permission to allow for further communication on the subject. But, on receiving the issue that included both interlocutors' critical texts, I was flabbergasted to discover Swedenburg's 'commentary' almost twice the length of my text (twenty versus thirteen pages) and extremely offensive in portraying my persona as ethnographer and citizen. I confess, I could never endure reading more than half of that venomous piece, which included misuse of personal information he received through a mutual acquaintance who had approached me professing some private interest.

Aware of my dismay, the editor, Fred Myers, responded in a letter (7 January 1993):

> Two things I should tell you: 1) People have responded very positively to that issue of the journal, and therefore the exchange has been productive. 2) Swedenburg's reply is so gratuitously hostile and extreme that it gives a good deal of weight to your implicit claim that there is something more than meets the eye with his 'commitment' ... In the end, what he wrote was not entirely uninteresting in its right, but he clearly illuminates what you objected to.

I assume that unusual encounter gave the *Cultural Anthropology* issue of November 1992 the colourful tone of a street quarrel scene, but it left me with a nauseating notion of déjà vu. Once again, my review of a problematic ethnographic report was treated in terms that violated the ethics and civility of academic comportment. Indeed, I was allowed to express my critical viewpoint, but at the price of an offensive attack on my work and persona conveyed on the pages of a reputable journal. Since then, I concluded, I will never voluntarily take part in an academic discourse engaging participants committed ideologically to their subject of interest, and the Israeli–Palestinian conflict in particular – a position I adhered to in the following case.

Daniel Segal–Shokeid Encounter

An unexpected experience awaited me when I was invited to present the Distinguished Lecture in Anthropology at Pomona College (February 2012). The lecture, as advertised, would address some methodological issues related to my work among gay people in New York. I was generously hosted, visited classes, and met with students. However, on the morning of the scheduled presentation, I was forwarded an email from Professor Daniel Segal of Pitzer College, addressed to the faculty of the seven colleges at the Claremont consortium. It informed his colleagues that he would not attend the guest's lecture, although he 'admired and have taught Shokeid's ethnography "A Gay Synagogue in New York"'. However, he claimed, my work on Israelis and Palestinians 'participates in a Zionist degradation and marginalization of Palestinians. He is speaking at Pomona at a moment when the State of Israel, under its extremist-right regime, is daily violating the human rights of our Palestinian sisters and brothers'. And the last sentence: 'Put simply: Professor Shokeid's representations of Palestinians are antithetical to what I believe – as an anthropologist, as a Jew, and as a person who seeks to live an ethical life in a complex and compromised world'.

I was astounded at that pompous and vile accusation raised by a 'good fellow Jew' (whom I had never met or communicated with before). When pressed by the Pomona Dean to substantiate his accusation, Segal referred to my early work on the preservation of the code of honour among Israeli Arabs (Shokeid and Deshen 1982), apparently assuming it reflected a Zionist-colonialist orientation on my part. Had he read any passage of that material, he would have seen its sympathetic symbolic implication. Indeed, has any past or present-day anthropologist working among Arab-Muslim people ignored the socio-political impact of their code of honour?

In any case, reminded of my past encounters with politically-ideologically committed anthropologists, I declined the suggestion of my Pomona colleagues to respond to Segal's accusations, to avoid a further display of academic self-righteousness. However, during the 2014 American Anthropological Association (AAA) meeting in Washington, Daniel Segal participated in a crowded BDS (Boycott, Divestments, Sanctions) panel. The official position claimed that the proposed boycott of Israeli academia was not aimed against individual professionals but was rather targeting Israeli institutions. Following the panel presentations, I took the opportunity to comment that I had already been personally boycotted by the honourable panel member. With no hesitation, Segal responded he had not stopped me from presenting my lecture.

It is impossible to know, of course, how many recipients of Segal's communique had therefore avoided my lecture, but the Pomona experience left a nauseous feeling about that sort of anthropological morality.

Munira Khayyat–Shokeid Flight Episode

On my way home from the AAA 2019 meeting in Vancouver, I boarded a flight going through Frankfurt. I had reserved an aisle seat in a front section, but next to me was seated a heavy-built man in a thick woollen sweater whose body was pressing against my shoulder, as he talked with a companion in (I gathered) an Eastern European language. Just before take-off, I asked a flight attendant if there was another vacant seat on board the plane that seemed fully packed. To my relief there was a nearby seat that was empty, between a man busy with his computer and a youngish woman who seemed disappointed at losing the comfort of a free seat beside her, in the densely seated tourist compartment.

I apologized to her for the inconvenience, pointing at the seat I had escaped from. To my surprise, I discovered we had both participated in the AAA meeting. When my neighbour revealed that she came from the American University in Cairo and was originally from Beirut, I was somewhat cautious about informing her of my own national identity. I was pleasantly surprised by her friendly response and her flattering appreciation of my work, given that Israel had invaded Lebanon and for many years occupied its southern part. For the rest of the flight, we were sharing personal and professional experiences. I discovered a young, ambitious, dynamic colleague who carried out research among villagers close to the Israeli border. Her subjects experienced the grave consequences of the enduring conflict, as the Israeli army retaliated to Hezbollah attacks on Israeli border settlements. Dr Munira Khayyat had earned degrees at leading American universities and had spent a year as a member of the Princeton Institute for Advanced Study (an institute familiar to me). We exchanged addresses and parted almost as old friends, as she invited me to visit her in Cairo – though I was unable to offer a similar invitation to Tel Aviv to someone holding a Lebanese passport.

During our flight conversation, I had told Munira about the forthcoming EASA (European Association of Social Anthropologists) Lisbon panel on 'exceptional experiences', and she responded warmly to my first email message:

> Dearest Moshe, it was indeed an exceptional experience, indeed! So very lovely to meet you and to talk about so many things of common interest.

You are a wonderful soul and an exceptional scholar who I am blessed by the twist of fate and an uncomfortable arrangement to have met. I very much look forward to seeing you in Lisbon. You are always welcome to visit me in Cairo.

In a later communication, I told Munira about my paper for the Lisbon panel and asked permission to mention her name and quote from her messages. I again received a warm response, allowing me the free use of our correspondence and expressing her wish to attend the Lisbon event.

For my part, I was overwhelmed by the fortunate circumstance that brought me together with a talented, generous, exceptional younger academic colleague, who was able to bridge the hostile borders of religion, nationality, and a continued armed conflict that separated us, as citizens of belligerent neighbouring nations. The first three cases in our presentation were all coloured by a declared or hidden sentiment, objecting to my work on the assumption that Israeli credentials tainted the legitimacy of a witness. I happily include this uniquely amicable collegial encounter among the exceptional experiences in my academic life.

In conclusion, disagreeable encounters are commonly experienced in the 'routine' daily life of academia. Many may agree with Henry Kissinger's claim: 'The reason that academic politics are so vicious is because the stakes are so low'. I have not met any happy sociology and anthropology departments, in Israel or elsewhere during visits abroad. Upsetting emotions are often the reflection of tensions related to appointments and promotions, of being taken advantage of by senior colleagues, and of disrespect of others' work, personal grudges, peculiar sympathies and antipathies. The incidents I describe here, however, relate to encounters between unacquainted professionals – cases of puzzling academic communication that, for better or worse, revolve around debated matters of ideology, ethnographic presentation, professional ethics and civil comportment.

However, a 'neutral' reader, unrelated to the tribe of anthropologists, may challenge my annoyed reaction and notion of personal degradation displayed in the above first three encounters, representing a member of the powerful partner in the Israeli–Palestinian conflict. Considering the ideological stance of my 'objectionable' interlocutors, one is reminded of Edward Said's (1996) description of the intellectual, the marginal man who tries to speak truth to power, who has to choose to support the weak over the powerful, and who is always challenged by the problem of primordial loyalties to the protestor's own community, nationality and religion. Thus, my antagonistic debaters may view their critical stance as exemplifying an 'out of the academic closet' noteworthy reaction against the university guise of political neutrality (e.g. Kaufman 1968; Thompson 1970; Bellamy 1997). Whatever my personal political position considering the ongoing conflict (Shokeid 2020), I share in their eyes the Israeli citizens' moral responsibility for the continuing occupation of Palestinian land and people. Nevertheless, in response to that valid quandary, I relate to Fassin's claim (2018: 8) cited above about the mission of public ethnography: 'What is at stake … is the sort of truth that is produced, established, and, in the end, told.'

Uncanny Encounters Exposing the Anthropologist in the Public Forum

Rabbi Meir Kahane's Funeral Event

An intriguing twist of circumstances caught me in an unexpected encounter during my research of the gay synagogue in New York. In the company of a leading congregant, I visited Brooklyn – home to various Jewish orthodox communities – in search of an expert to confirm the authenticity of a Torah scroll that had been donated to the synagogue. Unaware of the events taking place on that day (6 November 1990), we soon encountered an enormous crowd of mourners departing from the funeral of Rabbi Meir Kahane, founder of the Jewish Defense League in the US as well as the ultra-nationalistic Israeli party Kach, who had been banned as a racist by the Israeli parliament and who had been assassinated in exile in Manhattan. As we left a lunch counter, we noticed a group of men heatedly discussing the story with a reporter who was asking about the deceased and his accomplishments. Curious about the commotion, we lingered outside the dense circle of men, hearing words of praise and sorrow being expressed all around us. Suddenly the reporter turned to me (no doubt looking different from the mostly Orthodox crowd) and inquired about my identity and my reaction to the tragic event. A colleague told me the next day that he had learned of my presence in New York by reading a report in the New York Times (7 November 1990) that included the 'interview'. The article, by Ari. L. Goldman, titled 'Grief and Anger at Kahane's Funeral', closed with this paragraph:

> In front of a kosher pizza parlor, however, one visitor from Israel had a different sentiment. 'I don't think Kahane had something good to bring to the world', said Moshe Shokeid, an anthropologist from Tel Aviv who is spending a sabbatical in the United States. 'Kahane planted hatred in Israel. I will shed no tears'.

Unexpectedly, my academic identity and nationality was utilized by the reporter to magnify the significance of a commentator who, in contrast to the sorrow and anger engulfing the other participants, expressed an unsympathetic 'Leftist' position. Indeed, Rabbi Kahane represented the most extremist right-wing position in Israeli politics, supporting transfer of Palestinian residents and other measures leading to an apartheid regime. Had I known that my words at this impromptu street gathering would end up in print, I might have been more careful in my manner of speech. However, I do not regret this authentic expression of my feelings about the virulent teaching and harmful public impact of the deceased pundit and politician. Unprepared and totally unintentionally, I performed and was recorded acting in the context and perspective of 'public ethnography', and, as cited before: 'What is at stake … is the sort of truth that is produced, established, and, in the end, told' (Fassin 2018: 8).

Uncanny Incidents in the Construction of Ethnographic Reports

Close Informant's Secret Life

I have already reported in detail on the following event, reflecting on a mood of anxiety but also of great relief (2015: 29–46). 'Jeff', a man in his late forties whom I had met at the gay synagogue in New York about twenty years earlier, was one of my closest informants (1995/2003). Assuming the role of a dedicated guide, he taught me about the inner life of gay men and their popular sex venues. My relationship with Jeff was cemented years ago when he invited me to observe a monthly meeting of the Golden Shower Association, a group of gay men who shared erotic experiences together. It was a sign he considered me an intimate friend from whom he had no need to hide his most private sexual preferences. During the many years of our continued friendship, Jeff told me numerous details about his life: childhood, parents, employment, past boyfriends, and the continuing search for love and sex. He was acquainted with my writing and we had many a good laugh about the name I had invented for him, Jeffrey, as presented in my texts. This was one of our shared secrets.

In June 2008, I arrived back in New York for a few days' stay to participate in a professional meeting at New York University. I called Jeff and suggested that we meet. Jeff responded enthusiastically; he told me he planned to combine that visit with some other engagements he had in town. I willingly agreed to his request to stay over one night at the apartment I was renting in Chelsea. Jeff showed up in the late afternoon, and we enjoyed dinner at a nearby Italian restaurant. He told me about his recent affairs, starting a new job, getting involved in a new promising romantic relationship, and so on. However, by around 5:30 a.m. the next day, Jeff was awake with acute stomach or kidney pains. I realized he needed to go immediately to a hospital. I helped him get dressed, stopped a cab, and we headed to the nearby St Vincent's Hospital.

I stood next to Jeff as he provided the information needed for registration. As he was listing his past treatments and medications, he extracted from his bag a large container of pills. Suddenly, he raised his eyes towards me and said, 'You're not going to like this'. He continued with his medical report: 'I am HIV-positive'.

I was in no way uncomfortable at having been in close social contact with a man infected with the dreadful virus. Nor was I worried that the paramedic taking notes of Jeff's medical history might have assumed I was the cheated partner in a gay relationship. But I did feel betrayed at not being informed, by a friend I believed had shared his secrets with me. I refrained from any verbal comment and busied myself observing the doings of the crowded and hectic emergency room. After finishing my session at NYU a few hours later, I called Jeff. He was on the bus going home to New Jersey, having been treated for pain and discharged. When I called him a few weeks later from Tel Aviv, he told me the details of his infection, tracing it back to the late 1990s. I did not bring up his lack of disclosure about that misfortune, deferring the topic to a future occasion. I came to believe anthropologists sometimes develop a distorted perception of reality – assuming that their close informants are uniquely open to them, with no untold stories intentionally hidden.

A few months later (in November of the same year), I spent a few days in New York en route to the AAA meeting in San Francisco. I called Jeff and made plans to meet him for dinner on my last evening in New York. I wanted to find a way to access the untold story, which had left me wary of a relationship I considered so close and trusting. Jeff arrived at my place in the company of his boyfriend, and, as soon as they had seated themselves on the sofa, he announced, 'You see here two survivors!' In that cosy atmosphere I decided to ask Jeff directly why he had kept his HIV diagnosis a secret from me. It turned out he had also kept his health status secret from his boyfriend for a few months, afraid he might lose a man he loved more than anyone in the previous twenty years, as gay men normally keep that information secret even from one another. He had been 'afraid', he said, that I would stay away from him after learning his medical condition: 'I thought, here is my friend, an anthropologist who writes about the life of gay men. I should have told him about the suffering I go through and that of many others'. But he could not bring himself to risk losing the relationship – which seemed inevitable, in view of his observations of the frightened and brutal reactions of many gay men.

On my part, however, remained a troublesome question: Does this impromptu 'happy ending' to the story diminish my own uncertainty about the accuracy of ethnographic reports? More generally, how much do deception and naïve assumptions about the truth of our informants' reports enter into our scientific writings? That case formed an exceptional experience in my professional career, displaying the complexities of ethnographic work.

Close Informant's Loss of Faith

In the mid-1990s, I extended my field of interest to the Gay Community Services Center in New York City's West Village. The diverse cohort of voluntary associations meeting at the Center included Sexual Compulsive Anonymous (SCA), with a large membership of men and women (2015: 63–88). I regularly attended the weekly meetings of a few SCA groups. These meetings are open to everyone, and the discussions are presumed to be confidential. Though I never concealed my professional identity, I did not publicly announce my research interests. Many of the male participants described painful experiences they suffered, visiting various 'oases' of anonymous sex. Never satisfied sexually and emotionally, they felt they could not stop going back to these sites, which by their account seemed to ruin their lives.

One participant at these meetings was especially friendly to me: a sociologist in his mid-forties, who taught at a New Jersey college. Believing that our mutual sympathy reflected a professional kinship, I assumed he was acquainted with my gay synagogue ethnography. To my great surprise, however, it took him a few months to comprehend that I was conducting research. At a meeting one day, as I inquired about a particular issue, he burst out in a tone of dismay: 'Are you doing research?' When I responded matter-of-factly that I was, he reacted with words I cannot forget: 'I feel violated'. I guessed that he was so offended because the revelation of my professional interest had shattered the notion of a shared struggle that sustained our relationship. He must have assumed that I experienced the same existential predicament that seemed to wreck his life. I was shocked and deeply moved by this expression of a painful experience, and I never went back to meetings of that group or other SCA gatherings.

That unexpected manifestation of anguish and rage undermined my confidence in the ethics of my ethnographic practice and relationships. I considered a possibly heretical quandary: had not anthropologists, all along, employed an ethically flawed method? The 'natives' in most conventional field-sites, even if they welcomed the foreign anthropologist, rarely had any clear idea of the anthropologist's craft or forthcoming writings. Never before was I confronted with the challenge of my 'right' to explore and share (though anonymously) the social and personal way of life of one of my 'subjects'.

A Christian Saint on the Art-Cover of a Gay Life Ethnography

I would usually confirm the art-covers for my ethnographies as suggested by the publishers. In 2014, when I was spending a few months as a fellow at the Vienna Institute of Cultural Studies (IFK), the editor at PENN Press asked for my suggestions regarding the book jacket art for the forthcoming *Gay Voluntary Associations in New York* (2015). My stay in Vienna included art exploration during my free hours, enjoying the wealth of music, museums and architectural sites, among the finest in Europe. Thus, the next weekend, I spent many hours at the Kunsthistorisches Museum, roaming the familiar large rooms packed with paintings from top to bottom in densely cramped rows – art by old masters, amassed during the long reign of the Austrian monarchs and nobility. In a narrow side-room, I was intrigued by a painting of four adult men of different ages, one of them half naked, and a boy who watched them from a lower position. The scene seemed to show a friendly group engaged in a lively discussion, with the half-naked macho-looking guy taking the lead role. The image of a company of men engrossed in deep communication reminded me of the many hours spent in New York, observing not only the meetings of various gay voluntary associations whose often feverish, intimate exchanges performed as support groups, but also the moving sermons delivered in a variety of LGBT religious congregations.

Peering at the painting's title, I was stunned to read: *The Sermon of St. John the Baptist* by Bernardo Strozzi (among the great Baroque masters), dated 1644. St John, among the most revered personae in Christian mythology, appeared in Strozzi's portrayal as a kind of macho hunter, almost a gay depiction. I could identify, in particular, with the young boy listening to the older men, playing the role of the anthropologist and anxious to comprehend the men's discourse. The few lines in the museum catalogue outlining the life and work of the artist convinced me he was 'intended' for my book. A member of the Capuchin monastery in Genoa, Strozzi had fled to Venice in 1630, escaped his duties as clergyman, and under papal permission was granted the privilege of leading a secular life in the more liberal city of Venice. One wondered, was he gay?

To my great satisfaction, the PENN editor was impressed by my apparently bizarre choice of an Italian old master's 'religious' painting, and he sent me the graphic designer's sketch proposal that added New York's Hudson River, with the city's skyline in the background. I imagined it would be difficult to receive permission to transplant the image of a leading New Testament figure onto the cover of a book dealing with a subject taboo in Christian theology, especially with the sly addition of the New York landscape. But fortunately, the publisher's personnel gave permission to go ahead with the 'updated' Strozzi painting (figure 4.1).

Never before had I felt that the art-cover was an essential part of the ethnographic text. This time, however, it seemed to represent the spirit of the ethnography's social agenda. I was gratified when Jeffrey Ehrenreich, editor of *Anthropology and Humanism*, after seeing the book cover, during the AAA annual meeting book exhibit, adopted it for the cover of AH's June 2016 issue. That issue also included an article (pp. 39–43) telling the story of the seventeenth-century maverick painter, and a bio of the ethnographer who integrated the painter's creation into his report on LGBT New York. Actually, I cannot think about that anthropological endeavour without seeing the Strozzi figures as part of the ongoing mini-dramas narrated in the text.

Introducing the last three 'exceptional' experiences that took place during and after the phase of fieldwork, as well as in the final moment of exposing the ethnographic text (recruiting an old master's creative art as partner to the ethnographic project), not bounded by the time space or context that triggered its recording, seems to reflect a current growing

Figure 4.1. Book cover of *Gay Voluntary Associations in New York*. © Reprinted with permission of the University of Pennsylvania Press. Moshe Shokeid. Front cover. 26 October 2022.

trend of ethnographic freedom advocated in terms of the 'ethnographic present' (Sanjek 2013) – expanding the provisions of the 'normative' fieldwork endeavour.

Indeterminate in Academic Life

Concluding our saga of exceptional experiences in the arena of academic-professional life, I return to our introduction, and to Victor Turner, who enriched anthropologists' analytical conceptions and their comprehension of social life – both as collectives and as individuals. In particular, the exposition of 'liminality' and its impact on the terms of indeterminacy in social life. In our discourse: how do individual practitioners objectify an experience of disequilibrium that threatens their apprehending, not only of their own position as ethnographer and teacher, but even of their profession's operational and moral order?

The cases presented above displayed three areas of indeterminacy. The first related to the unexpected conflictual interactions, and the equally surprising supportive collegial relationships, with unacquainted anthropologists. My interlocutors – Van Teffelen, Diamond, Swedenburg and Segal – have shared and publicly revealed a political-ideological position on the Israeli–Palestinian issue. That position, I believe, affected the ethnographic interpretation of their field data and relevant academic discourses. Moreover, it influenced their discourteous comportment toward a colleague who expounded a different viewpoint related to their perception of facts and theory. For me, it was a stunning experience. I felt violated as an academic and a colleague in what I had considered civil society, especially as I actively participated in the Israeli public arena in support of the case of the Palestinians. How does one help the ill-fated residents of the occupied West Bank by referring to them, from the green lawns of a California campus, as 'my Palestinian brothers and sisters'?

Professor Max Gluckman, my Manchester School mentor, taught me before and after going to the field: 'Have your data right!' It was bewildering to encounter anthropologists who I determined have screened their field data and conclusions through a personal political perspective. However, as indicated above, I can at this late moment apprehend, though not empathize with the conviction they have fostered as protesting against the university-academic guise of political neutrality. On these occasions, I lost my personal identity characteristics, embodying instead, an 'Israeli delegate', representing the occupation regime's injustices committed in Palestine. Ironically, these days, one could define their stance in terms of public anthropology.

In contrast, my meeting with Munira Khayyat – an accomplished younger anthropologist for whom I must represent the 'enemy' in her experience of daily national life – revealed an authentic expression of academic collegiality and personal empathy. Her response was totally unexpected, even inspiring, coming after that of those veteran professionals (including two fellow Jews) who incriminated my work for moral deficiencies embedded in the fact of my national citizenship.

Another category of indeterminacy involved the anthropologist's spontaneous performance in the public forum. When my unplanned engagement among an angry funeral crowd was reported in a major newspaper, I was surprised to discover that some unrehearsed comments – becoming a sort of ethnographic notes – could carry some weight in the public arena.

The third category of indeterminacy relates to the quandaries, limits and ethics of ethnographic research. There were two cases of felt betrayal: my own discovery of a major existential component that had been kept a secret by a close informant; and the anguished protest expressed by a close participant, responding to the anthropologist's uninvited penetration into his intimate personal and social world. These unforeseen experiences in the ethnographer's work highlight a critical dilemma: are we sufficiently aware about the layers of truth that our subjects in the field allow us to uncover?

Finally, in contrast to the earlier cases, the Strozzi art-cover exceptional chronicle revealed the potential wider context and means available for the production of an ethnographic report, at least in the eyes and deep experiential certitude of the researcher.

Our list of some related and other unrelated surprising experiences exposed a chain of issues revealing professional concerns of method, records, interpretation, ethics and collegial relationships that might link to other ethnographers' personal experiences. That discourse seems also to represent some features of contemporary research trends, such as the strategies and domains of 'public ethnography' and the 'ethnographic present'. In any case, I feel that report helped me relieve some anxieties about the present state-of-art of the ethnographic project.

Moshe Shokeid is Professor Emeritus of Anthropology at Tel Aviv University. He received his PhD from the University of Manchester and studied diverse populations in various locations, concentrating on issues of migration, ethnicity and sexuality: Jewish immigrants from the Atlas Mountains in Israeli farming communities, Arabs in Jaffa, Israeli immigrants in the Borough of Queens and gay institutions in New York City. Major publications include *The Dual Heritage* (Manchester

University Press, 1971; Transaction, 1985); *The Predicament of Homecoming* (with S. Deshen, Cornell, 1974); *Distant Relations* (with S. Deshen, Praeger, 1982); *Children of Circumstances* (Cornell, 1988); *A Gay Synagogue in New York* (Columbia University Press, 1995; University of Pennsylvania Press, 2003); *Gay Voluntary Associations in New York* (University of Pennsylvania Press, 2015); *Can Academics Change the World?* (Berghahn, 2020).

References

Abrahams, Roger D. 1986. 'Ordinary and Extraordinary Experiences', in *The Anthropology of Experience*, Victor W. Turner and Edward M. Bruner (eds). Urbana: University of Illinois Press, pp. 45–72.

Bellamy, Richard. 1997. 'The Intellectual as Social Critic: Antonio Gramsci and Michael Walzer', in *Intellectuals in Politics: From the Dreyfus Affair to Salman Rushdie*, Jeremy Jennings and Anthony Kemp-Welch (eds). London: Routledge, pp. 25–44.

Dewey, John. 1934. *Art as Experience*. New York: Minton, Balch & Co.

Fassin, Didier (ed.). 2018. *If Truth Be Told: The Politics of Public Anthropology*. Durham, NC: Duke University Press.

Freud, Sigmund. 1958 [1919]. 'The "Uncanny"', in *On Creativity and the Unconscious: Papers on the Psychology of Art, Literature, Love, Religion*, Benjamin Nelson (ed.). New York: Harper & Row, pp. 122–62.

Jaeger, Gertrude and Philip Selznick. 1964. 'A Normative Theory of Culture', *American Sociological Review* 29(5): 653–69.

Kaufman, Arnold. 1968. *The Radical Liberal: The New York Politics; Theory and Practice*. New York: Simon & Schuster.

Said, Edward. 1996. *Representation of the Intellectual: The 1993 Reith Lectures*. New York: Vintage Books.

Sanjek, Roger. 2013. *Ethnography in Today's World: Color Full before Color Blind*. Philadelphia: University of Pennsylvania Press.

Simmel, Georg. 1959. *Essays on Sociology, Philosophy and Aesthetics*, Kurt H. Wolff (ed.). New York: Harper & Row.

Shokeid, Moshe. 1988/9. 'The Manchester School in Africa and Israel Revisited: Reflections on the Sources and Method of an Anthropological Discourse', *Israel Social Science Research* 6(1): 9–23.

———. 1992a. 'Exceptional Experiences in Everyday Life', *Cultural Anthropology* 7(2): 232–43.

———. 1992b. 'Commitment and Contextual Study in Anthropology', *Cultural Anthropology* 7(4): 464–77.

———. 1995/2003. *A Gay Synagogue in New York*. New York: Columbia University Press. Augmented edition, 2003. Philadelphia: University of Pennsylvania Press.

———. 2015. *Gay Voluntary Associations in New York: Public Sharing and Private Lives*. Philadelphia: University of Pennsylvania Press.

——. 2016. 'A Love Story: From Vienna to My Ethnography's Book Cover', *Anthropology and Humanism* 41(1): 39–43.
——. 2020. *Can Academics Change the World? An Israeli Anthropologist's Testimony on the Rise and Fall of a Protest Movement on Campus*. New York: Berghahn Books.
Shokeid, Moshe and Shlomo Deshen. 1982. *Distant Relations: Ethnicity and Politics among Arabs and North African Jews in Israel*. New York: Praeger and Bergin Publishers.
Swedenburg, Ted. 1989. 'Occupational Hazards: Palestine Ethnography', *Cultural Anthropology* 4(3): 265–72.
——. 1992. 'Occupational Hazards Revisited: Reply to Moshe Shokeid', *Cultural Anthropology* 7(4): 478–95.
Thompson, Edward P. (ed.). 1970. *Warwick University Ltd: Industry, Management and the Universities*. Harmondsworth: Penguin Books Ltd.
Turner, Victor. 1967. 'Betwixt and Between: The Liminal Period in *Rites de Passage*, in *Forest of Symbols*. Ithaca, NY: Cornell University Press, pp. 93–111.
Turner, Victor and E.M. Bruner (eds). 1986. *Anthropology of Experience*. Urbana: University of Illinois Press.
Van Teeffelen, T. 1977. *Anthropologists in Israel: A Case Study in the Sociology of Knowledge*. Amsterdam: Anthropology-Sociology Center, University of Amsterdam.
——. 1978. 'The Manchester School in Africa and Israel', *Dialectical Anthropology* 3: 67–83.
——. 1980 [1978]. 'The Manchester School in Africa and Israel: A Critique', in *Anthropology: Ancestors and Heirs*, Stanley Diamond (ed.). The Hague: Mouton, pp. 347–76.
Van Velsen, J. 1967. 'The Extended Case Method and Situational Analysis', in *The Craft of Social Anthropology*, A.L. Epstein (ed.). London: Tavistock, pp. 124–49.

Chapter 5

The Exceptionalism of Art as Disclosure of Deepest Truth
Stanley Spencer and the Look of Love

Nigel Rapport

Part One: A Kantian Thread

Tolstoy and the Ethics of Art

In 1897 Leo Tolstoy published an essay, 'What Is Art?' Art is misconceived if it is deemed simply a means to pleasure or catharsis, Tolstoy urged. It is rather a chief means of human union:

> Every work of art causes the receiver to enter into a certain kind of relationship both with him who produced or is producing the art, and with all those who, simultaneously, previously, or subsequently, receive the same artistic impression. (1994: 56)

Through art, human beings might consciously deploy 'external signs' to convey feelings and experiences such that others are 'infected' by the same feelings and experiences (Tolstoy 1994: 59).

Tolstoy admitted that not all art may be deemed of the same quality, however. Some art unites people but only at the expense of others who are disparaged. To this latter, Tolstoy gave the critical names of 'patriotic' art, also 'cultic', 'local', 'elitist' and 'voluptuous' art. Such art transmitted 'bad feelings': superstition, fear, pride, vanity and spleen. 'Sound' art, by contrast, evoked *necessary* feelings such as merriment, pity, cheerfulness, tranquillity, humour, delight and love.

Ultimately, nevertheless, Tolstoy was assured that by way of sound artistic appreciation a kindly communion could come to incorporate all humanity. Art was to be appreciated as a medium indispensable for progress towards 'wellbeing', both individual and collective, progress towards human beings finding 'loving harmony with one another' (Tolstoy 1994: 171–76). For by evoking an emotional unity between people under the 'imaginary' conditions of painting, literature and music, art trained them to experience such a unity in everyday life. Distances may be overcome between the most different of people, when, as if 'by an electric flash', former enmities and isolations were replaced by individuals' glad consciousness that others felt what they feel. There was an otherness to art – a quality of exception – which caused it to operate beyond the bounds of the merely customary. Art possessed the capacity to make brotherhood and love of one's neighbour 'the customary feeling and instinct of all' (Tolstoy 1994: 224), and to do so without the coercions of law and police, the organizings of charities and factories, the machinery of society and culture.

Simmel and the Truth of Art (and Tragedy of Society)

It was Immanuel Kant who, in the *Critique of Judgment* (1978 [1790]), sought to *define* fine art (*schöne Kunst*) in terms of it possessing an instrumental autonomism. The autonomism of art made it:

> A mode of representation which is intrinsically final, and which, although devoid of a purpose has the effect of advancing the culture of the mental powers in the interests of social communication. (1978 [1790]: 44/306)

More broadly, for Kant, aesthetics afforded a distinctive type of evaluation of the world (see Haskins 1989). Aesthetic production and appreciation represented an autonomous domain, not contingent upon history, society or culture; at the same time, this otherness enabled the producer and the audience alike to accede to a critical perspective on everyday life, the mundane and habitual. The Kantian insight echoed not only in the urgings of Tolstoy but equally in the sociological work of Georg Simmel, and in particular in his 1916 publication, *Rembrandt: An Essay in the Philosophy of Art*. Through the viewing of art-works there is the potential to remove oneself from the habitus of a purely conventional, cultural classification of the world, Simmel argued, and so to gain an exceptional, 'ironic', purchase on the life lived. To enter into a Rembrandt portrait, then, is to find honestly represented an individual life as *sui generis*. Rembrandt portraits provide 'unrefracted reflections' of the special, self-sufficient unity of form and content that is an individual human life (Simmel 2005 [1916]: 18).

The 'tragedy' of human life in society, however, Simmel went on (1971: 329), is that here, as against in art, the 'law' of individuality is sacrificed to exterior and extraneous concepts. Rather than seeing and engaging with the subjectivity of the unique other, life in society entails a traffic in static and fixed symbolic forms: languages (verbal and other) governed by grammars and syntax; laws, norms, conventions and customs of social exchange; symbolic classifications that categorize and emplace the world; material structures and boundaries whose inertia confounds movement and change. Albeit that symbolic forms are creations of the human spirit, their social distribution makes them autonomous of their creators: generalized, clichéd, adulterated. Social relations are tragic in that they operate by way of symbolic forms that come to replace individual identities with *a priori* cultural categories. Individual subjectivity may be the antithesis of standardized symbolic forms – in that subjectivity's uniqueness, vitality and fluidity – but in expressing itself socially subjectivity must 'pass through' form and become 'generalized, in some measure' (Simmel 1971: 9). Typification and generalization thus act as an *a priori* veil which both detracts from individuality – limiting, reducing, corrupting the individual as it is in itself and for itself – and also supplements that individuality – replacing it by what it is not. Albeit that society is never a thing-in-itself, an organism, and remains a sphere of individuals' 'reciprocal influencing', individuals come to belong as societal 'members' to the extent that in essence they do not belong (Simmel 1971: 19). Partaking in a collective name – a nation-state, a church, a profession, an ethnic group – individual members are represented as other than their true selves.

For Simmel, in short, life in society is one of 'distortion', of individual personalities forced to become inauthentic in their expression and public recognition. In the face of this alienation, art affords an exceptional, and ethical, compensation.

Nietzsche and the Compensatory Power of Art

Some years previous to his writing on Rembrandt, in 1907, Simmel had expressed an indebtedness to Nietzsche, including for the latter's insights into the relation between art and society: art as a means of individual expression and empowerment; also, art as a means of human progression. Nietzsche had written:

> [Art] is the great means of making life possible, the great seduction to life, the great stimulant of life. (1968 [1910]: 853.II)

Also:

> Truth is ugly. We possess *art* lest we *perish of the truth*. (ibid.: 822)

And again:

> It is only as an aesthetic phenomenon that existence and the world are eternally justified. (1967 [1872]: 52)

Nietzsche's position was complex regarding the nature of art and its relation to illusion (distortion) and reality. Human action in the world was at continual risk of being inhibited by nausea at what we knew of reality, Nietzsche contended, by the knowledge that the world was chaotic and could not be set in proper order, that action could not change anything in the eternal and impersonal nature of things. Human action therefore required certain veils of illusion (of deliberate ignorance) if motivation to act was not to be outweighed. But then possessing and practising a 'genius in lying' so as to make ourselves less vulnerable to the assaults of reality was not easy to come by. Art, however, achieved this mastery over reality for humankind by imposing meaning, coherence and value on the things of the world, ordering and transforming experience so that it appeared to accord to a pattern and a purpose. By way of art comprising a variety of kinds, human beings constructed illusions that were powerful enough to protect them from the truth, indeed to negate the truth. Deceived by our own artistry we overcome a sense of powerlessness, pessimism and fear in the face of the chaotic world.

Important differences existed, then, between the positions of Nietzsche and Simmel. But both could agree on the otherness of art, on there being a distinct aesthetic domain of production and appreciation whose exceptional qualities provide a particular perspective on a world of everyday necessities. For Simmel, art exposed the distortions by which life in society was every day lived by affording itself a true appreciation of the individuality of identity, while for Nietzsche, art effected those distortions or illusions by which everyday life could be maintained in the face of a reality without essential meaning, pattern or purpose. While Simmel would describe the distortions of stereotypical symbolic forms in social exchange as 'tragic', Nietzsche would see the illusions of art and the distortions of the nature of reality that it incurred as forms of empowerment, for individuals and for humanity alike: redeeming the world, enabling human beings to advance into life with purpose and direction.

But then this was not Nietzsche's final word. For in the figure of the Overman, Nietzsche construed the human being who was strong enough to confront truth and to love fate: *'amor fati'* (2003 [1883–85]). The Overman represented the potential that each human being possessed both to be the author of their life, to create it in their own image, and at the same time to recognize that their life was essentially a work of art: a construct, a beautiful sport. Nietzsche had the Overman *realize* – at once enjoy and look askance at – the illusionary character of the aesthetic truths that he or she created and deployed as means to self-empowerment. The Overman was ironical vis-a-vis his or her own 'will to power', seeing through the artifice of the aesthetic (art, religion, culture) and embracing reality and its necessities. In short, the distinct (Kantian) domains of the aesthetic and the mundane were experienced dialectically by the Overman, tacking, zigzagging, from one to the other as different moments of conscious being (Rapport 2005a).

Part Two: A Spencerian Vision

Stanley Spencer and the Look of Love

My intention now is to change register from art-criticism to art-creation. In the work of the British painter Stanley Spencer (1891–1959) there are intriguing overlaps with the themes we have considered, and significantly here the perspective is that of art as practice.

For Stanley Spencer, art was a moral vocation. His paintings were to be seen as lessons in love. They both derived from a particular loving looking at the world and they provided the viewer with insight into the world's truth. The look of love was revelatory of a reality immanent in the physical everyday but also distinct from it: more complete and spiritual. His paintings were primarily autobiographical, Spencer further explained, a matter of him placing himself in settings in which he felt 'cosy', loved, at home. But his paintings were also biographical and didactical: they portrayed a 'heavenly' love that was a miraculous novelty for any humans to feel – exceptional. And yet, any human being could be 'resurrected' into a world of love, their everyday life 'redeemed', should they look at life truly, 'lovingly'.

In a monograph, *Distortion and Love: An Anthropological Reading of the Art and Life of Stanley Spencer* (Rapport 2016), I attempted an understanding of the metaphysic behind Spencer's imagery, while also exploring how his images have been received by a viewing public. A particular focus was *The Stanley Spencer Gallery*, the first gallery in Britain to be devoted to the work of a single artist. Sited in the village of Cookham on the River Thames – Spencer's birthplace and the source of much of his inspiration – the gallery is run by volunteer custodians and supported financially by subscription, through the *Friends of the Stanley Spencer Gallery*. Visitors pay a modest entry fee – and may leave comments in a *Visitors' Book*.

Spencer's reputation has fluctuated widely, both during his lifetime and since: from being deemed a rustic eccentric to a national treasure. For some critics he is the most significant British artist of the twentieth century:

- *John Rothenstein*: I have known no more impassioned painter and draughtsman. Stanley was a genius. (1970: 51)
- *Fiona MacCarthy*: An incomparably committed, original and inspirational painter. (1997: 58)
- *Timothy Hyman*: The most fulfilled, courageous and irreplaceable British artist of the century. (1991: 33)

Spencer studied at the Slade School of Art in London, at the same time as Paul Nash, Mark Gertler, David Bomberg, Gwen Raverat, Ben Nicholson and Dora Carrington, excelling in this company and being prized (in the words of his teacher, Henry Tonks) as having 'the most original mind of any student'. At the same time, however, Spencer was marginalized – dubbed 'Cookham', since he insisted on returning to his home village each evening – and disparaged as someone for whom movements in modern art – the Impressionism of Roger Fry, Bloomsbury and Continental Europe – meant nothing. Picasso was an irrelevancy, Spencer insisted, given the grace of the mediaeval: 'I haven't got past Piero della Francesca yet!' (cited in G. Spencer 1974: 99). Spencer remained at home in his personal and individual world:

> I have always looked forward to seeing what I could fish out of myself. I am a treasure island seeker and the island is myself. (Cited in Collis 1962: 203)

Since his death in 1959, appraisal has more frequently been that Spencer may be regarded as a Modern Master. But classifying his artistic project has remained unsettled. Is he in the company of Fra Angelico and Giotto, or Cranach, or Blake, or Gauguin and Chagall, or Beckmann and Dix, or Rivera and Lowry? However eclectic the company, Spencer still appears a 'stranger', his art as an exception (Hauser 2001: 10).

Spencer's Genres

Spencer's art falls into different periods in his life and, more significantly, into different genres. He painted formal *portraits*, of himself and others, and *landscapes*. Spencer depended on these financially, they were perennially popular among the buying public, but he came to play down their personal significance, deeming them 'pot-boilers', empty of emotion and devoid of lasting significance. A third genre was the *nude* – primarily images of himself and his lovers – whose honest detailing of flesh and portrayal of human relationships led them to become key icons for those who followed in his wake, such as Lucian Freud and Francis Bacon (the latter feeling 'exhilarated despair' at what Spencer had accomplished). Fourthly, Spencer painted pictures of *wartime*. In the First World War he served both as a medical orderly and as a front-line soldier in Macedonia, and he transmuted these experiences most notably into a commission to paint a complete Memorial Chapel, at Sandham ['The finest complete work of mural decoration done in England within record' (Gordon 1943: 50)]. In the Second World War, Spencer served as an official War Artist, and went to Port Glasgow to record the building of warships on the Clyde. This resulted in a series of intricate tableaux celebrating man-at-work. Fifthly, a genre Spencer made his own were pictures of *redemption* and *resurrection*, as he termed them. These were stylized, 'visionary' paintings in which his native Cookham-on-Thames became a 'village in heaven'. All manner of miraculous and Biblical occurrences were transposed onto its streets, houses and graveyards, so that the lives, works, possessions and interactions of Spencer's Cookham contemporaries were envisioned as 'holy mundanities'. Figure 5.1 shows *The Dustman (or The Lovers)* (1934), in which a set of rubbish collectors are being 'redeemed' – their true value as individual human beings being recognized – through the loving attention of their wives and the neighbourhood children:

Spencer's Metaphysics
Of all these distinct genres, the paintings Spencer most valued were those envisioned depictions where he felt he had been able to effect a 'loving looking'. To be in love was to achieve harmony, and to compose an image 'with love' was to draw what he felt 'homely and happy with' (Spencer, cited in Leder 1976: 10). Love, according to Spencer, 'reveals and more accurately describes the nature and meaning of things [: it] establishes once and for all time the final and perfect *identity* of every created thing' (cited in Glew 2001: 165).

Spencer developed his own metaphysics concerning love – even cosmology – by which human life was redeemed and the world seen anew as heavenly and saturated with joy. Spencer was no conventional Christian or even believer in God, but his *métier*, he felt, his message and gift to humanity, was the painting of a world in which love between all things (animals and plants as well as people) revealed a heavenly bliss within reach of the everyday. Transformation was key to Spencer's painterly efforts, then: 'All things are redeemable in my opinion and I paint them in their redeemed state' (Spencer, cited in Hauser 2001: 69) – in a state of exception. He transformed the world around him – of war,

Figure 5.1. *The Dustman (or The Lovers)* by Stanley Spencer (1891–1959), 1934 (oil on canvas 115 × 123.5 cm). Source: Laing Art Gallery. © Estate of Stanley Spencer. All rights reserved Bridgeman Images.

conflict, dirt, ugliness, meanness and myopia – into an embodiment of 'loving resurrection'.

Spencer's Public

It would be true to say that during Spencer's lifetime, the viewing public did not entirely appreciate his vision of a world redeemed by love. The Royal Academy of Arts in London, the pinnacle of the British art world, saw fit to report to Spencer that its Hanging Committee did not appreciate the 'distortions and peculiarity' in his work, and considered his images caricature-like and poorly drawn. To show his work, the Committee concluded, would not be of 'advantage to your reputation or the influence of the Academy' (Collis 1962: 114–18). The 'peculiar mannerisms and distortions', wrote the *Sunday Times*, 'recall the experience of a nightmare'; surely the 'repellent shapes' with which Spencer dealt 'passed the bounds of good taste' and showed him to be faulty in the 'head and heart' even if not in the hand (cited in Daniels n.d.: 52).

Spencer's retort to these very public criticisms was that he, for one, quite lacked the 'herd instinct'. The apparent 'distortions' of his art were merely the residue of the public's habituation to the everyday superficialities of life in society. As he elaborated:

> Existing laws and conventions interfere to a serious degree with my paintings. My art depends on emotions and wishes. If they are interfered with my work suffers. I know the excellence of these wishes. I know the powers these wishes have. It is ghastly that my art should be made subject to what vulgarity happens to lay down in law and morality. Such values, applied to my pictures, are quite inadequate to elucidate their true meaning. I am not against anything I know of. I will examine a religious scale of values as carefully as a non-religious scale. I am prejudiced to the religious side. But I am not going to have the religionist telling me what to worship. ... I feel that I am actually discovering a hoard of significant meanings to life, but am being hampered in my task. The intention of all my work is towards happiness and peace. (Cited in Pople 1991: 381–2)

As summed up by art historian Keith Bell, Spencer's art was neither part of the recognized international avant-garde with its modernist emphasis on abstract form, nor 'realistic' according to popular taste. Hence, the 'serious accusation of distortion' continued (intermittently) throughout Spencer's career and 'evidently bothered Spencer badly' (Bell 2001: 374).

But this has not been the whole story. *The Stanley Spencer Gallery* opened in the village of Cookham in 1962, just three years after Stanley's death. Writing the Preface to the catalogue for the first exhibition in the newly opened Gallery, one of Spencer's prominent supporters, Lord William Astor, opined:

> This gallery is in its nature modest. ... But perhaps a great edifice would be less typical of Stanley than this gallery which is in scale with the rest of the village and reflects the nature of Stanley: small, cheerful, very special and deeply loved.

Moreover, the Gallery's visitors' books to which people have continued to contribute their opinions since the 1960s are replete with admiring commentaries – including much reference to 'love':

- The artist has had a great impact on my life – I have loved his paintings since childhood.
- Such a lovely human being.

- Great to see so many of Spencer's paintings in the place that he loved.
- Lovely melding of religion – everyday life.
- I love his people–very distinct characters!
- Love the humour in the paintings.
- I love his fun faces and quirky angles he sees people especially the colour and joy of life!
- Just like my weird dreams. Love the surreal faces.

The current President of the *Friends of the Stanley Spencer Gallery*, Dr James Fox, an art historian at Cambridge, may be cited in comparable vein:

> Spencer is in my opinion one of the most important British artists of the century. … But the real reason I love Stanley Spencer's work is that it is full to bursting with love. Love for his family and friends, for nature, and of course for Cookham, infuses every mark, every brushstroke, he ever made (2005).

Before reaching a closing discussion I want to examine in a little more detail this observation by Fox of Spencer's 'fullness': full of love and optimism. There is a key here to the otherness of art as Spencer conceived of it: to the exceptional qualities art possessed and might deliver.

Spencer's Heavenly Wholeness

In a number of his writings Spencer turned his attention to *The Dustman (or The Lovers)*, reproduced above. Spencer was distinctive in the way in which he reacted to his finished paintings and wrote extensively about them. He had 'given birth to them' and thus loved them, he explained. He had created new characters to populate the earth and he enjoyed watching them, talking to them, wondering how their lives apart from him would fare following the sad day when he would have to sell them. His painted people were the 'beloved' of his imagination:

> I love to walk up to one of my past selves – *The Dustman*, or the couples in *The Beatitudes*, which stand about in the land of me. My picture people are among my loves. They meet the Hildas, the Elsies. I love and feel and touch them. (Cited in Collis 1962: 155)

It can be said that Spencer was more successful in sustaining relationships with people he had 'brought to life' in his paintings than those actual others around him – such as his first wife, Hilda, his daughters Shirin and Unity, and the family maid, Elsie. As he even admitted to Hilda in a letter, it came to seem to him 'incredible that you exist in the flesh!' – so intensely had he related to the images of her he had created in paint (cited in Collis 1962: 127).

Of *The Dustman (or The Lovers)*, then, there are firstly the notes Spencer wrote for his London agent, Dudley Tooth, describing and 'explaining' the image as if for ease of sale. The painting, Spencer began, concerns 'the carried blessed':

> It is the glorifying and magnifying of a dustman. The joy of his bliss is epitomised in the union with his wife who carries him in her arms and experiences the bliss of union which his corduroy trousers and workday clothes intensify and quicken. They are gazed at by other reunited wives of old labourers on the left and right. All these old men and women are in an ecstasy at the contemplation of their reuniting and of their being about to enter their homes and enjoy the bliss of their bedrooms. ...
>
> Down the street the dustbins are ranged, some good, some not, some in old buckets, some in boxes that are supposed to be rubbish themselves. What is rubbish to some people is not rubbish to me and when I see things being thrown away, I am all eyes to know what it is. Some people are astonished at what others keep; that doesn't astonish me at all; what astonishes me is what people throw away. I never used to resent this; I was only puzzled, when overhauling the great mound of rubbish in Overy's farm when I was a boy, by this distributing of largess to any who liked to avail themselves of it and at Mrs Hatch's kindness in letting us carry off any things we liked, such as cardboard boxes, etc. But these bits of rubbish were bits of the lives of the people to whom they had belonged and expressed their characters. I used to like trying to imagine the kind of people these things had belonged to.
>
> These are relics – holy relics – of beings which, in my mind and imagination, are meanings and aspects of bliss in the same way as places and things are. So also here, the children, conscious of the joy of grown-ups and loving the things that grown-ups use (a child often loves what is made for grown-ups and won't be satisfied with what is made for children), in holding up their finds, do so in a sort of spiritual exultation, intended to emphasise the fact that the joy is a celebration of domestic life.
>
> Nothing I love is rubbish, and so I resurrect the tea-pot and the empty jam tin and the cabbage stalk and, as there is a mystery in the Trinity, so there is in these three objects and in many others of no apparent consequence.
>
> (Tate Archive Microfiche 16B)

Spencer likewise wrote about him painting *The Dustman* in a letter to his erstwhile Slade friend, the artist Gwen Raverat:

> I became so enamoured of the dustman that I wanted him to be transported to heaven in the execution of his duty – & so I got a big sort of wife to pick him up in her arms while two children in a state of ecstasy hold up towards him an empty jam tin, a tea-pot and a bit of cabbage-stalk with a few limp leaves

attached to it. This scene occurs (Cookham people will say "we have seen strange things today") a little away from the centre of the road in the village and the street goes away in perspective and the dustmen go all up the side of this, so to speak. (Cited in Glew 2001: 153–54)

Finally, here is Stanley looking back on *The Dustman* from some years' distance:

> I feel, in this Dustman picture, that it is like watching and experiencing the inside of a sexual experience. They are all in a state of anticipation and gratitude to each other. They are each to the other, and all to any one of them, as peaceful as the privacy of a lavatory. I cannot feel anything is Heaven where there is any forced exclusion of any sexual desire...
>
> The picture is to express a joy of life through intimacy. All the signs and tokens of home life, such as the cabbage leaves and teapot which I have so much loved that I have had them resurrected from the dustbin because they are reminders of home life and peace, and are worthy of being adored as the dustman is. I only like to paint what makes me feel happy. As a child I was always looking on rubbish heaps and dustbins with a feeling of wonder. I like to feel that, while in life things like pots and brushes and clothes etc. may cease to be used, they will in some way be reinstated, and in this Dustman picture I try to express something of this wish and need I feel for things to be restored. That is the feeling that makes the children take out the broken teapot and empty jam tin. (Cited in Pople n.d.)

Spencer spoke of being an artist as a 'sacred' vocation: 'I love to dwell on the thought that the artist is next in divinity to the saint. He, like the saint, performs miracles' (cited in Pople 1991: 126). The miracle was what the artist's vision enabled him to see, and his ability to compose that vision into a painted design. Since everything in the world was part of a divine creation, to paint 'miraculously' was to represent a heavenly wholeness. Spencer marvelled at his own ability. His painted compositions were miracles of otherness, of sight and of inclusivity, bringing a redeemed world to life:

> The harmony which I describe as falling in love, is one of the first to show itself, at least to me it was. If I saw something at all wonderful I wanted to be with it .... My desire to paint a picture was prompted by a desire to establish & celebrate a kind of harmony between myself & what I loved .... The first discovery I made really was the fact that I was loving desperately something. ... To be able to give shape & form & substance to the very thing I loved was to me like being able to perform miracles. (Tate Gallery Archive 825.22)

The artistic miracle was to see everything and to join with everything – to enter into a kind of marriage with everything (whatever may be the narrow conventions of marriage) – such that Spencer could claim, as above, that 'nothing I love is rubbish', and 'remote things join in me' (cited in Hauser 2001: 7). The artistic portrayal was exceptional while at the same time showing everything in its true, mundane identity.

In sum, the 'loving look' of art identified and cherished, for Spencer, what might be considered 'other' to everyday polite norms and conventions, making what was exceptional at the same time a revelation of what was most deeply true.

Part Three: Discussion

The Otherness of Art, the Exceptional Truth

I have wanted to explore some of the possible deliverances of 'art', using the voices of Tolstoy, Simmel, Nietzsche and Stanley Spencer as protagonists. Art, at least in a Kantian tradition, possesses an otherness that sets it against everyday realities – at an oblique angle – 'destabilizing' the habitus (Wulff 2018: 103). Three aspects of that otherness, in particular, are stressed: art as truth; art as compensation; art as ethical guide.

Art as Truth

Art was other, for Simmel, in its truthfulness to identity. In the portrait – paradigmatically those of Rembrandt – was a representation of individuality that was tragically lost in the systems of symbolic classification by which everyday life in society was conducted. There, the particular came to be distorted by the cultural capacity only to identify the conventional, habitual, general and stereotypical. But this individuality of life and existence was also something random and chaotic, observed Nietzsche. It was a truth difficult to comprehend and difficult to abide. To look the individuality of life in the face was too difficult, certainly, for those who must live a 'slave' existence, in thrall to the illusion that cultural cosmologies and conventions were true accounts of reality. Only an Overman, able to accept the necessities of 'chaos' and so to master their individual existence was able to see beyond the illusions, deceptions and distortions erected by aesthetic ventures such as religious metaphysics. The latter artifice stood in dialectical relation to truth. For Spencer, 'visionary' art distorted physical reality in order to represent the truth of the world. The norms occasioned by social structures and cultural conventions, that in turn sanctioned narrow lives, part-lives, people divided from one another and the world – ultimately sanctioning violence and war – must be seen through, and art provided this truthful perspective. At least, Spencer's own art did. Art was the representation of that feeling of joyful at-oneness with the world that comes from allowing a natural human capacity for love to flourish. The world possessed an intrinsic wholeness, and art that emanated from a loving-looking was able to portray the true individual identity of everything in the world and a true relationality.

Art as Compensation

To live with his art – to inhabit the worlds of people and places and relations created by his compositions – was for Spencer the greatest of compensations. The otherness of art gave it the power to offer an alternative way of being in the world; through art Spencer felt he could live in the world as he chose and have his own way. Not absolutely – he still must pay his way through his art – but the world it vouchsafed was one of supreme value. Here he could imaginatively, spiritually and phenomenologically overcome restrictive laws, intransigent human others, even death. For Simmel, the compensation of art was bitter-sweet; as with loving relations, it showed up the paucity of self-expression and communication in the everyday, the superficiality and alienation, when social exchanges that took place according to conventional cultural forms and institutions. Nevertheless, art did avert that 'tragedy' becoming phenomenologically overwhelming. For Nietzsche – as ever with him – contrary impulses must be appreciated. Art compensated for the ugliness of truth, and so seduced the viewer and stimulated them to act, enabling them to justify their existence to themselves and others. But ultimately human beings had the strength to look at life plainly and without artifice and so be masters of their destiny: to will the world to be as it was and to will their individual places within it.

Art as Ethical Guide

For Tolstoy, Simmel, Nietzsche and Spencer alike, finally, the otherness of art gave it the ability to offer insight into the human (and individual) condition of a significant ethical kind. Art was a necessary condition of human life and a fundamental and key means of human intercourse: educating humanity in the joy of a universal harmoniousness (Tolstoy). Art taught how to look and what to see: a loveable world of individual beings and things whose divine destiny was to be at one with every single other thing (Spencer). Art was a reminder of the *sui generis* nature of individual lives, and how a recognition and appreciation of their otherness was possible and necessary (Simmel). Art was a lesson in how human beings might empower themselves so as to reach a point in their lives where they achieved self-control. As Overmen, people could learn to choose an artistic form that most did justice to their original individual needs and most reflected their individual nature (Nietzsche).

The Otherness of Anthropology, the Exceptional Truth of the Cosmopolitan

Art's otherness in the above accounts is such as to offer a route to truth, to compensation for worlds of cultural obfuscation, and to an ethical vantage point upon life. Albeit that a line from Kant through Nietzsche, Tolstoy, Simmel and Spencer is not a necessarily straight one of cumulative argument or insight, I feel nevertheless warranted to describe the foundational ground of these conclusions concerning art as 'Kantian': the insight that through aesthetics human beings are afforded insight that is autonomous and not contingent upon history or culture.

But anthropology, too, was provided by Kant with an especial capability and role in this regard. Anthropology Kant foresaw as the scientific discipline that might endeavour to furnish a universal knowledge of human being as a singular subject and datum. Albeit that humanity manifested itself as 'polis', as individually particular and discreetly embodied human lives, lives circumscribed in time and space, nevertheless humanity represented one 'cosmos', one kind of world and nature, a single and distinct species-being. The project of anthropology was hence a 'cosmopolitan' one (Kant 2015 [1798]). Anthropology was to study how a human cosmos and an individual polis informed one another. There was a universal human nature: universal human capabilities and liabilities. These came to be uniquely substantiated in the conscious production and workings of individual human lives. The project of anthropology was empirically and objectively to elucidate the nature of human capacity as these came to be uniquely instantiated in individual consciousness and practice.

Nor did Kant's vision end there. For a cosmopolitan anthropology ought also to pursue a moral vision: to clarify the optimal conditions whereby individuals may live out their human potential for conscious experience and self-expression to the fullest. Finally, a cosmopolitan anthropology had an aesthetic identity, its proper practice being to inscribe a knowledge of human being in such a way that the recognition and appreciation of human dignity and of individual integrity were promoted. To the extent that such cosmopolitan insights were 'other' to the ways in which societies and cultures currently constructed their reality and sought to structure their members' lives, art and anthropology alike had vital, *exceptional*, emancipatory roles to play (Rapport 2012).

The conclusion of this chapter in particular, however seemingly paradoxical, is that the exceptional insight can also be construed as the *actual*, the factual one: it is the exceptional that is true. Human unity was the truth, Tolstoy declared, however distant union may seem in a warring world. It was the truth that could be viewed in a Rembrandt portrait, Simmel insisted, however exceptional such a representation within the habitus of cultural forms. The heavenly scenes of village life that he painted were, Spencer knew, true discernments of individual identity and human relations immanent within the superficies of life. Nietzsche's Overman was the exceptional individual who looked honestly at self and world, recognizing their own power to create a life as a work of art in a truly chaotic world – a capability practicable by all.

Ernest Gellner once offered the definition of a culture as 'a collectivity united in a false belief' (1995: 6). The exceptional escapes such an 'assent to absurdity', and the straitened lives that ensue. Such exceptionalism is within universal human reach, moreover: a transcendence of what is merely traditional by what is true.

Nigel Rapport is Professor Emeritus of Anthropological and Philosophical Studies at the University of St Andrews and Founding Director of the St Andrews Centre for Cosmopolitan Studies. He has also held a Canada Research Chair in Globalization, Citizenship and Justice. He has conducted ethnographic research in England, Scotland, Canada and Israel. His research interests include individuality, identity, freedom, creativity, art, humanism, cosmopolitanism, and links between anthropology, philosophy and literature. Among his books are *Diverse Worldviews in an English Village* (Edinburgh University Press, 1993); *I am Dynamite: An Alternative Anthropology of Power* (Routledge, 2003); *Anyone: the Cosmopolitan Subject of Anthropology* (Berghahn, 2012); and *Cosmopolitan Love and Individuality: Ethical Engagement Beyond Culture* (Rowman & Littlefield, 2018). His current work centres on Emmanuel Levinas and how his philosophy might align with anthropological science.

References

Bell, Keith. 2001. *Stanley Spencer*. London: Phaidon.
Collis, Maurice. 1962. *Stanley Spencer*. London: Harvill.
Daniels, A.J. [n.d.] 'Stanley Spencer: The Making of a Singular Man', unpublished manuscript.
Fox, James. 2005. 'Dr James Fox is New President of Friends', *Friends of the Stanley Spencer Gallery Newsletter*, November (mimeo.).
Gellner, Ernest. 1995. 'Anything Goes: The Carnival of Cheap Relativism Which Threatens to Swamp the Coming *fin de millenaire*', *Times Literary Supplement* 4811: 6–8.
Glew, Andrew. (ed.). 2001. *Stanley Spencer: Letters and Writing*. London: Tate Gallery.

Gordon, J. 1943. 'Stanley Spencer', *The Studio* 126 (#605, August): 50–53.
Haskins, Casey. 1989. 'Kant and the Autonomy of Art', *Journal of Aesthetics and Art Criticism* 47(1): 43–54.
Hauser, Kitty. 2001. *Stanley Spencer*. London: Tate Gallery.
Hyman, Timothy. 1991. 'Stanley Spencer: The Sacred Self', in *The Apotheosis of Love*, Jane Alison (ed.). London: Barbican Art Gallery, pp. 29–33.
Kant, Immanuel. 1978 [1790]. *The Critique of Judgment* (ed. J. Meredith), Oxford: Oxford University Press.
———. 2015 [1798]. *Lectures on Anthropology* (ed. A. Cohen). Cambridge: Cambridge University Press.
Leder, Carolyn. 1976. 'Recollections of Stanley Spencer', in *Stanley Spencer 1891–1959*, Duncan Robinson (ed.). Glasgow: Arts Council of Great Britain.
MacCarthy, Fiona. 1997. *Stanley Spencer*. New Haven: Yale University Press.
Nietzsche, Friedrich. 1967 [1872]. *The Birth of Tragedy*. New York: Random House.
———. 1968 [1901]. *The Will to Power* (ed. W. Kaufmann). New York: Random House.
———. 2003 [1883–85]. *Thus Spake Zarathustra*. Harmondsworth: Penguin.
Pople, Kenneth. 1991. *Stanley Spencer*. London: Collins.
———. [n.d.] The Art and Vision of *Stanley Spencer*. Retrieved 17 December 2022 from http://www.stanleyspencer.co.uk/The%20Lovers.html.
Rapport, Nigel. 2003. 'Stanley Spencer and the Visionary Metaphysic of Love', in *I am Dynamite: An Alternative Anthropology of Power*. London and New York: Routledge.
———. 2004. 'Envisioned, Intentioned: A Painter Informs an Anthropologist about Social Relations', *Journal of the Royal Anthropological Institute* 10(4): 861–81.
———. 2005a. 'Nietzsche's Pendulum: Oscillations of Humankind', *The Australian Journal of Anthropology* 16(2): 1–17.
———. 2005b. 'The Power of the Projected Self: A Case-Study in Self-Artistry', *Medical Humanities* 31(2): 60–66.
———. 2012. *Anyone: The Cosmopolitan Subject of Anthropology*. Oxford: Berghahn.
———. 2016. *Distortion and Love: An Anthropological Reading of the Art and Life of Stanley Spencer*. London: Ashgate.
———. 2017. 'The Inscrutability of Freedom and the Liberty of a Life-Project: The Case of Stanley Spencer', in *Freedom in Practice: Governance, Autonomy and Liberty in the Everyday*, Moises Lino e Silva and Huon Wardle (eds). London: Routledge, pp. 34–54.
Robinson, Duncan. 1994. *Stanley Spencer*. London: Phaidon.
Rothenstein, John. 1970. *Time's Thievish Progress*. London: Cassell.
Simmel, Georg. 1971. *On Individuality and Social Forms* (ed. D. Levine). Chicago: University of Chicago Press.
———. 2005 [1916]. *Rembrandt: An Essay in the Philosophy of Art* (ed. Alan Scott and Helmut Staubmann). New York: Routledge.
Spencer, Gilbert. 1974. *Memoirs of a Painter*. London: Chatto & Windus.
Tate Gallery Archive 825.22 'Written by Stanley Spencer in the 1920s and lent to R. Carline for transcription in 1929'.
———. Microfiche 16B 'Notes of Stanley Spencer to Dudley Tooth'.

Tolstoy, Leo. 1994. *What is Art?* (ed. W. Jones). London: Duckworth.
Wulff, Helena. 2018. 'Introduction to Part 2', in *World Literatures: Exploring the Cosmopolitan-Vernacular Exchange*, Stefan Helgesson, Annika Mörte Alling, Yvonne Lindqvist and Helena Wulff (eds). Stockholm: Stockholm University Press, pp. 103–6.

Part II

Literary Realms of the Exceptional

Chapter 6

Haunted Reading/Haunting Johnson

Petra Rethmann

There are scenes in Uwe Johnson's writings to which I have repeatedly returned. In his extensive oeuvre, these are small scenes, but they mark the hinge on which much of my interest in and regard for Johnson's writings depends. By and large, these are scenes in which people in the 1950s flee from Germany's East to the West. In *Ingrid Babenderede*, Ingrid and her friend Klaus Niebuhr flee from Wendisch Burg in Mecklenburg to Drensteinfurt in Northrhein-Westphalia.[1] In *Speculations about Jakob*, Gesine Cresspahl has already fled from Jerichow to Düsseldorf, where she works for NATO. In the same novel, Heinrich Cresspahl, Gesine's father, carries the suitcase of Mrs Abs to the train station when she decides to flee from Jerichow to Hannover. In *Anniversaries*, Gesine and Dietrich Erichson (dubbed D.E.), who like Ingrid and Klaus have fled from Wendisch Burg, become friends. And in 1958 the author Uwe Johnson himself packs his bag and steps out of the Berlin *Stadtbahn* or city railway to leave the GDR.[2] In each case it is the experience of flight (*Flucht*) that defines these figures. And this experience mattered to me because in and through it I began to search for the ways in which the trauma of and silence surrounding flight had begun to shape my family's life, as well as my own. In this chapter I want to trace my repeated return to Johnson's writing. In drawing on one of his own preferred narrative method and style, speculation, I track this return through four registers – ambiguity, nostalgia, victimhood and hope – that mark the haunting quality of Johnson's writing for at least this reader.

In recent years, an extraordinary amount of energy has been spilled over methodologies of reading. While as an inheritance of the New Criticism of the early twentieth century, close reading – a way of reading in which the sole focus is on the text, which tends to come at the expense of real lives and attention to them – has emerged as a tried and true literary methodology, more recently notions of paranoid, reparative, descriptive, surface and affective reading have moved to the fore (Sedgwick 1997; Felski 2008, 2020; Best and Marcus 2009; Love 2010). While I am not able to do justice here to the complexities of these notions and their debate, for now suffice it to say that each of these notions has opened up debates of reading by variously introducing wisdom, insight, pleasure and stimulation as important marks of reading. In being inspired by this scholarship, as well as work on resonance (Rosa 2019) and attunement (Stewart 2011), I suggest the notion of haunted reading – by which I mean a reading in which the ghosts of one's own past and those of an author enter into responsive relation. Or, to be more concrete, my own sense of what was either assumed, half-forgotten or unspoken in the house in which I grew up returned me to Johnson's writing again and again in the hope of finding in it nuggets of illumination regarding my family's history – to grasp something of the way in which sadness infused the fabric of that house's life.

I grew up in the 1970s in a house which my grandfather had bought in 1958 with money from the *Lastenausgleich* (equalization of burdens). Coming into law in West Germany in August 1952, the equalization of burdens indicated the need to balance the assets between Germans who had lost land in the Second World War and those who had been able to maintain (more or less) their possessions. It also offered a strong incentive for East German refugees, as well as German repatriates and expellees, to leave either the Soviet Occupation Zone (1945–47) or the East German Republic (1947–89). On 17 March 1953, my grandfather and mother became two of approximately three million East Germans who between 1947 and 1989 fled the GDR. In the evening of that day they packed a small suitcase in the little town of Hecklingen and walked all night across muddy fields to reach the train station in Zerbst, from where they then took a train to Berlin Ostbahnhof, travelled on with the Berliner *Stadtbahn* across Friedrichstrasse (the border between East and West Germany) to Berlin-Marienfelde, where they stepped out and walked to Marienfelde refugee transit camp.[3] There they met up with my grandmother and aunt who had arrived the day before. For a few months the family languished in refugee camps in West Berlin, Hannover and Unna-Maasen, and was then assigned a one-room apartment in Dortmund-Deussen in the industrial Ruhr Valley, close to the city's port from which coal and ore were shipped to the North Sea. My grandfather felt lucky to obtain work as a carriage driver for the *Dortmunder Kronenbrauerei* (local beer brewery), my grandmother worked as a cleaner and my seventeen-year-old mother as a nanny and then in the office of a steel factory named *Hüttenunion*. When in 1958 my grandfather was able to purchase a house in Selm at the northeastern edges of the Ruhr Valley, the family felt that they had found a new home.

I vividly remember how on any given Sunday afternoon, my grandparents would get together with another East German family who had also fled. On these afternoons a coffee set decorated with Japanese cherry blossoms, which had been gifted to my grandmother by one of the families for whom she had cleaned, would sit on a rickety table, inevitably served with sheet cake. Smoke from the cigars that my grandfather and his friend smoked billowed through the air. They did not so much talk as move verbal fragments back and forth. In Hecklingen my grandfather had owned a twenty-eight-hectare farm: two oxen, a few horses, cows, goats, turkeys and geese, fields of turnips, poppy and wheat. Even if by the standards of agricultural reforms that between 1945 and the mid-1950s transpired in East Germany this did not amount to much, government officials had told him that his farm would be absorbed into the socialist collective farm system. As a farmer my grandfather had also been obliged to meet agricultural production quotas several times higher than what the land could give. This, and the establishment under Walter Ulbricht of a socialist regime in which 'the party was always right', was given as a reason for the flight. And in those afternoons, all of this – history, dictatorship, flight – became condensed in one expression: 'the land'. *The land* marked the loss my grandparents and their friends have never been able to shake.

As a child and young woman I wanted more stories, more information, more explanations. Frustrated with the dearth of narrative details I assumed that my grandparents, their friends, my mother and aunt were just poor storytellers. They might have had the kind of rich and felt experience that Benjamin (1986 [1936]) proclaimed as one indispensable condition for all great storytelling, but the richness of words that marks such an experience was not forthcoming. Today it strikes me as far more likely that my grandparents, mother and other refugees I knew might have just wanted to forget about the ordeals of the flight, the years of uncertainty that followed, their shunning by West German neighbours, and the pain of separation from family in the East. Their reluctance to speak was not just related to a reluctance to remember, but also an effect of trauma and loss. It may even have been the case that the absence of words, their quietness and silence, was their way to protect them from their own pain.

To trace some of the elements of what I call here haunted reading I have divided this chapter into two parts. In the first part I introduce the author Uwe Johnson through the readerly lens of ambiguity. Ambiguity is a trademark of Johnson's writing, and in his oeuvre it evinces a political stand more interesting and nuanced than then-West German ritualistic condemnations of East German politics and ideology – condemnations at work in my family as well. In briefly looking at Johnson's novel *Mutmassungen über Jakob* (here referred to as *Speculations*), I introduce ambiguity as one guiding principle in Johnson's writing. In centring on the registers of loss, victimhood and hope in the second part I juxtapose autobiographical circumstances of my own life with Johnson's writings. I end with a short mediation on memory and trauma.

Ambiguity: The Author

Ambivalence or ambiguity, it seems, was the only way in which Johnson knew how to deal with Germany's political separation into a socialist East and a capitalist West. Born in 1934 in the Pomeranian town of Kammin (in today's Poland), Johnson spent his first ten years in the agricultural town of Anklam. In 1945 he fled – just a few steps ahead of the advancing Red Army – to Recknitz/Güstrow, where he joined other members of his family. When in 1952 he enrolled for German philology at the University of Rostock he hoped to become a teacher of literature and language, but in 1954 these hopes were thwarted when he spoke up in support of the *Junge Gemeinde*[4] and was forced to leave Rostock. Between 1954 and 1956 Johnson continued his studies at the University of Leipzig, where he worked with anti-fascist and independent-minded Marxist literary scholar Hans Mayer and attended lectures by philosopher Ernst Bloch. When in 1956 he sought to publish his first novel, *Ingrid Babenderede*, based on the trial of the *Junge Gemeinde*, he was barred from continuing studies towards a PhD. He was also unable to find future employment. In 1958, a few weeks before the West German publishing house Suhrkamp Verlag – which published all of Johnson's works – brought out his first novel, *Speculations*, he moved to West Berlin.[5] In 1970 he published the first volume of his four-volume novel, *Anniversaries: From the Life of Gesine Cresspahl*, and then in rapid succession in 1971 volume two, and in 1973 volume three. Suffering from writer's block and a host of personal problems, in 1974 he moved to the town of Sheerness on the Isle of Sheppey in the UK. In 1983, a few months after he published the fourth volume of *Anniversaries*, he was found dead at his home, with his death being diagnosed as the effect of excessive alcohol consumption.

Wahrheitsfindung or 'truthfinding' may be one of Johnson's stated goals, but ambiguity – the recognition that no certainty can be had – is the theme that runs through all of his work. In *Speculations about Jakob*, ambiguity sits in emblems of perceptual hardship: the thick morning fog that makes it hard to distinguish the figure of Jakob or the train that kills him; the difficulty of reading an old map of the Jerichow region, in which water, flatland and mountains are all indicated by the same colour; the effort by a philologist to reconstruct old speech patterns from fragmentary and incomplete linguistic evidence. Each emblem is marked by ambivalence, and conjecture appears to be the only interpretive mode. Formally situated at the level of an investigation, *Speculations* is not so much about the reconstruction of Jakob's life, but about the effort to piece together, from fragments and different units of perception, a life. In this multivocal effort – narrators include Jakob's colleague Jöche, Gesine and Heinrich Cresspahl, Stasi agent Mr Rohlfs, and Jakob's friend Jonas Blach – factual details are increasingly called into question. The novel's reader, too, has to rely on conjecture to piece together a number of independent details, weigh often contradictory evidence with very little guidance, and deduce narrators from their relationship to Jakob and the context. *Speculations* creates a narrative world in which nothing is certain, nothing clearly knowable, and perhaps no one trustworthy. Rather than unfolding into a psychological or narrative solution, the novel thwarts a reader's need for a single vision, plot and order, and forces them to deal with ambivalence, fragmentation and disjunction.

When I first read *Speculations*, I was struck by the jarring complexity of Johnson's style. But I was equally struck by the haunting of his writing: a haunting in which truth does not lie in the factual realm but in a more fictional or intuitive understanding. In *Speculations* Johnson marshals a number of mechanical aides to perception, such as photographs, tapes, films and official documents. But although these aides evince much accurate and factual information, there is not a single shred of evidence that would provide either narrators or readers with a sense of certainty, of right or wrong. *Speculations* marks a narrative world in which authorial control moves toward scepticism, openness and variety. This novel is not the work of an author who believes in intentional mystification, but the work of an author who believes that linguistic tools or language, and especially syntactical and lexical rules, have become insufficient to articulate reality. Speculation, scepticism and doubt are the perceptual grids on which reality rests.

Haunting: The Reader

Loss

As I mentioned above, in the house in which I grew up, my grandparents' sense of loss was everywhere. It hung in rooms, in the folds of curtains, the smoke of cigars. It was present in verbal fragments, the politically dismissive tone when my grandfather mentioned the work brigades hunting for blight-spreading Colorado Beetles that American planes had allegedly dropped on his potato fields and in which my mother worked, and in stories through which relatives flitted like ghosts. It was also in the packages that every three months my grandmother sent to relatives in either Besenstedt (family of my grandmother) or Spremberg (family of my grandfather). These packages were put together in the same punctilious fashion that marks Johnson's writing. They were not allowed to weigh more than five pounds, and their content was debated with an obsession that at times seemed to border on paranoia. A few days before they were sent, a pair of scales appeared on the kitchen table, and food items – coffee, especially Jacob's Krönung, biscuits, sugar and other stuff – were weighed back and forth. My grandmother refused to send packages to the daughters of one of my grandfather's cousins because he had been betrayed by his wife when he attempted to flee and received fifteen years in prison. According to my grandmother this man had been friendly and kin, but his daughters had sided with their mother.

As a writer Johnson has sometimes been accused of nostalgia (Lennox 1989), as if he was longing for a time and place that could no longer be had. I consider such an assessment to be mistaken. Or, to be more exact, in my estimation such an assessment happens to emerge when literary critics are too concerned with the critical forces of exposure and demystification, and cannot understand or see the pain that accompanies deep loss. In *Begleitumstände*, a series of seminars and talks that Johnson delivered in 1979 at the University of Frankfurt, he speaks of the 'loss of home, fleeing, and the uncertain arrival in a strange place'. Famously reserved as a person, this might be the only time he may have articulated his own loss as clearly. But there also exists a photograph that shows him in June 1982 as part of a British tourist group travelling to the GDR. Apart from the places to which he travelled – Berlin, Rostock, Güstrow, Warnemünde and Leipzig – nothing appears to be known about why he travelled, but I assume that he felt compelled to return because he had no choice. Trauma seems to work that way. You cannot help but revisit the memory or place of your wounding until your memory has healed (see also Raffles 2020).

For my grandparents and mother, as for Johnson, this wounding was profound. Perhaps so profound that no amount of writing or speaking could have domesticated this wound. As Patrick Wright (2020: 29) writes in his biography of Johnson, East German refugees were often marked by a 'low status', and in the house in which I grew up this seemed to be true in both social and psychic terms.[6] For as long as I can remember, loneliness felt like the basic condition of my grandparents' and mother's lives.

In the world in which I grew up, to be defined as a refugee meant to be isolated and excluded. It meant having the wrong religion (most refugees were Protestants in a place that was largely Catholic), speaking with the wrong accent (in this case one marked as Saxon accent), and eating mutton and caraway (*Kümmel*) like the Turkish *Gastarbeiter* (habitually translated as guestworker). We all lived at the edge of town because that's where those who did not belong to Selm's Catholic centre lived. In my grandmother's voice her sense of abjection was palpable when she described the atmosphere at the wedding of my parents – my father was disinherited when he married my mother, and his parents and sister refused to speak to my mother – 'like a funeral'. I have come to accept that I have inherited some of their sadness. And I have come to believe that I recognize the same sadness in Johnson.

Victimhood

In April 2015 I visited the Marienfelde Refugee Center Museum at the southwestern edge of Berlin. In walking through the almost empty museum, I tried to imagine the overcrowded conditions and swarming of people of which my mother spoke when she talked about Marienfelde. Bodies of men, women and children pressing against each other. Men and women clutching hard-sided suitcases or bags that carried passports, papers and deeds. I tried to imagine my grandparents, filling out forms, answering questions about their reason for the flight. I imagine that in the stories my grandfather told to West German government officials he spoke of an East German 'Workers and Peasants State' that had no respect for farmers, that the 'accelerated construction of socialism' was killing him because you cannot accelerate agricultural production unless you change crop cycles and/or are prepared to use chemical substances, and that he had spent a few days in prison because he could not afford to part with farm produce and wheat to ease the economic strain in the cities. I also imagine that my grandfather offered this explanation with the conviction of certainty of somebody who had been wronged.

Johnson has sometimes been accused of not liking very much 'the people of Marienfelde'.[7] I could not find a single sentence that would affirm such an assertion, but I do think it fair to say that Johnson would have taken issue with the kind of victimizing narrative most likely offered (either as performance, out of conviction, or both) by my grandfather and others. I assume that this would have been the case for one key reason. Unlike my grandfather who needed the money from the *Lastenausgleich* that would allow him and his family to settle in West Germany (really, anywhere), Johnson walked straight into a West Berlin apartment because publisher Peter Suhrkamp had already arranged for his papers and apartment. There I detect a bit of haughtiness in Johnson when he says that he insisted on fending for himself because he did not want to have to say thank you 'for the loans, credits, and working places available' (Wright 2020: 35).

I have struggled in writing the previous two paragraphs because in writing them I have entered difficult terrain. In imagining what my grandparents might have said in Marienfelde I imagine how they imagined themselves as victims. As a young woman who grew up in West Germany, I imagine them from the perspective of someone for whom the term 'victim' meant anyone who was killed in the Holocaust and German death camps, or anyone who was a victim-survivor with all of the suffering and horror that came with that status. I was then concerned – and continue to be concerned – with the way in which the term victim might easily have been appropriated by German victims and used in German-focused narratives of dispossession to emphasize a lost *Heimat* (home), and *only* German suffering and not the suffering of others. I surmise that Johnson would have not denied the suffering of Germans, but would have rejected what I call here the 'equalization of suffering' as a political position that so many Germans then adopted – as if German deaths and trauma as a result of bombings and dispossession makes German victims no different from Jews who died in the camps. Specifically, I think, Johnson would have been suspicious of the ways in which dispossession and loss would have allowed Germans to cathect themselves as bereft victims, and in which the destruction of German and European Jewry would lose its distinctiveness as a particular act of genocide against Jews and against other groups chosen for death, and thus been blended into an undifferentiated evil of war.[8] The danger for Johnson would have been that the historical specificity of the Holocaust and the Nazi teleology of genocide are erased. I did and do share his suspicion of relativizing in which the suffering of everybody is the same.

How can the difference between victims be articulated? Contemporary German authors (Kempowski 1992; Sebald 1999; Kluge 2014; Grass 2015; Hansen 2015) writing on the issue of German victimization have begun to explore the ways in which the language of victimhood locates itself between two historical positions. On the one hand, there are the narratives, literary texts, autobiographies, museums, films and photographs of the death camps and the destruction of German and European Jewry during the Third Reich. On the other hand, there is a German civilian population, particularly at the end of the war, that is traumatized from constant air raids, firebombing, flight, homelessness, starvation, statelessness and – especially in Germany's East and the memory of my grandmother – the raping of women that characterized the advance of the Red Army. In such narratives, Germans are victims of human – and socialist – indifference to life rather than of particular historical moments and political decisions. As Hanna Arendt noted in her 1950 *Report from Germany*, even 'educated and intelligent Germans will proceed to draw up a balance between German suffering and the suffering of others, the implication being that one side cancels out the other'.[9]

Hope

When, in 1984, the British miner's strike ripped across the UK – where Johnson then lived – in the Ruhr Valley in which I lived, many mines had already started to close. Here are some that I remember: Zollern in Dortmund-Bövinghausen (1898–1966); Minister Stein in Dortmund-Eving (1856–1987); Gute Hoffnung in Dortmund-Löttringhausen (1954–65); Germania in Dortmund-Marten (1855–1971); Zollverein in Essen-Katernberg (1847–1986) Minister Achenbach in Lünen-Brambauer (1900–92); Erin in Castrop-Rauxel (1970–83); Graf Moltke in Gladbeck (1871–1971); Waltrop in Waltrop (1903–79); Ickern in Castrop-Rauxel (1877–1974); Recklinghausen in Recklinghausen (1864–1974); Graf Schwerin in Recklinghausen (1867–1983); Ewald in Oer-Erkenschwick (1900–78). Apart from the closing of Zollverein, which is now marked as a world heritage site, none of these closings had been monumental. In the Ruhr Valley there was no leader such as Arthur Scargill, the head of the National Union of Mineworkers, who was then viciously harassed by the Tory press and the state, but who also condemned the emergence of *Solidarnosc* and continued to defend Stalin even in his most recent stance as a communist Brexiter who would like to see a workers' state reopening Britain's mines, mills and factories. Arthur Scargill would have been my family's nightmare.

At times, I may have been as well. In 1979 in West Germany I joined the youth organization of the German Communist Party (DKP), which – more than ten years after the German Constitutional Court had banned the Communist Party of Germany as extremist in 1956 – was then still operated illegally. (It was legally acknowledged in 1986.) At that time I read Johnson but also workers' literature from the Ruhr Valley, especially Max von der Grün.[10] I joined the Communist Party because I wanted to learn more about East Germany (as if Communism would provide me with such knowledge), and was vehemently opposed to the so-called NATO double-track solution, which offered the Warsaw Pact countries (Albania, Bulgaria, Czechoslovakia, East Germany, Hungary, Poland, Romania, Soviet Union) a mutual limitation of medium-range ballistic missiles while also deploying more medium-range nuclear weapons in Western Europe. My comrades and I organized anti-nuclear power demonstrations – and attended performances by jazz musicians like Pharao Sanders and Carla Bley. In 1983, when I attended a regional party meeting that felt far too Stalinist for my taste, I left.

Johnson has never been a member of the East German Communist Party, but he clearly harboured a utopian hope for what most commonly has been described as a 'socialism with a human face'. Johnson's utopian sense may have been inspired by the lectures of Ernst Bloch that he attended between 1954 and 1956 in Leipzig. Like Johnson's academic advisor Hans Mayer, Bloch was an independent Marxist thinker. Although he then taught in the GDR, for him utopia did not mean a state-socialist blueprint, but 'a place and state [to which no one] has yet been' (1986: 1376). In Johnson's writing this utopian impulse can most sharply be seen in the last paragraph of *Anniversaries IV*. In this paragraph Gesine Cresspahl, who throughout the volume has – like her author – hoped for a 'socialism with a human face', observes the Soviet take-over on 20 August 1986 in Prague. Her reaction is one of grave disappointment. The question is whether this event should also spell the end of hope. Johnson does not seem to think so, and neither do I.

Epilogue

It is hard to say what Johnson would have made of the fall of the Berlin Wall and the GDR. It is also hard to say if he would have continued living in Sheerness, where – as Colin Riordan (1989) has suggested – the English language had started to become the medium in which he was able to articulate some of his woundedness more freely. Johnson was interested in literature as a form of history and documentation, as well as a form of intermediation. Perhaps he would also have started to think of literature as a particular form of reconnaissance? In 1981 literary critic Fritz J. Raddatz might have thought as much when he told British radio listeners that Johnson had written something very beautiful. In particular he said that nobody who ever left their country did so 'without writing a letter; a letter to the country'. Johnson's work, Raddatz suggested, should be understood as 'a long, long letter addressed to the country, which means to the problems of the country'. This seems to me a good way to put it. As Johnson might have said, for 'persons living in both parts of Germany', writing and reading as part of a reflection on traumatic pain is perhaps the only way to gain a measure of healing.

In 1990 my grandfather and my mother travelled to Heckligen to see the farm that for thirty-eight years they had not seen. My grandmother said that she was too afraid to see what had become of the family's former house and barn, and declined to travel with them. When later I spoke to my mother on the phone, she said that for an entire day my grandfather had walked silently along and across fields, looked for a long time at the barn that had once harboured tools, oxen and cows, and that they even knocked at the door of the house in which they had once lived. They were lucky that its now-occupants were friendly and let them walk through all of its rooms. My mother reported this in a tone of concern for my grandfather, who for the duration of the trip barely spoke a word. But neither did my mother speak about her feelings related to the trip. Both my grandfather and my mother might belong to generations that Françoise Meltzer (2019: 4) calls 'tight-lipped', but I imagine a flurry of emotions surging.

When, a few years ago, my grandfather was diagnosed with Alzheimer's, the memory of his life in West Germany was eroding. And then it was completely erased. He could only remember his life in East Germany – life before the flight. At the time of his death, Johnson had been planning to write a book about the life of Heinrich Cresspahl, who makes his first appearance in *Speculations* and, born in 1888, had lived between 1925 and 1933 in England. Perhaps walking back in memory and time is the only option for those who felt that they have never fitted into their present.

Petra Rethmann is Professor of Anthropology at McMaster University and Director of the Institute on Globalization and the Human Condition. She is the author or editor of three books, and the author of numerous articles that have appeared – among others – in *American Ethnologist, American Anthropologist, Anthropologica, Anthropologie et Sociétés* and *Sinij Divan*. She has held guest professorships at the University of St Petersburg, University of Cape Town and Aleksanteri Institute/Helsinki. She is currently working on an ethnographic memoir entitled *Less Than/A Dream*, a book on ethnography and form, and one preliminary entitled *Liberal Wounds*.

Notes

1. As a reader, I cannot set aside my admiring recognition of Johnson's stylistic innovations and aesthetic daring (Baker 1999; Hell 2002; Leuchtenberger 2003). Yet what makes reading this author so exceptional to me is his ability to articulate some of my own emotional, political and historical perceptions. Psychoanalytically schooled analysts (Schwab 2010) may call this transference.

2. Apart from Johnson himself and the fictive figures I've listed above, other refugees – too – populate his writings. For example, *Anniversaries I* introduces Holocaust survivor Mrs Ferwalter. Refugees also populate a number of shorter stories and fragments that Johnson did not incorporate into novels. See, for example, *Osterwasser*, in *Karsch, und andere Prosa*. It thus seems all the more surprising that, to my knowledge to date, Johnson scholarship has not examined the issue of refugee-ness in this author's writings.
3. The suitcase that my grandfather carried in the night contained a black suit and a white shirt for him, and a frilly dress for my mother. The story they had concocted was that they were travelling to a wedding in Spremberg, a small town at the Polish border, where my grandfather's brother lived. According to my grandmother, this brother was *ein Überzeugter* (somebody who was ardently convinced that the East German socialist system was rightful and good). My grandfather's brother could not imagine leaving, but he must have loved my grandfather enough that he agreed to support his story.
4. The *Junge Gemeinde* was a Christian student congregation whose members in the early 1950s were lined up for a show trial and jailed for distributing leaflets which demanded freedom of speech.
5. Johnson had originally sought to publish his novel under the pseudonym Joachim Catt, but decided against it because the Stasi would surely have found out.
6. Wright here is talking about the expellees that came from Eastern Europe, but much of what he says also holds for refugees from Eastern Germany. In any case, in the West Germany in which I grew up these were often lumped together.
7. See, for example, Wright (2020: 93) in *The Sea View Has Me Again*.
8. This is also the argument made by Eric Santner in *History Beyond the Pleasure Principle: Some Thoughts on the Representation of Trauma*.
9. This concern also holds today. For example, as Ian Leveson and Sandra Lustig note, the national memorial Unter den Linden in Berlin (erected in 1993, nine years after Johnson's death in 1984), is dedicated 'to the military and civilian victims of Second World War, the Shoah, and Stalinist persecution in East Germany all at once, without differentiation'. All of the various victims are remembered and monumentalized together, all together, for all time. Clearly, such a form of remembrance is ahistorical and ethically problematic. What, exactly, is the Berlin monument of 1993 commemorating? On whose terms, and from which perspective?
10. In 1961 a group of initially local writers from the Ruhr Valley met in Dortmund to form Gruppe 61. The organizers were Fritz Hüser, a city librarian, and Max von der Grün, a miner with literary ambitions. From its inception there was a fundamental disagreement amongst the membership as to whether it was writing as workers for fellow workers, drawing on a long-established local tradition, or whether it was to broaden the narrow base of West German literature.

References

Arendt, Hannah. 2004. *Hannah Arendt/Uwe Johnson: Der Briefwechsel*. Frankfurt a. M.: Suhrkamp.
——. 1950. *The Aftermath of Nazi Rule: Report from Germany*. In *Commentary* X/10.
Baker, Gary L. 1999. *Understanding Uwe Johnson*. New York and Columbia: University of South Carolina Press.

Benjamin, Walter. 1986 [1936]. 'The Storyteller: Observations on the Works of Nikolai Leskov.' In *Walter Benjamin. Selected Writings. Volume 3: 1935–1938.* Howard Eiland and Michael W. Jennings (eds). Cambridge, MA: The Belknap Press of Harvard University Press, pp. 143–66.

Best, Stephen and Sharon Marcus. 2009. 'Surface Reading: An Introduction', *Representations* 108: 1–21.

Bloch, Ernst. 1986. 'The Principle of Hope'. Cambridge, MA: MIT Press.

Felski, Rita. 2008. *Uses of Literature.* Malden: Blackwell.

———. 2015. *The Limits of Critique.* Chicago: University of Chicago Press.

———. 2020. *Hooked: Art and Attachment.* Chicago: University of Chicago Press.

Grass, Günter. 2015. *Im Krebsgang.* Göttingen: Steidl.

Hansen, Dörte. 2015. *Altes Land: Roman.* München: Albrecht Knaus Verlag.

Hell, Julia. 2002. 'The Melodrama of Illegal Identifications, or, Post-Holocaust Authorship in Uwe Johnson's *Jahrestage. Aus dem Leben von Gesine Cresspahl'*, *Monatshefte* 94(2): 209–29.

Hirsch, Marianne. 1981. *Beyond the Single Vision: Henry James, Michel Butor, Uwe Johnson.* York, SC: French Literature Publications Company.

Johnson, Uwe. 1959. *Mutmassungen über Jakob.* Frankfurt a. M.: Suhrkamp.

———. 1964. *Osterwasser*, in *Karsch, und andere Prosa.* Frankfurt a. M.: Suhrkamp.

———. 1970–83. *Jahrestage: Aus dem Leben von Gesine Cresspahl.* Vol. 1–4. Frankfurt a. M.: Suhrkamp.

———. 1986. *Begleitumstände: Frankfurter Vorlesungen.* Frankfurt a. M.: Suhrkamp.

Kempowski, Walter. 1992. *Mark und Bein.* München: Albrecht Knaus Verlag.

Kluge, Alexander. 2014. *Air Raid.* Trans. Martin Chalmers. New York: Seagull.

Koepnick, Lutz. 2021. *Resonant Matter: Sound, Art, and the Promise of Hospitality.* London: Bloomsbury.

Lennox, Sara. 1989. 'History in Uwe Johnson's *Jahrestage'*, *The Germanic Review* 64(1): 31–41.

Leuchtenberger, Katja. 2003. *'Wer Erzaehlt, muss an alles Denken': Erzaehlstrukturen und Stragegien der Leserlenkung in den fruehen Romanen Uwe Johnson's.* Gottingen: Vandenhoeck & Ruprecht.

Love, Heather. 2010. 'Close But Not Deep: Literary Ethics and the Descriptive Turn', *New Literary History* 41(2): 371–91.

Lustig, Sandra and Ian Leveson. 2006. 'A Response to Diana Pinto', in *Turning the Kaleidoscope: Perspectives on European Jewry.* New York: Berghahn.

Meltzer, Françoise. 2019. *Dark Lens: Imaging Germany, 1945.* Chicago: University of Chicago Press.

Neumann, Bernd. 1994. *Uwe Johnson.* Hamburg: Europäische Verlagsanstalt.

Raffles, Hugh. 2020. *The Book of Unconformities: Speculations on Lost Time.* New York: Pantheon.

Riordan, Colin. 1989. *The Ethics of Narration: Uwe Johnson's Novels from 'Ingrid Babenererde' to 'Jahrestage'.* London: Modern Humanities Research Association.

Rosa, Hartmut. 2019. *Resonance: A Sociology of Our Relationship to the World.* Trans. James C. Wagner. Cambridge: Polity.

Santner, Eric. 1992. 'History Beyond the Pleasure Principle: Some Thoughts on the Representation of Trauma', in *Probing the Limits of Representation: Nazism and*

the 'Final Solution', Saul Friedlander (ed.). Cambridge, MA: Harvard University Press, pp. 132–54.
Schwab, Gabriele. 2010. *Haunting Legacies: Violent Histories and Transgenerational Trauma*. New York: Columbia University Press.
Sebald, Winfried G. 1999. *Luftkrieg und Literatur*. Frankfurt a. M.: Fischer.
Sedgwick, Eve Kosofsky. 1997. 'Paranoid Reading and Reparative Reading; or, You're So Paranoid You Probably Think This Introduction is About You', in *Novel Gazing: Queer Readings in Fiction*, Eve Sedgwick (ed.). Durham, NC: Duke University Press, pp. 1–37.
Stewart, Kathleen. 2011. 'Atmospheric Attunements', *Environment and Planning D: Society and Space* 29(3): 445–53.
Wright, Patrick. 2020. *The Sea View Has Me Again: Uwe Johnson in Sheerness*. London: Repeater Books.

Chapter 7

Sacred Muses
The Lake Goddess in Flora Nwapa's Literary Worldmaking

Paula Uimonen

Introduction: Literary Worldmaking and the Lake Goddess as a Sacred Muse

We were cruising slowly along the Urashi river, when a mindblowing experience jolted my appreciation of the wonders of life, well beyond intellectual reason. The environment itself was pristine, the brownish water flowing slowly amidst lush vegetation on the riverbeds. As I scrambled to the front of our small boat, I asked the driver to turn off the engine, so I could listen to the surroundings. Serene silence, sprinkled with the sounds of insects and birds. It was one of the most beautiful environments I had experienced in my travels around the world. But what made this so exceptional was the unexpected sense of spiritual connection. As I surrendered myself, I felt the presence of my loved ones who had passed on, sharing my joie de vivre. It was as if the extremes of being in this world embraced my inner core, connecting the living with the dead, in the eternal cycle of life. I have written about this elsewhere, referring to it as a magical (Uimonen 2020), and spiritual (Uimonen 2022) experience. In this chapter, I use this exceptional experience during fieldwork as a starting point for exploring spirituality in art and creativity, by way of the Lake Goddess in Flora Nwapa's literary worldmaking.

It was Flora Nwapa's literary creations that brought me to Oguta, her hometown in Southeast Nigeria, with its magnificent Oguta Lake and the adjoining Urashi river. My first visit was in December 2016, together with Flora Napa's oldest daughter Ejine Nzeribe and her only son Uzoma Nwakuche, who accompanied me on the boat trip. By then we had travelled around Nigeria for several weeks for the Efuru@50 literary festival, in celebration of the 50th anniversary of Flora Nwapa's novel *Efuru* (Nwapa 1966). This was the first internationally published novel in English by a black African woman writer. The Efuru@50 festival was a national celebration, organized in five different cities across the country: Lagos, Maiduguri, Abuja, Enugu and Owerri. I had attended the event as part of my research on African women writers, an intense period of fieldwork that introduced me to Flora Nwapa's aesthetic worlds.[1]

In this chapter I deliberate on the Lake Goddess in Flora Nwapa's literary worldmaking as a sacred muse. The Lake Goddess was a recurring character in Flora Nwapa's literary oeuvre, from her first novel *Efuru* (Nwapa 1966) to her last, posthumously published novel *The Lake Goddess* (Nwapa 2017). In Nwapa's literary worlds, the Lake Goddess appeared under various names: Ogbuide, Uhamiri, Woman of the Lake, Mammy Water and Great Mother. This fictitious character was in turn inspired by a prominent deity in traditional Oguta cosmology, commonly referred to as Ogbuide or Uhammiri, as documented in Sabine Jell-Bahlsen's extensive ethnography (2008, 2014). A water goddess, often known as Mammy Water or Mami Wata, is also worshipped in many other places, and has inspired artists in other parts of Africa and the world (Drewal 2008).

By conceptualizing the Lake Goddess as a sacred muse, I wish to bring attention to spiritual dimensions of art and aesthetics, thus thinking through the *exceptional* from a somewhat unusual angle. In arts, the exceptional is often associated with something superior, especially in the aesthetic valuation of beauty. In the anthropology of art, it is well known that Gell argued against aesthetics and defined art as a technical system, elaborating on the 'enchantment of technology', in recognition of 'the power that technical systems have of casting a spell over us so that we see the real world in an enchanted form' (Gell 1992: 44). Gell refuted the emphasis on aesthetics in dominant art theory, instead accentuating the relation between art and magic, yet he insisted on methodological philistinism. Although Gell's emphasis on enchantment offers interesting pointers to the exceptional, perhaps his refusal to think beyond art as objects and technical activities blinds us to the very magic in art that he so poignantly recognized? At the time, materialism may have served as a productive antidote to the emphasis on beauty in aestheticism. But perhaps it would be erroneous to desacralize instances when art makes us see the real world in its enchanted form?

When appreciated as a form of aesthetic worldmaking, literature offers valuable insights into some exceptional forces in the continuous making of our world. In the emergent anthropology of world literature, scholars have approached literature from a variety of angles, from transnational migration and travel writing to literary festivals and women writers (see, for example, Helgesson et al. 2018). Drawing on my recent work on Nigerian women writers, I take this opportunity to probe deeper into topics that I have struggled with for some time. When trying to make sense of spirituality in Flora Nwapa's writing (Uimonen 2020), I have come to understand the challenges of approaching spirituality with sufficient epistemological and ontological openness. Trained as an anthropologist in Sweden, I have feared the label of going native when discussing spiritual matters in African contexts. Even though the book that impressed me the most during my undergraduate studies was *In Sorcery's Shadow* (Stoller and Olkes 1987). Having lived in Tanzania for years, I have become used to daily invocations of God, and my second hometown Bagamoyo is known for witchcraft. Meanwhile, African scholars have made me acutely aware of Eurocentric misrepresentations of local cultural contexts, which I painstakingly try to avoid. Hopefully we can all learn something from probing alternative ways of approaching literary worldmaking *with* the Lake Goddess.

The Lake Goddess and Literary Imagination

> 'We are the Lake People' ... 'We live on the Lake. We call the Lake Goddess Uhamiri or Ogbuide. We sometimes call her Mother. She is the Mother of all of us. Our forefathers discovered her while they were fishing many years ago. They were fascinated by the Lake's blue waters, fishes, depth and volume of water. They had not seen anything quite like that before, so they worshipped her for she was a great Goddess. The blue waters of the Lake were awesome and a source of wealth for our forefathers. We believe that the Goddess protects us and inspires us to great heights. We believe that no invader from any part of the world can destroy us. We believe that the deity is a beautiful and ageless woman who is partial to women. We believe that she intervenes in the lives of the people, both men and women, but more especially women'. (Nwapa 2017: 186–87)

This passage in *The Lake Goddess* captures the cultural significance of the lake and its goddess for the Oguta community, here described as the Lake People. In this fictitious dialogue, the father of the main character Ona explains to her husband about the Lake Goddess, so that he may understand why his wife can no longer live with him. The husband, Mr Sylvester, is from another town and thus not fully acquainted with the customs and beliefs of Oguta people. At this point in the novel, it has become clear to the father, Mgbada, that Ona has been called by the Lake

Goddess to serve her as a priestess, which means she has to sever the relationship with her husband. Mgbada, who is also a traditional healer, clarifies: 'It is a divine call, and it is for life, and when one is called, one must obey. Failure to obey means disability or even death' (Nwapa 2017: 187). Eventually Mr Sylvester accepts Ona's calling, understanding that it brings her security, power and peace, since she is destined to serve Ogbuide and by extension, the whole community of the Lake People.

Through the goddess and other characters in *The Lake Goddess*, Flora Nwapa introduced readers to a captivating literary world, inspired by the social and spiritual worlds of the Oguta community, yet crafted with the artistic liberty of writers of creative fiction (Jell-Bahlsen 2007). When creating her literary worlds, Flora Nwapa drew on stories she had heard when growing up in Oguta, such as stories that women told of the Lake Goddess. Later she did her own research on the goddess and her worshippers. Nwapa herself came from an elite family of early Christian converts, which limited her interaction with the water deity and her followers. But through her fiction she could establish a closer relationship with the Lake Goddess, thus engaging with sacred forces by way of literary worldmaking.

The crafting of literary worlds offers valuable insights into worldmaking through storytelling and imagination. A leading world literature scholar has suggested that the world as we know it has a 'narrative structure', it is 'formed by the telling of stories' (Cheah 2014: 325). Comparatively, a leading anthropologist has suggested that 'the world is a conversation', underlining that 'in this conversation lies *ontogénèse*, the becoming of being' (Ingold 2018: 169, emphasis in original). Since the world is always in a state of becoming, literary storytelling epitomizes the creative process of worldmaking through imagination. In his book, *Imagining for Real*, Ingold argues that modern rational science's separation of reality and imagination, fact and fable, has had 'fateful consequences for human life', to the point where 'life itself appears diminished', the loss of creative impulse leading to a loss of wonder, hopes and dreams (Ingold 2021: 62). With examples ranging from medieval reading to indigenous ontology, Ingold demonstrates that imagination is not only real, but gives us indispensable insights into reality, constituting a way of knowing and being in the world through participation in and interaction with the world. Writers play their part in this interaction through 'entextualization', which Barber describes as 'the art of making things stick', a creative practice of 'laying down the means for new creation' (Barber 2007: 33).

Returning to the Lake Goddess, we can appreciate how Flora Nwapa engaged in worldmaking by not only depicting the world, but also by intervening in its creative transformation. For starters, in writing about the Lake Goddess, Flora Nwapa made her stick, to use Barber's words. Through entextualization, the Goddess was recast in literary form, both emplaced in and dislodged from the local community and its natural environment. Through her literary work, Nwapa made this local deity known to readers around the world, her books mediating a wider web of relationships with the goddess. Moreover, she described the Lake Goddess as our Mother, an ageless woman who nurtures and protects the Lake People. The Lake Goddess was thus depicted as the community's source of life, a maternal force vital to its very existence, her role in creation underlining the value of women and motherhood.

Written in the context of religious colonialism and patriarchal politics, Nwapa's literary engagements with the female water deity were controversial in many ways. At the time, religious colonialism had turned Christian converts against traditional spiritual practices, resulting in tensions and violent conflicts, which are still ongoing (Jell-Bahlsen 2008; Uimonen 2020). Colonialism also brought more patriarchal political structures and gender hierarchies that degraded the position of women, while undermining the cultural ideals of gender complementarity (Ogunyemi 1996). In a postcolonial context, these political developments have been exasperated by neo-colonial dependency and global power relations, which have undermined the status of women even further. Addressing such social transformations, Nwapa offered role models for women through her literary characters, a creative practice that can be understood in terms of womanist worldmaking (Uimonen 2020). While many of her female characters were strong and resourceful women, the Lake Goddess was exceptional in the powers she conveyed.

Since this chapter deals with sacred muses, the spiritual dimension to the Lake Goddess in Flora Nwapa's aesthetic worldmaking deserves more attention. As noted in the citation above, Flora Nwapa wrote that 'We believe that the Goddess protects us and inspires us to great heights' (Nwapa 2017: 187). In Flora Nwapa's case, the Lake Goddess certainly inspired her to great heights, starting with her first novel *Efuru* (Nwapa 1966), which assured her place in literary history and canons, while establishing her as the Mother of modern African literature. The Lake Goddess reappeared in many of her literary works. In one of her first children's books, *Mammywater* (1979), the goddess of the lake and her river husband were visually illustrated in their underwater world. In Flora Nwapa's novel about the Biafran war, the Lake Goddess played a decisive role in protecting Oguta from invading troops. With the telling title *Never Again* (Nwapa 1986 [1975]), this was the first novel about the civil war written by a woman writer. It was also the only novel in which Flora Nwapa wrote in the first-person, and it carries the dedication 'For the mysterious and beautiful ... Uhamiri'. Having herself lived through the horrors of the civil war, scholars have appraised it as Flora Nwapa's most auto-biographical novel, one that also signals the spiritual relationality of her literary worldmaking (Uimonen 2020: 175–77).

We can thus glean how Flora Nwapa captured the divine interventions of the Lake Goddess in the Oguta community, and in so doing channelled the agency of the goddess. Recast in literary form, the goddess was no longer spatiotemporally confined to her natural environment, but released into the world at large, inspiring readers around the world to imagine the world anew. As a sacred muse, the Lake Goddess emerged in all her glory in Nwapa's creative fiction, extending her sphere of influence well beyond the Oguta community into a larger world in the making.

Sacred Muses and Water Goddesses

> Ogbuide, we thank you
>
> Queen of Water, we thank you
>
> Great Mother, we thank you
>
> Good and kind Mother
>
> Come closer
>
> Mother and water are the same
>
> Without water
>
> Who can live?
>
> Without Mother
>
> Who can live?
>
> Our beautiful Mother
>
> Come closer
>
> (Nwapa 2017: 229)

These were Flora Nwapa's last words in *The Lake Goddess*, published some twenty-five years after completion. They recount the main character Ona singing praises for the Lake Goddess, accompanied by two female fish-sellers. By then Ona had dedicated her life to serving Ogbuide, as a devoted priestess. Ona's fate was similar to that of Efuru, the main character in Nwapa's first novel (Nwapa 1966), thus affirming certain leitmotifs in her oeuvre, centred around the Lake Goddess.

So why did Flora Nwapa write about the Lake Goddess, over and over again? What made her such an influential sacred muse? Let us pause at the centrality of water and mother in these poetic lines to think through sacred muses.

Water deities and sacred muses have appeared in different contexts at different times. In his seminal text *H_2O and the Water of Forgetfulness*, Illich elaborates on the prominence of water in Ancient Greek mythology, which he traces through Mnemosyne (well of remembrance/Goddess of memory), a female Titan birthed by Gaia (Mother Earth), also known as the Mother of the Muses (Illich 1985: 31–32). Elaborating on the significance of the Mother of the Muses in the Ancient Greek world, he concludes that water 'became the source of remembrance, the wellspring of culture and acquired the features of woman' (Illich 1985: 32). Comparatively, in Igbo and Oguta cosmology, we find a gender-neutral supreme god and creator, *Chi-Ukwu/Chukwu*, along with a pantheon of female and male deities, including the supreme earth goddess and the supreme water goddess (Jell-Bahlsen 2014). The water goddess is particularly powerful, since she 'controls the crossroads and eternal transitions between life and death' (Jell-Bahlsen 2008: 80). Elaborating on the crossroads in the Oguta wordview, Jell-Bahlsen (2014: 27) recounts that individuals cross a river twice, to enter and exit this world, which she compares with ancient Greek mythology where a ferryman takes the dead across a river into the underworld, although in Oguta, this crossing is managed by a ferry*woman*. Seeing that most myths of creation conjure water (Illich 1985), and that sacred water beings have a central role in many stories of cosmogenesis (Strang 2021), water is clearly of great significance for the creation and recreation of life. For human lifeforms, the power of recreation is channelled through the reproductive power of women, our mothers.

Nowadays the muse is often dislodged from her divine origins, but it is worth paying closer attention to other ways of appraising the source of creativity in arts. For contemporary writers and artists, the muse is commonly thought of as a person, or a mysterious force that inspires the individual artist. But creativity is much more than individual innovation, it can be appreciated as cultural improvisation, which is generative, relational and temporal (Hallam and Ingold 2007). Emphasizing its social and cultural essence, anthropologists have underlined that 'creativity is a profoundly social fact' (Hastrup 2007: 193), while reminding us that people ascribe creativity to different sources in different cultural contexts (Barber 2007). As outlined above, in the ancient Greek world, creativity was ascribed to the Muses, goddesses of inspiration. In Igbo culture, creativity is also ascribed to spiritual powers, more specifically *chi*. In her analysis of Nigerian women's literature, Ogunyemi describes *chi* as 'the individual's quintessence, the creator god's unique, or personalised, gift ensconced within' (1996: 36). She notes that writers are inspired by their *chi* to tell a story, which is a collective undertaking, since 'writing, like storytelling, is intercessory, with the artist melding the group's artistic gifts and collective experience to present the novel to those willing to read or listen' (Ogunyemi 1996: 43). While this line of thought resonates with the anthropological appreciation of the social relationality of creativity, it is noteworthy that in this cultural context, the generative force is ascribed to spiritual power. As Ogunyemi underlines: 'From a literary perspective, *Chi* as inspiring muse gives the writer the courage and determination to institute, identify with, or counter a discourse' (Ogunyemi 1996: 40).

In an Igbo cultural context, it makes little sense to dislodge creativity from its divine origins, which makes the Lake Goddess a powerful sacred muse. To the literary scholar Ogunyemi, who has analysed Nwapa's writings through her African womanist theory, there is no doubt about the Lake Goddess' creative powers. She postulates that when Nigerian women write about the water goddess, they actually *incarnate* the goddess (Ogunyemi 1996: 34).

When the source of creativity is ascribed to spiritual power, art acquires a powerful essence, transcending human life worlds in exceptional ways. Far from being reducible to technologies of enchantment, art is released from the material constraints of everyday life, its appraisal curtailed only by human imagination. This is why an anthropology of art cannot be reduced to the production and circulation of art objects, as in Gell's theory of art as a technical system. Nor can aesthetics be confined to valuations of beauty, since art, just like aesthetics, takes different forms in different contexts. But if we open our minds to recognizing not only the materiality and sociality of art, but also its spirituality, perhaps we can get a fuller grasp of those enhanced experiences of and through art.

Let us now turn to the gendered dimension of creative agency, since the examples I draw upon in this chapter are female goddesses, the Muses in Ancient Greece and the Lake Goddess in Oguta. Can we discuss art and creativity in terms of generative forms of cultural improvisation without recognizing the centrality of gender, in this case femininity? The goddesses I have introduced here are representative of maternal forces, from the Muses that descended from Mother Earth to the Lake Goddess aka Queen Mother. This matricentricity of creative agency is rather remarkable, seeing that mothers are essential to human reproduction. Creativity can thus be related to the very essence of human existence, especially the power of female agency in the creation of human life. Ogunyemi (1996) has even hypothesized *chi* as the mother within, thus accentuating female power in African writers' literary practices.

The sacred muses discussed here are also related to water, pointing to the cultural significance of water throughout human history. Strang (2021) has shown how the worship of water beings, including Mammywater, supports a form of conviviality between humans and the environment, which maintains highly sustainable lifeways. The worship of various water beings recognizes the generative powers of water, which is often reflected in cosmogeneses of powerful nature deities. She contrasts the worship of water in different parts of the world with the development of modern hierarchical societies that assert patriarchal dominion over nature. In such technically instrumental societies, nature worship is replaced with religions that humanize deities and with secular worldviews dominated by science. It would seem that Flora Nwapa captured something essential about human life when she pointed out that water is life, just like mother is life. So let us now explore divine inspiration in relation to creation.

Divine Inspiration, Literary Ontology and the Force of Creation

Can we recognize divine inspiration as a reality, just as real as the writing of literary worlds? We would probably not hesitate to accept sacred muses as social facts, deliberating on them as social constructs, but could they exist in their own right, as spiritual forces? Let us return to Gell, who discussed the relation between art and magic with ethnographic examples from the Trobriand Islands. Elaborating on technical virtuosity in the carving of canoes or gardening, he reflected on magic as the ideal technology, noting a convergence between objects produced through art and magic. He argued that this convergence related to the sense of art objects 'transcending the technical schemas of their creators', which Trobrianders attributed to 'divine inspiration or ancestral spirit' (Gell 1992: 59). Gell concluded that the kind of awe we may experience when marvelling at a masterpiece, unable to explain how 'such an object comes to exist in the world', is similar to Trobrianders' fascination with the efficacy of their technologies (Gell 1992: 62). Thus he argued that both art and magic can be understood as technologies of enchantment. But surely there is more to the enchantment of art and magic than technical systems?

Reflecting a common stance in social science, when Gell insisted on methodological philistinism, he argued that it was as important for the study of arts as methodological atheism was for the study of religion. He drew on Berger's work on religion, which underscored that regardless of the scholar's own religious convictions, or lack thereof, 'theistic and mystical beliefs are subjected to sociological scrutiny on the assumption that *they are not literally true*' (Gell 1992: 41, emphasis added).

By comparison, in a well-known passage in his classic study of witchcraft and magic among the Azande, Evans-Pritchard stated 'Witches, as the Azande conceive them, clearly cannot exist' (1976 [1937]: 18). This oft-cited statement seems to affirm the methodological atheism that Gell appealed to, asserting that witches are not literally true. But Evans-Pritchard himself reflected on the philosophical challenge involved: 'We do not think that witchcraft exists, but we have been taught that God does' (1976 [1937]: 244). He noted that for atheists, both witches and God would be an illusion, but for those who believed in God, it all came down to faith. Interestingly he also reflected on the issue of anthropologists going native, concluding that 'If an anthropologist is a sensitive person it could hardly be otherwise' (Evans-Pritchard 1976 [1937]: 245). Despite Evans-Pritchard's cautionary reflections, in anthropological studies of religion, atheism has been a common epistemic premise, while religion is typically approached as cultural belief (Winzeler 2012).

In recent years, scholars have moved beyond this epistemological impasse, towards an appreciation of spirituality as integral to the human condition, beyond belief. Challenging the scientist underpinnings of modernist ontology, Escobar has pointed out how 'The Western realist episteme translates non-Western reals into beliefs, so that only the reality validated by science is real' (Escobar 2020: 15). In his quest for a pluriversal world, a world in which many worlds fit, he emphasizes relational ontologies of radical interdependence as viable alternatives to the dualist ontology of modernism. In addition to his insistence on multiple realities, Escobar recognizes 'emotions, affect and spirituality as vital forces that contribute to building the worlds in which we live' (2020: 24). Scholarly deliberations on political ontology thus challenge the rational and secular claims of social science, including the conceptualization of religion as a system of beliefs.

Upon closer scrutiny, what is categorized as religion or belief in non-Western contexts tends to contain a much higher degree of complexity. African scholars have lamented the one-dimensional appraisals of religion in African cultures, from the colonial idea that 'Africans were pagans, a people without religion' to the 'counter discourse' that their worldview was 'profoundly religious' (Oladipo 2005: 355). Such misrepresentations are often related to the use of Western concepts, which fail to capture the complexities of worldviews in African cultures (Imbo 2005: 364). Oladipo has argued that religion in Africa is not only a matter of belief, but also an attitude, articulating an 'ontological ultimacy' of non-human powers and agencies (Oladipo 2005: 357).

By comparison, de la Cadena (2018: 31) introduces *not only* as an ontological opening, to underline divergent ways of knowing and not knowing. Her deliberations are ethnographically grounded in conversations whereby her interlocutor 'Mariano would insist that what to me *was* (for example, a mountain) was *not only* that. And it was possible that I could eventually *not know* what *it* not only was' (de la Cadena 2018: 28). Such epistemic uncertainty has often been rationalized by anthropologists, foreclosing them as practices of worlding. For instance, Gell deliberated on 'magic as an accompaniment to uncertainty', not as opposed to knowledge, but as a reflection of the uncertainty of knowledge of the world, concluding that 'the magical attitude is a by-product of the rational pursuit of technical objectives using technical means' (Gell 1992: 57). Thus, rather than acknowledging that magic may capture a multifaceted world of *not only*, he relegated it to a by-product of reason in technical systems.

Let us now shift our focus to literary ontology. Escobar notes that 'ontologies often manifest themselves as narratives', such as myths and rituals, which have been extensively documented by anthropologists (2020: 25). When it comes to literature, Cheah has elaborated on its 'peculiar ontological status', arguing that literature communicates directly with a force that enables the constitution of reality, and he describes literary worlding as 'a process that keeps live the force that opens up another world, a force that is immanent to the existing world' (Cheah 2008: 35–36). By conjuring other possible worlds, literature thus occupies an exceptional position in narrative manifestations of ontology, in what I have conceptualized as a *pluriverse of aesthetic worlds* (Uimonen 2020). Not only does literature offer fictitious representations of different beings and becomings, it also creates new aesthetic worlds, thus intervening in the very worlding of a world of many worlds.

When appraised in terms of worldmaking, literary ontology points to the force of creation. Drawing on Derrida, Cheah (2008) described the force of literature as analogous to birth, which takes us from creativity to creation. Ingold (2021) elaborates on creation, rather than creativity, in relation to the continuous becoming of the world. He notes that in a prose-poem from the first century BCE, a Roman author addressed Nature in the feminine as the 'creatress of things', thus comparing her generative capacity to that of giving birth, which reflected the original meaning of creation, as in begetting a child (Ingold 2021: 15). Some five centuries later, when the Old Testament was translated into Latin, the word creation was given a whole new meaning with the opening words 'in the beginning, God created heaven and earth', thus implying the creation of the world as something from nothing. During the Renaissance, creation jumped from world to mind, as artists appealed to divine creation as a measure of their genius. Ingold elaborates on creation in theology and art, to reinstate creation as something crescent, just like the work of art is always crescent. Drawing on Bergson's work, he argues that to invent is 'not to create a world, but actively to participate from the inside in the world's ceaseless creation of itself' (ibid.: 27). Interestingly, he asserts that this process of creation does not belong to individual human beings, even less so to their brains, rather it 'belongs to the world, to existence, perchance to God' (ibid.: 27). Through Ingold, we can thus recognize Cheah's force in literature as the force of creation, even divine creation, denoting ontogenesis, the ongoing generation of being.

Following this line of thinking, it should not be inconceivable to appreciate the Lake Goddess as a sacred muse in Flora Nwapa's literary worldmaking. When creating her aesthetic worlds, Nwapa participated in the world's creation of itself from within a world of divine inspiration. Far from representing a world created from nothing by God the Father, Nwapa created other possible worlds through other forms of divine invention, especially that of the Goddess our Mother. In retrospect, it is not impossible that divine forces even intervened in her creative writing in rather surreptitious ways. In the Igbo world a 'human being receives his/her life force, *Chi*, from the supreme God *Chukwu*, the God of Destiny, before birth', along with his/her destiny, but 'an individual's destiny is challenged and *can* be changed, by the supreme water goddess' (Jell-Bahlsen 2014: 27, emphasis in original). What if the supreme water goddess changed Flora Nwapa's destiny? Could it be that through divine intervention in Flora Nwapa's life force, the Lake Goddess wanted to send a message to humans around the world that another world is indeed possible (Uimonen 2020: 210)?

Concluding Reflections on the Sacred Wonders of Our World in the Making

When I first experienced the wonders of the Urashi River, I had been exposed to the Lake Goddess through Flora Nwapa's first novel *Efuru*. Her stories of the Woman of the Lake, the mysterious Uhamiri, had intrigued me, captivating my imagination. As I write these words by the lakeside in Oguta, five years after my first visit, I can but conclude that Flora Nwapa made the Lake Goddess stick, thus channelling her creative agency. For years, I have appreciated that the beautiful Oguta Lake is *not only* a lake. And it seems that her sacred muse compels me to write about the lake's spiritual essence, while directing me to other water spirits in other parts of the African continent (Uimonen and Masimbi 2021).

'If you have a clean heart, the lake will be good to you', the Priestess N'Dr Stella Akuzor Anozia, Ezeugegbe 1 (Queen Mirror One) told me, when sharing her story a few years earlier. At the time, we had just met and she had explained to me how Ogbuide had called her to serve her as a priestess, her life story reminding me of Ona's fictitious story in *The Lake Goddess*. From then on, I knew that the lake would be good to me, and she has indeed inspired me to great heights. Just like she has inspired so many other human creations, along with her fellow sacred muses around the world.

As I now revisit Oguta in December 2021, my memory of the Priestess is framed by grief, as I face her recent passing in September. As a small token of comfort and compassion, I give a copy of my book to her daughter Joy on my first day back in town. 'I had planned to give her this myself, but she will not see it ... at least through this book the world will know Our Mother'. We hug and cry. Then she tells me of the circumstances of her mother's passing. It is a story that cannot be divulged in this text. But I take great comfort in knowing that Ezeugegbe 1 remained true to her calling, serving the water deities and the community through her power of healing, refusing to engage in anything but good deeds. 'She wanted to die a saint', Joy reflects, 'even if it killed her'. I recall our sister Idenu's words on Facebook: 'May She Rise in Power'. And I know, our mother will rise again, reincarnated in another form. Just like I know that other priestesses will continue serving the Goddess of the Lake, so that she may protect and inspire us, like she has since time immemorial. End of story.

Paula Uimonen is Professor of Social Anthropology at Stockholm University. She specializes in digital anthropology as well as anthropology of art, visual culture, transnationalism and world literature. Her recent publications on world literature include the monograph *Invoking Flora Nwapa: Nigerian Women Writers, Femininity and Spirituality in World Literature* (Stockholm University Press, 2020), and the book chapter 'One World Literature with Chinua Achebe and Flora Nwapa', in *Claiming Space: Locations and Orientations in World Literatures* (Bloomsbury Academic, 2021). She has also co-edited a volume on visual digital heritage, *Connect to Collect: Approaches to Collecting Social Digital Photography in Museums and Archives* (Nordiska Museets Förlag, 2020). Paula's new research project, 'Swahili Ocean Worlds' (2022–24) explores relationships with the sea and sustainability in fishing communities in Tanzania. The project is funded by the Swedish Research Council.

Note

1. The research project 'African Women Writers' was part of the multidisciplinary research programme *Cosmopolitan and Vernacular Dynamics in World Literatures* (2016–21), coordinated by Professor Stefan Helgesson at Stockholm University and supported by Riksbankens Jubileumsfond. See https://worldlit.se/.

References

Barber, Karin. 2007. 'Improvisation and the Art of Making Things Stick', in *Creativity and Cultural Improvisation*, Elizabeth Hallam and Tim Ingold (eds). Oxford: Berg, pp. 25–41.
Blanes, Ruy Llera. 2006. 'The Atheist Anthropologist: Believers and Non-Believers in Anthropological Fieldwork', *Social Anthropology* 14(2): 223–34.
Cheah, Pheng. 2008. 'What is a World? On World Literature as World-Making Activity', *Daedalus* 137(3): 26–38.
——. 2014. 'World against Globe: Toward a Normative Conception of World Literature'. *New Literary History* 45(3): 303–29.
de la Cadena, Marisol. 2018. 'Earth-beings: Andean Indigenous Religion, but *Not Only*', in *The World Multiple: The Quotidian Politics of Knowing and Generating Entangled Worlds*, Keiichi Omura, Grant Jun Otsuki, Shiho Satsuka and Atsuro Morita (eds). London: Routledge, pp. 21–36.
Drewal, Henry John (ed.). 2008. *Sacred Waters: Arts for Mami Wata and Other Divinities in Africa and the Diaspora*. Bloomington, IN: Indiana University Press.
Escobar, Arturo. 2020. *Pluriversal Politics: The Real and the Possible*. London: Duke University Press.
Evans-Pritchard, Edward E. 1976 [1937]. *Witchcraft, Oracles and Magic among the Azande*. Oxford: Oxford University Press.
Gell, Alfred. 1992. 'The Technology of Enchantment and the Enchantment of Technology', in *Anthropology, Art and Aesthetics*, Jeremy Coote and Anthony Shelton (eds). Oxford: Clarendon Press, pp. 40–63.
Hallam, Elizabeth and Tim Ingold. 2007. *Creativity and Cultural Improvisation*. Oxford: Berg.
Hastrup, Kirsten. 2007. 'Performing the World: Agency, Anticipation and Creativity', in *Creativity and Cultural Improvisation*, Elizabeth Hallam and Tim Ingold (eds). Oxford: Berg, pp. 193–206.
Helgesson, Stefan, Annika Mörte Alling, Yvonne Lindqvist and Helena Wulff (eds). 2018. *World Literatures: Exploring the Cosmopolitan-Vernacular Exchange*. Stockholm: Stockholm University Press.
Illich, Ivan. 1985. H_2O *and the Waters of Forgetfullness: Reflections on the Historicity of Stuff*. Dallas: The Dallas Institute of Humanities and Culture.
Imbo, Samuel. 2005. 'Okot p'Bitek's Critique of Western Scholarship on African Religion', in *A Companion to African Philosophy*, Kwasi Wiredu (ed.). Oxford: Blackwell Publishing Ltd, pp. 364–73.
Ingold, Tim. 2018. 'One World Anthropology'. *HAU: Journal of Ethnographic Theory* 8(1/2): 158–71.

———. 2021. *Imagining for Real: Essays on Creation, Attention and Correspondence*. London and New York: Routledge.
Jell-Bahlsen, Sabine. 2007. 'Flora Nwapa and Oguta's Lake Goddess: Artistic Liberty and Ethnography', *Dialectical Anthropology* 31: 253–62.
———. 2008. *The Water Goddess in Igbo Cosmology: Ogbuide of Oguta Lake*. Trenton, NJ: Africa World Press.
———. 2014. *Mammy Water in Igbo Culture: Ogbuide of Oguta Lake*. Enugu: Ezu Books Ltd.
Nnaemeka, Obioma. 1995. 'Feminism, Rebellious Women, and Cultural Boundaries: Rereading Flora Nwapa and Her Compatriots', *Research in African Literatures* 26(2): 80–113.
Nwapa, Flora. *Efuru*. 1966. London: Heinemann.
———. 1979. *Mammywater*. Enugu: Flora Nwapa & Co.
———. 1986 [1975]. *Never Again*. Enugu: Tana Press Ltd.
———. 2017. *The Lake Goddess*. Oguta: Tana Press Ltd.
Ogunyemi, Chikwenye Okonjo. 1996. *Africa Wo/Man Palava: The Nigerian Novel by Women*. Chicago: The University of Chicago Press.
Oladipo, Olusegun. 2005. 'Religion in African Culture: Some Conceptual Issues', in *A Companion to African Philosophy*, Kwasi Wiredu (ed.). Oxford: Blackwell Publishing Ltd, pp. 355–63.
Stoller, Paul and Cheryl Olkes. 1987. *In Sorcery's Shadow*. Chicago: The University of Chicago Press.
Strang, Veronica. 2021. 'Elemental Powers: Water Beings, Nature Worship, and Long-Term Trajectories in Human–Environmental Relations', *kritisk etnografi: Swedish Journal of Anthropology* 4(2):16–34, special issue on Water: An Anthropological Contribution, ed. Karsten Paerregaard and Paula Uimonen.
Uimonen, Paula, and Hussein Masimbi. 2021. 'Spiritual Relationality in Swahili Ocean Worlds', *kritisk etnografi: Swedish Journal of Anthropology* 4(2): 35–50, special issue on Water: An Anthropological Contribution, ed. Karsten Paerregaard and Paula Uimonen.
Uimonen, Paula. 2020. *Invoking Flora Nwapa: Nigerian Women Writers, Femininity and Spirituality in World Literature*. Stockholm: Stockholm University Press. Open access. Retrieved from: https://www.stockholmuniversitypress.se/site/books/m/10.16993/bbe/.
———. 2022. 'Oguta – Sjögudinnans Stad i Sydöstra Nigeria', in *Platser i Världen: Tolv Litterära Besök*, ed. Anette Nyqvist. Stockholm: Appell förlag, pp. 61–75.
Winzeler, Robert L. 2012. *Anthropology and Religion: What We Know, Think, and Question*. 2nd edition. California: AltaMira Press.

Chapter 8

Experiential Literary Ethnography
How Creative Writing Techniques Can Capture the Cultural Value of Live Arts-Based Experiences

Ellen Wiles

I ran as fast as I could from the train, with an absurd gait thanks to my heavy rucksack, panted into the gallery's book-lined reception, ploughed up the stairs, and was cautiously ushered into a space that roared with quietude. It was a full house: about fifty people, most of them in their early twenties, were sitting around at small tables. A few were tapping at laptops, most were writing in notebooks, others were scrawling on loose sheets. A slab of spring sunshine fell from the arched window onto the herringbone floor. And there she was, on the other side of the room: the poet Eileen Myles, with her greying bob and WEST TEXAS CLOUD APPRECIATION SOCIETY t-shirt, pencil in hand, writing. She did not make eye contact.

I slipped into the last spare seat and pulled out my notebook and pen – I did have my laptop with me, but did not feel like working at a screen, not here. A quick check that my phone was on silent, then I buried it in my pocket. A siren wailed in the distance. A passing lorry grumbled, its vibration faintly rattling a window. The air smelled of polish and lemon detergent and old wood, and the rose body spray of someone on my table. It felt good to slow my breath, to smooth out a new page and write the date at the top, to contemplate the grain of the paper, then look around briefly, knowing that I had a golden nugget of time here, now – that *we*, this group of people whom I would never know individually, and would never speak to, but who had all planned our days around coming to this write-in event, had a golden nugget of time here, now – just to be in the moment, to daydream and to put words down in hushed concert. Whatever burbles emerged in the spidery mess of my own handwriting, and however useless the resulting prose proved to be for any future purpose, I already knew that I was going to enjoy the process, and I was grateful. And now, whenever I see the name Eileen Myles, or read one of her poems, I am right back at the Camden Arts Centre in Northwest London, in that raucously peaceful moment.

And that is the thing with experiences – with real, multisensory experiences, especially live performance events involving a gathering of other bodies to share time in a way that cannot ever be repeated – experiences that feel out-of-the-ordinary, that move us, that inspire us, that make us dwell more actively in the present. We remember them. And they change the way we think. They change us.

This might seem obvious; but in an age of digitalization, when an infinite amount of information and entertainment is now available to us on screen at the utterance of 'hey Siri', cognitive scientists have found that such embodied experiences have even more impact on us than they used to, and more value in shaping how we make judgements and decisions – they have revealed that at live, in-person performances our hearts beat together, and our brains tick together (Sharot 2017; Richardson et al. 2018).

Futurologist James Wallman has argued that, in contrast to the materialism of the twentieth century, we have entered an era of 'experientialism' in the twenty-first: that a premium value has been placed on experiences that succeed in immersing us in the present moment, in a particular place or story, and that create lasting memories (Wallman 2015).

And yet, in the wake of Covid, arts organizations and performers all around the world who bring us the most remarkable live, in-person experiences have come under serious threat. Many have folded completely under the pressure. Others' incomes been decimated, leaving them vulnerable. In this context, digital alternatives to in-person events have become ever more feasible and are often cheaper to run. This makes live, in-person experiences even more fascinating and urgent to think and write about than they already were.

But it does not make it any easier to capture in writing, or otherwise, why any given event is exceptional, or why the experience of it is valuable, relative to any other – and why an in-person experience of an event might be more valuable than a digital alternative. This has always been a challenge – and as anyone who loves the arts can attest, no summary can encapsulate the experience of any decent artwork.

In an age of big data, metrics and impact assessments, though, arts organizations are increasingly required to prove the value and impact of what they do, in order to survive – just as academics are. And the danger is that short-term economic data, like ticket sales and audience numbers, are relied on as default measures of value. We all know that those figures are reductive, and do not amount to fair means of judging the value of any arts-based experience. So how can the value of such an experience be understood and written about in a way that meaningfully communicates its particularity and its value?

This is a core question that I wrestled with when I approached the subject of live literature events, such as literary festivals and salons, for my latest research project – now a book (Wiles 2021): how to interrogate, and express in words, their cultural value as performance experiences.

The problem with writing about arts-based experiences, which have a significant aesthetic dimension, is that the more 'exceptional' they appear, the more complex and challenging they can seem to write about. That challenge is only increased in the context of a live performance event, like a festival, play or concert, which only takes place for a short time in a particular place. Any single event, attended by a large or diverse audience, can mean a panoply of different things to different participants. The scale of the challenge is no doubt part of the reason why, in the realm of anthropology and the social sciences, the quality and value of arts-based experiences has been relatively neglected over the years.

Scholarly caution around the notion of experience, more generally, has roots plunging way back down into the Enlightenment – in outdated theories like Cartesian dualism, and in the idea that humans (white, male, privileged, Western humans, anyway) are capable of detached, rational judgements, and purely analytical thinking; that emotions are women's domain; that the senses are irrelevant. Throughout academia, the measurable, the quantitative, and the supposedly rational and objective, have long been prioritized at the expense of the immeasurable, the qualitative and the subjective.

But the more we have learned from science about our brains and our bodies and our behaviour as a species, the more it has become clear that our emotions and senses, and the multi-faceted quality of our experiences, not only underpin our memories, but shape our value judgements, and our decision-making. Contemporary scholarship needs to address both the multifacetedness and the significance of experience in both substance and also, crucially, in style. Writing in the traditional academic vein – in purportedly-objective, 'scientized' language (Sword 2017; Moran 2018) – is particularly unsuited to the task; it is likely to result in prose that might appear intelligent and scholarly on the surface, but is ultimately lacking in liveliness, in sensory and emotional depth, in creativity. When applied to arts-based experiences, such writing is certain to miss their experiential essence, to feel reductive in terms of their complexity, and, ultimately, to fail to capture their value.

Fortunately, within the contested field of anthropology, there is a wildflower meadow of inspiring anthropologists-as-writers who have been brave enough to be creative and experimental with language in order to help to bring human experience, and scholarship, to life, particularly after the 'writing culture' debate blew up in the late 1980s (Clifford and Marcus 2010 [1986]). Anthro-writers who inspired me in this direction include: Paul Stoller, with his ideas about 'sensuous scholarship' (Stoller 1989) and the 'taste of ethnographic things' (1997); Ruth Behar, with her openness to emotions in anthropology (Behar 1997); Michael Jackson, with his poetic take on 'lifeworlds' (2017); Anand Pandian and Stuart McLean, who embraced some of the possibilities for experimental ethnographic writing in their edited volume, *Crumpled Paper Boat* (2017); and Helena Wulff, whose pioneering anthropological research over the last two decades has foregrounded the relationship between writing, emotion and anthropology (Wulff 2007, 2016, 2021).

Emboldened by these scholars, as well as those working in performance studies and exploring questions of liveness (e.g. Fischer-Lichte 2008; Reason and Lindelof 2016), those working on matters of cultural value (e.g. Belfiore 2015; Walmsley 2018), and also drawing upon my own background experience in fiction writing (Wiles 2017), in musical performance, and in cultural anthropology (Wiles 2015), I decided to experiment with a new ethnographic approach to writing about live literature events in order to capture and interrogate their value as experiences.

When I started this research project – back in 2013 – it seemed that most of the existing scholarship around live literature events was focused around their economic and marketing functions within the publishing industry. Wulff's work on Irish writers' performances at literary events (2008) was a rare and rich example of the anthropological potential of exploring such events as performance experiences. I wanted to explore further in this direction: to show how different kinds of literary events – which range hugely from big festivals to intimate bookshop gatherings – can be valuable for their participants in different ways; and how the distinct and particular value of one event might be communicated and examined in conjunction with another.

After much reading across disciplines, experimentation and reflection, I devised 'experiential literary ethnography': an approach that has the capacity to both evoke a particular experience, using literary writing techniques through narrative, and to interrogate it, through an ethnographic process. It can be defined by several core elements.

First: the use of literary writing techniques to evoke the experience of participation in an event, including descriptions of particular, resonant details, observed in situ. Anthropologists will be familiar with the idea of 'thick description', which is another way of putting this – though the degree of 'thickness' will ideally be proportionate to the relevance of the thing being described. In a literary event context, evocative description might incorporate things like the shape of the building or tent, features of design, imagery, branding, staging, audience arrangement, background music, temperature, smell, atmosphere – it might include the apparent range of demographic features among the audience, the performer's body language, dress, posture, gesture, accent, voice, pitch and pacing. After having spent time conducing ethnographic research on this subject, it was clear to me that all those things contributed to the value of the experience – and part of that was evidenced in the way that they imprinted themselves on participants' memories afterwards.

But it is not enough just to pack in multi-sensory details in description. There is also the matter of active scene-setting; the literary technique of describing elements of an experience in such a way that it feels natural and immersive, and so that the narrative appears to bring the reader through the scene itself, observing those elements organically along the way.

Next, there are the questions of voice and point of view to consider. In my live literature research, I did not want my event ethnographies to focus on my subjective experience alone; I needed to wrestle with the matter of plurality – this goes to the heart of the cultural value of arts-based experience, and is part of what makes such experience so difficult to write about. Not only is experience inherently complex and multifaceted, it is also infinitely variable and inevitably subjective. Every participant's experience at one live, in-person performance event will be different – although, vitally, some aspects of it will be shared, and that sense of sharing the experience goes to the heart of its value. So how can a piece of writing capture that plurality, while also remaining coherent, and enabling persuasive arguments to be made?

This brings me to the second key element of experiential literary ethnography: interweaving participant conversations. During the research process, in order to capture a sense of how different people at a literary event were experiencing and valuing it, I would go around speaking to as many participants as I could – including both reader-audience members and author-performers. I would ask questions about how they were experiencing the event and what they valued about it. I prefer to refer to these exchanges as conversations rather than interviews, because I deliberately set out to keep them very informal and unstructured, so as to allow me to be responsive and alert to nuance and particularity, and to enable participants to impart with as much freedom as possible what the event meant to them. My background as a barrister felt useful as I went about this: the techniques I had learned about asking open rather than closed questions, and in shaping a conversation in such a way that it felt natural to the other person and encouraged them to impart resonant details.

During the process of narrative composition, extracts of these conversations can be incorporated within the ethnographies by being interwoven, apparently naturally, into the scene. Again, my aim in doing this was the enable the reader to feel as if they are present at the event, participating in this conversation as well as in the experience itself. This process of initiating and incorporating participant conversations enables the ethnographic narrative to illustrate the variety of experiences, and gives it a polyphonic quality – a richer texture. It enables the ethnography to acknowledge the significance of the writer's own point of view, but to situate it among other points of view. The polyphonic quality of the resulting narrative helps to make the case for the value of live arts-based event experiences by embodying the idea that their capacity to mean such different things for so many is a core part of their value. This incorporation of dialogue, and a variety of voices, also gives the ethnographic narrative a more varied rhythm, which helps with reader engagement.

The third key element of experiential literary ethnography, particularly relevant for an arts-based performance, is to find a way to represent the texts performed in some way in the narrative, so that the particular aesthetic qualities of the art form are recognized and taken into account. Simply summarizing facts about a particular event, like the name of the author or performer, or the blurb on the back of the book that they are going to talk about and read from, is not enough to give a reader a sense of what the experience of encountering this text was really like. For that reason, when writing about literary events, I sought to transcribe and include quotations from readings and performances. Literary narrative skill needs to be deployed in weaving those quotations organically into the scene, in order to make them feel alive, and an integral part of the experience being interrogated.

A fourth element is the inclusion of reflections on wider cultural patterns and tendencies that contextualize the event in its cultural landscape – a kind of zooming-out. In the case of a literary festival, for instance, this might include reflections on the origin of the festival, the person or people who conceived of it, and the growth and dynamics of literary festivals nationally and globally. To maintain the immersive effect of the narrative, ideally such contextual factors will again be woven in organically, perhaps between conversations and scene descriptions, and as and when each factor becomes relevant.

A fifth element is theoretical commentary and analysis, with reference to relevant scholarship, in order to ground the piece in the network of critical ideas. This material can be difficult to weave into the narrative organically, but needs to be balanced, positioned and expressed in harmony with the experiential effect of the rest of the narrative. A sudden transition to conventionally formal or technical academic prose is best avoided.

Finally, all these elements should lead naturally to an extraction of certain key insights towards the end of the narrative: a conclusion, conventionally enough, but one that leaves the reader with a sustained sense of the experience being explored.

To create a coherent and dynamic whole, it is important that the language used throughout the ethnography is lively and expressive, as well as being clear and accessible, even in the more theoretical sections. Creative writing techniques are useful here – aspects of the craft such as imagery, form, style, register, metaphor and dialogue.

Of course, experiential literary ethnography is just one possible way of approaching the challenge of interrogating the value of arts-based experiences; there are many others, both existing and potential.

Ultimately, all ethnography, all anthropology, and all scholarship, is about storytelling. Experiential literary ethnography offers an approach to telling a story about an experience that evokes its multifaceted, multisensory qualities; that crafts a compelling narrative which reflects the temporal quality of the experience; and that extracts and interrogates key details, quotes and ideas along the way, in order to reveal its distinctive meaning and its value as fully as possible. It allows readers to gain a virtual form of the experience, and to gain insights and perspectives on the experience from multiple points of view.

My book, *Live Literature* (Wiles 2021), includes two extensive experiential literary ethnographies, one exploring the Hay Festival – perhaps the world's most famous festival, and one of the biggest – and the other exploring the Polari Salon, which is an intimate LGBTQ+ salon based in London. The process of researching and composing these narratives enabled me to reveal how these two events are experienced and valued in very different ways by their participants.

Hay is a huge annual festival, which (save for during Covid) takes place in a cluster of white tents in a lush green field surrounded by hills in rural Wales. It showcases the most famous and bestselling authors around in any given year. If you go there as an audience member, you are likely to have to plan a long journey around it – a pilgrimage, as many regulars see it – and you become one of thousands of others milling ant-like along its walkways around the tents. The 'density' of this festival, as Victor Turner would put it, and its geographical situation, far removed from most people's everyday lives, creates a buzz of collective participation in the space, and a feeling of 'liminality' (Turner 1995; 1967). Regular Hay-goers are unlikely to recognize each other, as there are simply so many participants, save for the faces of the people they choose to go with – and many people do go to Hay as a regular group holiday with friends and/or family. Others, though, like to go to Hay on their own. One woman I spoke to talked passionately about how it is her salvation to travel there solo each year, leaving her husband and children behind for one week only, to immerse herself in books and ideas. There are so many events at Hay in the course of its ten days that people can book themselves into a huge tent to see someone famous perform one hour, and the next hour can walk around the corner into a small tent to discover someone they have never heard of before – perhaps an author from a European country, writing in another language, whose literary work has just been translated into English. This potential for exposure to big names and personalities, and to a wide variety of stories and ideas, is key to Hay's appeal among most audience members. The format of literary events at Hay is often standardized: each event tends to last 50 minutes, including a 30-minute discussion between one or two authors and a chairperson, sometimes – but not always – punctuated by a very short reading from the newly published book that is being featured, followed by 20 minutes for audience questions. Events during the daytime span fiction, non-fiction and children's fiction, and all books featured are either by very well-known and/or acclaimed authors, or are the publishers' top titles, in which they have invested the most money. In the evening, musical performances often take place in the bigger tents. The intimate ritual of book signing after a literary event – which, at Hay, often requires standing in a very long queue snaking out of the big bookshop tent – gives individual audience members a sense of gaining a heightened and intimate connection with the writer who has just performed on stage. This is quite likely to be a famous writer whom they revere, and whom they would never otherwise have a chance to meet one-on-one.

Here is an extract from my ethnography of Hay (Wiles 2021: 44–55), to give you a sense of the way the experiential ethnographic narrative works.

> Colourful flags and celebratory bunting flutter ahead to mark the entrance, and a huge banner announces the HAY FESTIVAL above the strapline, *Imagine the World*, with several large sponsorship logos displayed alongside it, most prominently *The Telegraph*'s. Large, white marquees rise up behind. In the entranceway, I pause to look into a thrumming box office tent, and a *Telegraph*-branded tote bag is waved at me: free with today's paper. I accept one, take a programme from another steward, and walk on through.
>
> I circuit the site to find my bearings. Not a difficult task, it turns out; in comparison to most music and cross-arts festivals I've been to, this site is exceedingly neat and geometric, with all the tents arranged in an orderly manner around a large rectangle of metal walkways. It might be situated in

a muddy field, but no wellies are necessary. It feels slightly reminiscent of a trade show I once went to in London's Exhibition Centre – but the regular glimpses and constant sense of the hills and trees around the site is a reminder of Hay's distance from urban centres of commerce. Greenery pervades the site, too, albeit in a manicured iteration of the surrounding countryside. In between the walkways are perfectly mowed lawns dotted with deck chairs and picnic benches for audiences to relax, mingle and read. In the centre of one lawn is a quaint shepherd's hut on wheels, advertising itself to would-be writers as rooms of one's own. Another lawn features a giant, multi-coloured HAY sign that children can climb on and be photographed, ideally smiling widely, and in the sunshine. There's a shop selling Hay Festival merch, an Oxfam second-hand bookshop, and a Festival Bookshop selling the new titles of featured authors and presenters. Food and drink options are plentiful; there's a food hall-style tent, a fancy restaurant tent, several cafes, a tapas bar… Wait, is that the towering form of Stephen Fry walking past the press tent?

...

I spot someone I recognise on a deck chair, tall, slim, black-haired – yes, it's Jo Glanville, Director of English PEN: an NGO that supports writers at risk, freedom of expression and literature in translation. She will be chairing several international fiction events over the next few days. I go over to introduce myself, and happily she's very welcoming, so I sit cross-legged on the grass to chat to her. I am slightly surprised to hear her opinion about the rise of literary festivals: it is 'utterly baffling'. 'I'd be very interested if you find out the key to their popularity', she adds. 'I think the literary event in itself is a really *peculiar* thing, because, just because someone can write a book, it doesn't mean that they can stand and *talk* about it, and talking about the book in public isn't the same as reading a book which is a very *private* act … and when you're reading a great piece of literature, we all know what an *extraordinary* experience that is … you enter some extraordinary *world*, and you *leave* your real world to enter this other world.' I'm intrigued by the way she evokes the idea of otherworldly liminality, just as Victor Turner described it. 'And obviously, aesthetically, depending on what you're reading', Glanville continues, 'you're enjoying extraordinary *language* … So the concept of a festival, actually – and the popularity of events where a writer is standing up and speaking – is actually *really* baffling to me. It's a conundrum! The paradox of literary festivals.'

...

It is time for me to head to the first event I've circled in my programme, which is lined up for one of the smaller tents, named the 'Starlight Stage': a conversation between Philip Gross, the T.S. Eliot prize-winning poet, and artist Valerie Coffin Price. They collaborated to create *A Fold in the River*: a poetry and art book inspired by the Welsh river Taff. Gross used to live by and walk regularly along this river, and transformed his journals into a poetry collection. For this book, Price retraced his routes to develop prints and drawings, and the result was published by Seren: a small indie press.

The tent is decorated with a web of tiny fairy lights over the ceiling, and the stage is painted black. A gentle, slight and bearded persona on stage, Gross reads softly but engagingly from his poems, which are moving, exquisite, and apt for the geography and climate of Hay:

> Enough now. Wind back the reel;
>
> spool in the river, right up to the source
>
> which is no one where
>
> unless you hold it cupped
>
> in the all-angled lens of a raindrop – that
>
> or the quivering globe of all this
>
> for the most part sea …

Price's projected illustrations make the experience of listening to the poems more immersive, reflecting their spirit and helping focus attention. After a sequence of readings by Gross, Price eagerly introduces her work, and the two take turns in explaining how the project developed. Gross speaks somewhat hesitantly, but articulately, warmly, and in a calmer manner than his illustrator. While not a charismatic performer, in the extrovert sense, he is clearly more used to speaking in front of audiences. The event is not chaired, and this seems to give it an intimacy and informality, but also a slight awkwardness in turn-taking. Most of their conversation is about process: their respective processes of making, and their collaboration.

After the event, I speak to Stan and Kira, a British-American couple in their mid-thirties, who are married and both work in Christian ministry. I ask how they found the event. 'Fascinating', Stan tells me, beaming. 'Especially hearing about the ways people produce art. I have been interested in music before, but poetry is a bit of a side thing for me'. Kira tells me that she'd studied English, and had come to Hay a couple of times before. 'What I loved', Kira says, was 'the fact that both of them were so *absorbed* in this river, even though it doesn't sound like a particularly beautiful one'. They both enjoyed the 'play-off' between poetry and images in the event, and in the concept of the book. When I ask what they felt they gained from hearing a writer like Gross reading his work aloud at an event, rather than reading it themselves on the page, Kira says that the *meaning* becomes much clearer, for her. 'Sometimes you don't understand something until you hear someone read from it.'

*

Polari is a very different species of literary event. It is a cabaret-style night out, taking place roughly every month in London (with occasional tours to venues outside the city). It features performed readings from literary works that are either by writers who identify as LGBTQ+ or that engage with LGBTQ+ experiences in some way. The format eschews the panel conversations and audience Q&As that often feature at literary events, and this enables the salon to foreground the texts as performances, and allows the power of literary narratives to represent the variety of LGBTQ+ experience, and to connect the participants through the act of collective listening and empathizing. It also enables the event to maintain a fun, performative vibe – even when, as often, some of the stories being told are raw and painful. At the interval participants, many of whom are London-based regulars who recognize each other, mill around, chat and have a drink. Every salon features a range of author-performers, from new and inexperienced to well-known and critically acclaimed, which fosters a sense of support for those at the grassroots who have been traditionally neglected by the mainstream publishing industry. The event was created by its host, Paul Burston, in a Soho gay bar, as a reaction to that neglect. Its name, Polari, derives from the name of a secret language that was used among gay men when homosexuality remained illegal in the UK (Baker 2002). A few women participants told me that they experienced it as still primarily targeted at gay men, due to the undoubtedly camp aesthetic and the nature of some of the jokes cracked on stage. But, for most people I spoke to – men, women, trans and others – the event creates a tangible sense of inclusive, emotional community (Maffesoli 1996).

This extract of my ethnography of Polari illustrates the same narrative approach adapted to a very different context (Wiles 2021: 139–53):

> Behind a low stage illuminated in flamingo pink, still empty but for a small wooden podium at the centre, ceiling-high windows display a spectacular backdrop of the Millennium Wheel, mere metres away. It's glowing emerald – though, as I watch, it begins to shift to a brilliant orange like a giant reverse traffic light installation. Behind the wheel is a sparkling black ribbon: the Thames, underlining the Houses of Parliament. The view could almost be computer-generated, but this is really what London looks like from the fifth-floor function room at the South Bank Centre. Screens on either side of the stage show a 'real' computer-generated image of the same Millennium Wheel backdrop, but with a larger-than-life man lounging in the foreground, sporting a top hat garnished with a feather and a purple sparkly tie reminiscent of Willy Wonka, and holding a paperback which he is regarding with an exaggerated expression of gleeful shock, half looking at the camera. Several other books float and flit around him like butterflies amidst sparkles of magic dust.
>
> A full-house of about 150 people has gathered here on this chilly January evening, to a soundtrack of feel-good funk, and the chatter is noisy and ebullient. Some are queuing for drinks at the little bar, exclaiming at how good it is to see each other, hugging, jostling, joking, chatting. The majority seem to know several others and act like regulars. Seats are quickly filling up. I'd say there is a mix of men and women here, ranging in age from twenties to sixties. As the

music volume ramps up a notch, the man from the screens takes to the stage in the flesh, wearing a flamboyant combination of white sunglasses, a silver top hat – which turns out to be the same hat in which he once posed nude for a gay magazine cover – a candy-floss suit jacket and a boldly-patterned tie. 'Welcome!' he grins. 'I'm Paul Burston and I'm your host for this evening. Now, are there are any Polari virgins in the house?'

A scattering of hands cautiously ascend as members of the audience 'come out' as Polari virgins – I estimate about a third. Burston regards them for a moment, before slyly semi-reassuring them: 'we'll try to be gentle with you'. He explains to us that his tan is thanks to his trip to Rio last week – assuming a general familiarity with his normal appearance, I note, which further suggests the presence of a regular community of audience members. 'I was lying there on the beach, imagining you all in budgie smugglers', he adds with a lewd grin – a comment that I presume applies only to the men in the room, so probably about two thirds of the audience.

...

During the interval, I ask a lady sitting near me if she'd mind speaking with me for my research, and she immediately replies: 'of course!' – an attitude that will be reflected in almost all my Polari participant conversations, and seems to match the relaxed, enthused vibe of the event. Robin is a petite 52-year-old South Londoner with a short blond bob, dressed in a check shirt and jeans, and is here for the fourth time with a group of friends. The venue, she tells me, was her initial attraction: 'I've been coming to the Southbank since I was a child. As a venue, it's really one of a kind' – but Polari also appealed because 'you hear new stuff and get to chat to other people', and because it's 'pretty much the only event of its type in London which is just … gay and lesbian'. This is fascinating; while I had been aware of divisions within the LBGTQ+ community, I had not realized how far that translated into the existence of shared arts and cultural spaces, and how rare Polari was perceived to be by those who attended it.

I ask Robin if she is here at Polari more for the community and social side or the literature. 'The literature first', she says, 'but *obviously* because it's gay and lesbian – and the social aspect to it probably second.' The queer perspective of the writing by the featured authors is important to her, she explains, and more so than their individual identities as authors – but the two do interrelate. 'Most of the writing at Polari touches on gay and lesbian issues', she says, and even if that's sometimes 'quite indirect … that's fine. Really it's just interesting to hear whatever the subject matter might be about, from a lesbian or gay perspective. Even if it's fictional.'

The quality of writing at Polari is 'pretty mixed' in her view, but she praises its range and diversity. Coming here has prompted her to read books she wouldn't otherwise have read, including poetry by Stella Duffy (who is performing later tonight) and it has caused her to put lots of other writers on her to-read list – though she can't recall any names off the bat. The kind of writing that works best in performance, she thinks, is 'observational humour'.

She grins as she says this. 'People always like to laugh don't they? – so I think any writer that can choose something from their work that can make people laugh and is about observation and human nature, that can cut across all sorts of things – that's going to work really well.' She finds the standard of performances at Polari to be mixed, too – but she clarifies that she doesn't necessarily *expect* writers to be good performers: 'that's not their forte; they might be writers but that's a very different thing.' This echoes my conversations with reader-audiences at Hay: the idea that a 'good' performance, in a live literature context, won't necessarily be theatrical or dramatic; and that a sense of *authenticity* in performance can be more valuable.

I hope these extracts illustrate the way in which experiential literary ethnography works, incorporating the elements that I outlined earlier – including style, language, and narrative pacing; the use of literary techniques such as characterization, dialogue and setting; and the incorporation of critical reflection, analysis and patterns of insight gained through the research and writing processes. My hope is that the combination of all these elements allows the distinctive value of each event to be revealed and also makes for engaging reading.

It would delight me if experiential literary ethnography and comparable creative approaches to narrative were taken up more widely by scholars and practitioners seeking to research and communicate the rich and multifaceted experience, value and impact of arts-based events in an increasingly digital world in which, especially post-Covid, many performance arts organizations are struggling to survive. I hope that the academy will continue to nurture innovative approaches that seek to interrogate and reveal why arts-based experiences matter, particularly when funding for the arts is thin on the ground.

Ellen Wiles is a novelist, anthropologist and curator. She is the author of three books that explore the relationship between creative writing and ethnography in different ways. She teaches creative writing at the University of Exeter, UK. Her website is https://www.ellenwiles.com.

References

Baker, Paul. 2002. *Polari: The Lost Language of Gay Men*. New York: Routledge.
Behar, Ruth. 1997. *The Vulnerable Observer: Anthropology That Breaks Your Heart*. Boston: Beacon Press.
Belfiore, Eleonore. 2015. '"Impact", "Value" and "Bad Economics": Making Sense of the Problem of Value in the Arts and Humanities', *Arts and Humanities in Higher Education* 14(1): 95–110.

Clifford, James and George Marcus (eds). 2010 [1986]. *Writing Culture: The Poetics and Politics of Ethnography*. Berkeley: The University of California Press.
Fischer-Lichte, Erika. 2008. *The Transformative Power of Performance: A New Aesthetics*. Trans. S. I. Jain. London: Routledge.
Jackson, Michael. 2017. *Lifeworlds: Essays in Existential Anthropology*. Chicago: The University of Chicago Press.
Maffesoli, Michael. 1996. *The Time of the Tribes: The Decline of Individualism in Mass Society*. Trans. D. Smith. London: SAGE.
Moran, Joe. 2018. *First You Write a Sentence: The Elements of Reading, Writing ... and Life*. London: Penguin Books.
Pandian, Anand and Stuart Mclean (eds). 2017. *Crumpled Paper Boat: Experiments in Ethnographic Writing*. Durham, NC: Duke University Press.
Reason, Matthew and Anja Mølle Lindelof (eds). 2016. *Experiencing Liveness in Contemporary Performance*. New York: Routledge.
Richardson, Daniel C., Nicole K. Griffin, Lara Zaki, Auburn Stephenson, Jiachen Yan, John Hogan, Jeremy I. Skipper and Joseph T. Devlin. 2018. 'Measuring Narrative Engagement: The Heart Tells the Story', bioRxiv preprint, 20 June 2018, https://doi.org/10.1101/351148.
Sharot, Tali. 2017. *The Influential Mind*. London: Little Brown.
Stoller, Paul. 1989. *Sensuous Scholarship*. Philadelphia: University of Pennsylvania Press.
——. 1997. *The Taste of Ethnographic Things: The Senses in Anthropology*. Philadelphia: University of Pennsylvania Press.
Sword, Helen. 2017. *Air and Light and Time and Space: How Successful Academics Write*. Cambridge, MA: Harvard University Press.
Turner, Victor. 1967. 'Betwixt and Between: The Liminal Period in Rites of Passage', in *The Forest of Symbols: Aspects of Ndembu Ritual*. Ithaca: Cornell University Press, pp. 93–111.
——. 1995 [1969] *The Ritual Process: Structure and Anti-Structure*. New Brunswick: Aldine Transaction.
Wallman, James. 2015. *Stuffocation*. London: Penguin Books.
Wiles, Ellen. 2015. *Saffron Shadows and Salvaged Scripts: Literary Life in Myanmar Under Censorship and in Transition*. New York: Columbia University Press.
——. 2017. *The Invisible Crowd*. London: HarperCollins.
——. 2021. *Live Literature: The Experience and Cultural Value of Literary Performance Events from Salons to Festivals*. New York: Palgrave Macmillan.
Wulff, Helena (ed.). 2007. *The Emotions: A Cultural Reader*. London: Routledge.
——. 2008. 'Literary Readings as Performance: On the Career of Contemporary Writers in the New Ireland', *Anthropological Journal of European Cultures* 17(2): 98–113.
——. 2016. *The Anthropologist as Writer: Genres and Contexts in the Twenty-First Century*. Oxford: Berghahn.
——. 2021. 'Writing Anthropology', Cambridge Encyclopedia of Anthropology. Retrieved 1 February 2023 from https://www.anthroencyclopedia.com/entry/writing-anthropology.

Part III

Exceptional Visual and Practice Experiences

Chapter 9

Lighting Praxis
Lighting Aesthetics and Creativity Narratives in Professional Cinematography

Cathy Greenhalgh

Introduction

In this chapter I draw out several elements which correlate translations between the everyday and the exceptional as displayed in the accounts of professional cinematographers. The examples I use bring up questions of performativity and rhetoric in professional creative domains, storytelling as a structuring device in freelance artistic / industrial careers, and practice language and aesthetic organization in collaborative work. I draw on my experience as a cinematographer and director, as a teacher of students of diverse cultural heritage and on long-term ethnographic research with feature film cinematographers.

I focus here on narratives found at the *Camerimage International Festival of the Art of Cinematography*, held annually in Poland, particularly those pertaining to lighting and experience of light. The festival is an unusual environment where cinematographers share stories about creative collaboration, aesthetics and technique. These can involve breakthroughs in solving problems through planning and testing or declarations of epiphany and revelation and how specific conditions, spontaneity or serendipity might have led to their occurrence. These moments can be claimed in this sharing with compadres, and responses from listeners can help to serve careers, as much as for the betterment of the profession.

My examples are situated in relation to theories of storytelling in organizational modes, such as with a film crew and freelance work, and as they arise within collaborative creativity and distributed knowledge systems. I align with notions about practice and creativity in anthropology, film and media studies and sociology. How stories of cinematographers' work become part of their praxis is expounded on here; and how lighting is a particularly rich font of exceptional experience which seems to promulgate this growth.

What a fieldworker learns over time is an 'interpretive skill related to the culture of interest', writes Van Maanen (1988: 101), in suggesting a need to highlight the 'poetic dimension of ethnography' (ibid.). He writes:

> Impressionist tales typically highlight the episodic, complex and ambivalent realities that are frozen and made too pat and ordered by realist confessional conventions. Impressionist tales, with their silent disavowal of grand theorizing, their radical grasping for the particular, eventful, contextual, and unusual, contain an important message. They protest the ultimate superficiality of much of the research published in social science – ethnographic or otherwise. Fieldworkers are sometimes conscious that the art they practice is to provide an account of or even a paper of a deeply uncertain world. The pen as camera obscura. Impressionist tales of the field bring such matters to light, for they attempt to be as hesitant and open to contingency and interpretation as the concrete social experiences on which they are based. (ibid.: 119)

What I like here, as it is a common trope, is the use of a photographic / cinematographic metaphor, the 'camera obscura', to encapsulate the issue at hand. Van Maanen seems to suggest that traditional writing is too much like a camera and echoes photography as realism. But an impression is like looking into a dark chamber, peering through a hole into a box and observing a projected image via a mirror and a lens. It is at one remove and has been set up, 'framed' with an aesthetics and composed poetic intent in mind. So there is a purpose to this kind of storytelling from the field. It may allow a difference in sensory input. Indeed, writing may be accompanied by sound recording, photographs, film, collage, drawing and online mixed media outputs. But the idea that the visual fixes too much and that the visual is evidence is of course contestable and illusory and may perpetuate the assumption that seeing cinematographically follows a certain pattern, habit and procedure.

Light as Experience, Expertise and Substance

I first thought of light as expanding the complexity of the conundrum of translation into material and articulating how this happens, when I asked French cinematographer Robert Alazraki a question at a press conference at *Camerimage* in 1997, after he showed his latest film, *A Summer in La Goulette* (1996), which had been shot in Tunisia. I asked him to tell me why lighting seemed to contain more of what one would call the individual signature of a cinematographer's work on a film. Cinematographers' work is not described usually in the manner of an individual as with an artist or photographer, because this is collaborative work and most critics cannot be certain exactly where the cinematographers' input can be seen in a film – that is: who made aesthetic decisions; was the cinematographic 'look' created by the cinematographer, or heavily influenced by the 'director's vision', and their work 'merely' a well-crafted translation? This was also during the early years of the festival, before interviews were appearing online and when there was still only speculative description of the medium involved. It is fairly straightforward to copy composition and framing and camera movement (except hand-held movement, which is an individual choreography), but it is hard to copy lighting exactly, even with the same equipment used by another cinematographer and crew following a template.

Look at the various ways in which Caravaggio and his contemporaries, or painters copying or working in a guild or workshop in the style of Velasquez paint light and shadow in paint. One can usually tell that they are not the original artist. There is much that is reminiscent in the work, yet something of the style of the imitator as well. Even when there are several cinematographers working on the same television series and they have a lighting look or template, one can see subtle differences between one episode and the next. These are what distinguish an artist and which audiences seem to feel, as well as notice. This is why certain cinematographers become the virtuoso ones. This is much more than 'style' and points to how the meaning and storytelling in the film are somehow 'imbued' with the materiality of the maker as well as the materials, even in collaborative work. The light itself has an agency, an energy, and is inflected by the manipulator of its 'substance'. A unique look in the lighting (as well as framing and camera movement) is something that cinematographers seek and is part of the mystery (and mystique), of the art as well. In fact, in Los Angeles, on the bigger films, all the camera operating is carried out separately to the Director of Photography, because of union rules. So it is the light that distinguishes the DP's work.

Alazraki rolled his eyes, smiled and looked upwards to that notional (paradisical, heavenly?) inspirational space. Then he looked at me, and twisted and rubbed his fingers into wisps of air and said: 'How can we say ... It's like cooking, or music ... the same ingredients go into a recipe, but everybody makes it taste different. Everybody plays an instrument or sings differently. We don't know why.' Lighting for the cinematographer is the quintessential element of their art and what separates the best work, the 'enlightened' from the mediocre. This story also highlights the difficulty of articulating lighting as a practice. Yet it contains a praxial statement – that lighting may have a recipe and set ingredients, but that with each cinematographer, the dish (film) will turn out differently. Certain cooks have a developed taste palette, a speed of working, an imagination for food combinations, excellent observation of procedural details and timing and make inspired decisions, with calculated risk. The story implies what may be at play, understanding of process and sets of procedures, but also the ability to visualize or to 'listen to the material', the agency of light and observation of the circumstances and physical situation where the encounter with it takes place.

One term I have used in fieldwork that it seems cinematographers have immediately related to is Cristina Grasseni's 'skilled vision'. She aligns this notion with both sensory ethnography and the anthropology of practice. She posits the cultural nature of vision and explores it 'as a ductile, situated, contested and politically fraught means of situating oneself in a community of practice' (Grasseni 2009: 2). She classes as 'virtuoso' 'those practitioners who daily go about defining and creatively extending the "visual environments" of their practice' (2009: 3). Her work stresses:

> [t]he disciplined and disciplining aspects of memory and sensibility that are not spontaneous, personal and subjective but rather *embedded* in mediating devices, contexts and routines. (2009: 4; original emphasis)

She notes 'the role of informal, mostly tacit knowledge in expert conduct, apprenticeship and professional identity, taking into consideration the role played by peer-to-peer negotiation, hierarchical relations and the management of contexts, narratives and artefacts in the social construction of skilled visions' (ibid.: 4).

The professional cinematographer community is an example of what Grasseni describes as '"sharing a worldview" [which] means learning to inhabit ecologies of vision, taken as "the public organization of visual practice within the worklife of a profession"' (Goodwin, cited in Grasseni 2009: 11). The question is where does creativity arise within these strictures? What interests me about Alazraki's statement is that it suggests a realm of the spontaneous, serendipitous, or 'magical', as much as the aesthetic, critical and engineered aspects of lighting.

The following story by American cinematographer Ed Lachman relates to cinematographic skilled vision expertise and incorporation of the agency of light in nature and naturally occurring colour as part of a film narrative. Lachman was at the press conference and seminar at *Camerimage* in 2002 with Sandy Powell, the production designer, after the screening of director Todd Haynes' film *Far from Heaven* (2002). The film is influenced by Douglas Sirk's films and is a comment on the nature of melodrama and portrayals of race, sexual orientation, gender and class in 1950s' America. Lachman (and Powell) are regular collaborators with Haynes. Haynes is known for using a 'lookbook' for each of his films, which outlines the visual influences.

In filmmaking, light effects can be used to organize what the viewer sees and feels; directing attention, revealing shape and form, establishing relationships between characters, orienting space and time, creating rhythm and embellishing textures of settings and faces. Lachman often employs strong colour palettes in his work and *Far from Heaven* contrasts idyllic autumnal colours in the outdoor locations and warm orangeish lighting in the home interior, with colder colours, blue and garish greens and purples in night cityscapes and clubs. The coldness increases as the characters' world, with friction with societal norms, falls apart. The production design echoes the colour palette in the settings and costumes. There are several outdoor scenes where trees have particularly intense yellow, brown, red and orange and a little green colour and the women are dressed in similar pastel or saturated hues. The shoot had been scheduled in autumn in upstate New York to take advantage of the fall (autumn) colours, but they had also added lighting to the daylight on the trees and actors to intensify and spotlight some areas. It is a disturbing beauty and represents the control the wife and main female character tries to maintain.

A member of the audience asked whether Lachman had used camera filters, as are often employed in such scenes, such as coral or tobacco or straw filters. The answer was surprising, and I had not read about this in any of the technical accounts of the film. Though the air is normally quite clear in the area they were shooting, the sky was not blue or grey, but in fact very orange / yellow / brownish during the days they were shooting. Lachman, 'figured out that this was something like ash smoke in the sky, as this was just three weeks after 9/11 when we were shooting, do you remember ... we were also very intense, just like the film story' he nodded at Powell (Lachman 2002). He was convinced this acrid effect was from the World Trade Center catastrophe. He had no need to use any filters or digital grading of the colour on the sky backgrounds in the film, because what was naturally occurring was a unique situation and effect that fitted the story they were telling. It also gave a unique memory to the shooting experience for the crew, which then 'colours itself' into the retelling of the making of the film. This is the sort of detail that comes out in a story, that then gets reified for the cinematographer audience, and is about an accident, not a technique. In general it is not the kind of detail that a film critic or film theorist notices or has access to as information from which to interpret their reading of the film at hand.

This agency of the light material was not brought into or found normally in weather and seasonal conditions at the shooting location, but caused by an extraordinary world event a few weeks before. There are numerous accounts in recent years of strange effects of skies going orange, because of volcanoes in Iceland, St Vincent and La Palma, and the Australian and Californian bush fires. This colouring is both beautiful, sublime and ominous. Lachman's story here is not so much about great cinematography, though it confirms his expertise in adapting to circumstances and making decisions that work with the film project, but about those wonderful things that happen in the course of one's life as a cinematographer. These experiences make one think not only more deeply about light as the cinematographers' material, but about its physics and enchantment, in a philosophical manner.

Creativity, Constraint and Organization in Filmmaking

Practice theory in various disciplines encompasses attempts to get under the surface of descriptions of what people initially appear to be doing. Schatzki suggests: 'Whereas philosophers and social investigators once cited mental entities such as beliefs, desires, emotions and purposes, practice theorists instead highlight embodied capabilities such as know-how, skills, tacit understanding, and dispositions' (Schatzki in Schatzki et al. 2001: 7).

There is a matrix of material conditions and finance, production culture, workflow and community of practice hierarchies, as well as changing technology that continuously affects professional cinematographers. Employment is often precarious and discontinuous (see Curtin and Sanson 2016) and there is a historical construction of the cinematographer / director of photography's role (see Regev 2018). Praxis often exists undercover as lived experience and is rarely explicitly theorized. Wenger characterizes a community of practice as a special type of community which understands its group identity as a 'joint enterprise', involving 'mutual engagement' in a 'shared repertoire' (Wenger 1998: 73). The community 'sustains dense relations ... organized around what they are there to do' (ibid.: 74). Meaning is 'continuously negotiated in practice' and 'modes of belonging' are 'reified' by levels of specialists and gatekeepers within the community (ibid.: 84).

Collaborative creativity characterizes film production, which also has to operate within the crew hierarchy on a film set. John-Steiner claims:

> The very effort to work together, to risk an undertaking that is so different to the norm, is a creative act ... the achievement of productive collaborations requires sustained time and effort. It requires the shaping of a shared language, the pleasures and risks of honest dialogue, and the search for common ground. (John-Steiner 2000: 204)

Csikszentmihalyi seeks examples of the 'kind of creativity that leaves a trace in the cultural matrix' (1996: 27). He believes that whilst the person who brings in novelty may be seen as possessing talent, this only becomes visible via 'a culture that contains symbolic rules ... and a field of experts who recognise and validate the innovations' (6). It requires 'domains of knowledge and action' (36) within 'fields of accomplishment' (41). To reflect upon what Csikszentmihalyi calls the state of 'flow'experience, it is helpful for a person to have a 'sensory advantage in knowing the domain' (53) and they should be able to 'harbour opposites' (68). '[W]ithout a good dose of curiosity, wonder, and interest in what things are like and how they work, it is difficult to recognise an interesting problem' (53). Creative people are able to gauge who the gatekeepers in their field are and are able to be 'original, without being bizarre ... the novelty they see is rooted in reality' (63). They are 'rebellious and independent and also traditional and conservative at the same time' (72), 'able to change constraints into opportunities' (152).

I began to notice at *Camerimage*, but especially from the 2010s onward, that some of my cinematographer interlocutors spoke in a different way at the festival press conferences and seminars than in the trade press and in interviews with me. They were communicating in a wider way about their work and responding with accounts that were 'praxial' in character when talking about creative technique, that is, with the aim of cementing some element of practice as well tested in the industry in their work for the specialist audience. Often though, they would be firstly establishing something unique about their own legacy. Secondly, there was an air of passing on tips for professional survival as well as information about a technological solution or technique of working. In other words, there was as much information about handling professional life and working relationships as professional expertise about the actual cinematography practice.

Sometimes situations on location or in the studio seem to align with decisions, technique and available technology, due to both planning and the ability to recognize serendipity. This synchronicity often happens in stories about inspiration, where there has been a lot of planning, but everyone is in an intensified situation of observation and working together, such as with regular collaborators Haynes, Powell and Lachman. Then when something occurs which fits that they all agree on, it gives impetus, enthusiasm and energy to the crew and to the making of the project and will often gift the film with a unique flavour in its look. Lachman's fifth collaboration with Haynes on *Wonderstruck* (2017) was shot on both 35mm film and digital, with scenes in both colour and black-and-white. The film, based on the novel by Brian Selznick about two characters, one who is deaf and the other who loses his hearing, has dual storylines set in 1927 and 1977. The film was shot in Peekskill, Brooklyn and New York where there are some period buildings left. Lachman describes the look:

> 'In *Wonderstruck*, we were creating visual metaphors for deafness. It was a film about hearing with your eyes. *Wonderstruck* was a combination of the gritty street look of the Seventies, with the raw camera movement and naturalistic lighting, contrasted to the black and white studio chiaroscuro lighting and balanced formalism and orchestrated camera movement of the silent movies of the Twenties. We were mirroring the deafness of a young girl as she was growing up – her mother was a silent movie actress – so what better way to show that world than to show it through the cinema of the silent period which also mirrored her own deafness.' (Lachman in Heidsiek 2018)

They were shooting some tests of the young girl walking down the street. They were looking for hard clear light that slashes through the gridded streets at midday. Lachman related at a talk after showing the film at *Camerimage*, 'The sunlight came out from behind cloud for a few seconds and glowed on the young girl as she was walking along the street ... and this became a turning point in the film, it wasn't quite scripted that way' (Lachman 2017). It was something that happened in collaboration, that the cinematographer noticed, was observed by the director and then incorporated because it fitted the metaphor for the whole film, but it was not something planned in advance. It was a naturally occurring typical event, which then became a 'miracle' event, a realization for the character, which then became a central metaphor for the story.

The telling of this story by Lachman at *Camerimage* is for him to draw attention to how one needs to be very observant to one's surroundings, notice how natural light itself can give you cues and, in this case, an abundance of what was needed for the story. The audience are predominantly cinematographers and student cinematographers. So on the one hand, Lachman is a virtuoso cinematographer, and he has a plan. But he's attentive all the time to what light is just there, and what it is doing. An event occurred right in front of them. It then becomes a story of the ritual of working, an everyday something which might have a serendipitous happy outcome for the project.

In a Swedish ethnographic study on film sets, Soila-Wadman found that the professionals she interviewed: 'emphasized the value of unexpected, even troublesome, situations in filmmaking, to accentuate artistic expression. The challenge is being able to "keep your cool"' (Soila-Wadman in de Monthoux et al. 2007: 81). She surmises:

> the artistic expression-in-becoming in filmmaking practice is bringing out, bursting out, organizing itself in an ongoing negotiation process between the involved actors in the film team in front of the camera and behind the camera. In the collaborative team ... They are thinking, watching, feeling, acting. They are talking about how to find solutions. For example, what is the solution for a situation when you have hail when, according to the script, you should have sun? ... Actors in film production use 'circus' or 'battlefield' to describe the turbulent characteristic of a shooting phase of a film project. (ibid.: 79)

My point is that Lachman's story is a way in which the cinematographer 'reifies' the everyday into an extraordinary revelatory moment, making a ritual marker. It makes something memorable and shows how that is a part of the normal way of incorporating inspiration into the art form. One is not particularly expecting something will happen, but if you are attentive to circumstances, then it does happen, it reifies the 'magic' of one's profession, and supports material substance and structure of the film narrative and the vision the director has for the film. Here the simplicity of the sun's action, the agency of light, becomes a reminder, an acknowledgement, a 'thank you' from nature (see also Greenhalgh 2018, on cinematographers' response to natural light and colour). Pope sees this 'continuous becoming' as a kind of 'shapeshifting' that is found in notions of creativity as myth, story, metaphor, metamorphosis and transformation (Pope 2005: 134).

Communication, Performativity and Professional Rhetoric

The idea of the lone auteur or creator is usually applied to the director in filmmaking, but this is not how the role works in practice. The way the director 'runs the set' for the producer, with the assistant director barking the orders, can have any kind of mood, from the communal to the dictatorial. As Sherry Ortner describes it in her ethnographic work: 'A set in production is always spoken of in the possessive case, relative to the director: it is his/her set'. Chaos and organization on a set are largely down to the '"tone" set by the director' (Ortner 2013: 205). Discussing cultural capital on film sets, Lantz notes the 'director is persistently mystified in texts' (Lantz in de Monthoux et al. 2007: 64). In other words, it has taken years to accumulate the status of the cinematographer as a model of 'aesthetic leadership' (ibid.) and this has recently been threatened by digital workflow and the emerged growth of the role of the visual effects supervisor. Indeed, the 'positioning of the cinematographer as central collaborator can be viewed as the discursive product of stakeholders who themselves helped to produce a romantic idea of "cinematography". Critical here was the anxiety to move away from a mechanical gear-grinding view of practice to something more akin to a labour of love' (Clarke 2017: 109).

In 'Shooting from the Heart: Cinematographers and their Medium' (Greenhalgh 2003: 149–53), I made a number of observations in relation to the debate about co-authorship and cinematographers. Briefly: collaborative work confuses the authorship (auteur) debate in film theory and criticism, and it is easier for film industry producers to identify one person, the director, as figurehead and the principal cast of actors to promote films. World cinema's strong style is attributed primarily to directors. Cinematographers are notoriously taciturn and refer to the director's vision to keep their jobs. Whilst storytelling for feature film and major television series cinematographers, it is a major trope for them to say that their work 'serves the story' the director wants. Contracts sometimes require secrecy about special looks created for films. Emphasis on story and acting detracts from the image and relegates discussion of it to 'beauty' or spectacle. The split between technology and aesthetics demotes the cinematographer from artist to a 'creative technician'.

Many cinematographers are uneasy about the distinction between 'craft' and 'art' in terms of how their expertise is viewed. Cinematographers need the consistency of working with a particular director over several films – a 'body of work' gets work noticed (it takes time to achieve this unless one is lucky at the beginning; this particularly affects women who need to break through and may have to choose career longevity over relationships and family possibilities). Copyright and union laws affects ownership of the image (these vary from country to country). Digital manipulation of the image is now diversified across post-production (visual effects), taking image control away from the aegis and milieu of the cinematographer. In addition, in trade magazines, cinematographers may make space to promote particular manufacturers' lenses, lights, film stock or digital services they have been supported or sponsored by. It is very rare to find negative portrayals of people or working situations in print or online. Cinematographic authorship only becomes articulated through the external visibility of cinematographer partnerships with directors and communication of shared dialogue and vision.

Since I wrote these observations, the online world has considerably expanded the accounts from cinematographers about their work. There are also more women and cinematographers of diverse black and brown heritage, previously less represented, now gaining virtuoso status. All these conditions do still apply, but some cinematographers have become more interested and adept at using social media to mould their brand or stamp a personality on their work and discussion of it. I would suggest, therefore, that these accounts must be considered as functioning within a professional rhetoric which has the above parameters. There is performance of a role, accompanied by a professional 'form of talk', as Goffman would put it (Goffman 1981). One has to be very careful of attending to a romantic way of speaking that cinematographers tend to have, especially about the subject of light. Anthropologist Anand Pandian analyses one cinematographer's attitude on a film shoot in Tamil Nadu in his book *Reel World: An Anthropology of Creation* (Pandian 2015: 107–20). This is a poetically written account and gives interesting insights into the relation between the Indian cinematographer and his traditional Indian philosophies of light influences and the creative decisions being made. I believe, though, that Pandian falls for some of the professional rhetoric common in cinematographer parlance.

Amongst the technical and aesthetic information provided, one has to unpack the way of speaking, glean the production conditions and processes and try to find what is tacit evidence and what knowledge might be revealed underneath an explicitly articulated and sometimes rhetorical or repeated cliche description. Epstein describes a similar but more extreme situation with regard to actors: 'No matter how ungratifying the work may be, actors, in their videotaped interviews, publicity appearances and acceptance speeches at award ceremonies are expected to portray their acting as a form of spontaneous art' (Epstein 2005: 305).

> The 'value of pseudopraise ... flattery, already the coin of the realm, is further institutionalized in Hollywood in the interviews conducted with actors, directors, producers, and writers during every major production for inclusion in 'The Making Of' featurettes that are furnished to the media. In these interviews, participants are not expected to divulge their actual evaluations of the performances of co-workers ... it is common for them to describe one another, over and over again, as a 'brilliant' performer, 'consummately talented' and 'a genius'. (ibid.: 305)

The *Camerimage* festival promotes the collaborative work of directors with cinematographers in particular. In Eastern-European countries, but particularly in Poland, this artistic duo combination is particularly revered, and criticism of films, film school training and the stature of film artists in society reinforces this more concretely than one would find in the UK or US, for example. This is a festival and trade fair where many stories of what really goes on in the industry are told in the cities bars, festival parties, seminars and press conferences. What goes wrong in collaborations does not get reported in the trade press and is not known or cared about by film critics. Successful partnerships are eulogized and difficulties smoothed over in reported narratives. Yet how to handle these collaborative dynamics is crucial in a cinematographer's career biography and in teaching would-be camera crew and cinematographers in both confident and diplomatic behaviour.

Camerimage, for those cinematographers especially interested in the art form, has become one of the places to appear within the circuit of getting one's work as well as professional demeanour and articulacy displayed. I have seen reputations develop and grow as well as fade here (having attended for twenty-five of the thirty years the festival has been in existence at the time of writing (2022), accompanying over four hundred of my students). Top cinematographers and several visiting directors, producers and actors, those on the way up and all levels of crew and students from MFA, MA and BA cinematography courses worldwide, attend every year. It has become one of the venues in which many issues are discussed, both those on and 'off the record'.

When I first attended the festival in 1995, there were a handful of Polish journalists and presidents of national cinematography societies who wrote reports in their guild presses. On the first visit there were few foreign (non-Polish) students there and this included women and those of diverse backgrounds. Now the festival has five thousand attendees (though somewhat curtailed by the Covid 19 pandemic in 2020 and 2021) and reporters from mainstream broadcast and film media present. Being female, a cinematographer / director and a teacher, and carrying out an ethnography with, not all, but predominantly, male interlocutors, brought up numerous questions of a personal, social, cultural and political nature in fieldwork. Continuous discussions have been had on the state of cinematographic art, the nature of the film business, maverick means of survival, cultural film practices in different countries represented in competition, gender and diversity issues. I am grateful for the most thought-provoking discussions I've had which were often with my own students and other teachers attending *Camerimage*, especially other regular attendees, as much as with cinematographers and industry delegates.

The Last Black Man in San Francisco (2019), directed by Joe Talbot and scripted from a story by its principal actor Jimmy Fails, narrates a tale about race and gentrification set in San Francisco's striking Victorian wooden house neighbourhoods. American cinematographer Adam Newport-Berra had prior experience as a skateboarder, and movement in the film was influenced by his abilities to move the camera in unusual ways. The director and main actors were less experienced at filmmaking, but as San Francisco natives, were very familiar with the light and feel of apartments in the houses. There is a strong western sunlight through large windows across spaces, which picks out figures against typically dark wood-panelled walls. At a seminar after screening the film at *Camerimage*, Newport-Berra explained: 'San Francisco is like every place, it has its own spirit ... We wanted to elevate the city to a mythological proportion in the film. We chose a colour palette with a lot of "rose", and a patina and textures that would work with the [black] skin tones' (Newport-Berra 2019).

Newport-Berra was one of the most experienced people on the low-budget feature shoot, shooting on a digital camera. He understood the scheduling and hierarchy of crew procedures on set better than those around him. This took some of his cinematography time, so he had to 'pick my battles carefully ... I wanted to make the film easier for Jimmy ... as this film was a big leap for him ... we were mixing real actors with non-actors, real people' (ibid.). The director and main actor wanted to be frontally lit. This is an unusual thing to do and can flatten out and lighten up skin tones too much. It is not the way that has been built up carefully of lighting skin tones for dramatic difference in features in the last decade. This technique is sometimes used in Bollywood cinema, for giving the main characters a glowing, spotlit diva look, which artificially pulls them out from the chorus in singing and dance numbers. It looks like the painting technique used by Pre-Raphaelite painters to pick out main figures in the light, such as the painted woman and child in Ford Madox's Brown's painting *The Pretty Baa-Lambs* (1851). From 'day one, I said no but in the end it worked with the actors lit from the front ... for this film, it adds a little magic', he said (Newport-Berra 2019). He had 'an epiphany ... I've learned from this film that we're motivated to "control", set up for success in everything you do ... but spontaneity in terms of risk can prove really magical. I'm humbled to be part of that and Joe's vision was clear ... he was a complete cinephile' (ibid.).

This story shows both invention on the spot with lighting, but also deference to actors and directors. It's a tricky balance. There are only a few technical articles on this film and none mention this mismatch of experience and taking risk. This is the kind of story relayed to both buoy up and (as he found) impress upon an audience with student members coming up a few years behind. But it also brings up the wider question of historical habits and cultural interventions in lighting. Lighting technology has seen rapid change in the last few years with use of digital lighting systems, incandescent lighting mixed with LED, and new reflective surface invention, and smaller lighting unit 'green shooting'. LUTs (digital menu look-up tables on cameras) enable use of very specific colour palettes in digital filmmaking and ever greater expression with light. Lighting varied human skin tones in contemporary storytelling featuring more people of colour and women's (and non-binary) narratives provoke decolonizing of traditional ways of lighting (see Greenhalgh 2020 on lighting and skin tone). As Krista Thompson writes: 'the use of light produced though visual technologies generates distinct aesthetic, synaesthetic physiological, and phenomenological effects; creating and denying types of viewership in particular performative and spatial context'. (Thompson 2015: 14).

Conclusion

Reflecting on their construction of 'artistic citizenship', Elliot and Silverman declare:

> From our perspective, praxis is a multidimensional concept that includes active reflection and critically reflective action guided by an informed ethical disposition to act rightly, with continuous concern for protecting and advancing the well-being of others. It is action dedicated to personal and collective flourishing, grounded in commitments to transform and enrich people's everyday lives. Praxial art making thus consists of thoughtful and careful (i.e. 'care-full') artistic practice, of artistic action that is embedded in and responsive to ever-changing social, cultural, and political circumstances. (Elliott and Silverman 2016: 90)

> Praxis integrates critical reflection and ethical action. Hegel, Marx, and Freire, among others, modified significantly Aristotle's concept of praxis. As such 'praxis' is inclusive of critical thinking and action, as well as emotions, techniques, motivations, aims, values, ethics, and all their interactions. (ibid.: 6)

Stories are performed with viewers and listeners in mind. Stories about the everyday use of light in the practice of cinematography and striving for the exceptional are performed within a defined professional milieu. Hong Kong based cinematographer Christopher Doyle writes in one of his memoirs:

> The image exists. It's our job to find it … .It's not just a script that makes a film 'good' or 'bad,' it's knowing what you really want to do and finding a way. Nothing is as important as knowing how to think on your feet. If you're clear about what a scene should say, you can adapt to any situation. You can change lines or locations, you can shoot days in the rain instead of on a clear moonlit

night. So even with all the rehearsals, and all the discussions directors and actors go through, films are made day-by-day and shot-by-shot, just as they should be. (Doyle 1998: 107, 99)

Here Doyle alludes to the spontaneous, expressive, adaptive process of thinking and working and resolving as one goes along, that is, praxis. Prior documentation, such as the script, storyboards, budget and pre-production planning need to be flexible to shooting conditions and personnel. Whilst cinematographers do not speak in other environments so much, *Camerimage* is one of the few places they share stories with some freedom from other institutions. Doyle and Lachman have been regular attendees over many years. Whilst cinematographers are not healers, of course, I have often heard their work described stereotypically, sometimes romantically amongst themselves, as if they must perform as a magician or shaman. This is a status to have to live up to. Trinh T. Minh-ha captures the idea of stories as transformation with that beneficence:

> The story as a cure and a protection is at once musical, historical, poetical, ethical, educational, magical, and religious. In many parts of the world, the healers are known as the living memories of the people. Not only do they hold esoteric and technical knowledge, but they are also kept closely informed of the problems of their communities and are entrusted with all family affairs. In other words, they know everyone's story. Concerned with the slightest incident, they remain very alert to their entourage and heedful of their patients' talks. They derive their power from *listening* to the others and *absorbing* daily realities. (Trinh T. Minh-ha 1989: 140; original emphasis)

Interpretation though lighting and how it is handled as an intellectual and physical process is key within the cinematographer's role. American cinematographer John Bailey puts it thus:

> Cinematographers have an especially magical tool to facilitate self-expression and discovery. It is light, at once lambent and elusive, and also static and solid. Our work, our experiments in space and time, our aesthetic statements, are encapsulated by it. And ultimately, it is one key to our unique personal history. (John Bailey from *American Cinematographer* magazine cited in Greenhalgh 2003: 97)

Cathy Greenhalgh is an independent filmmaker, lecturer, media anthropologist and writer. She has thirty years' university teaching and management expertise (latterly as Principal Lecturer in Film and Television, University of the Arts London) and fifteen years as a professional cinematographer, directing films using choreography, essay / ethnographic documentary for cinema, gallery and museum spaces. She also makes collages and writes poetry.

References

Alazraki, Robert. 1997. Press conference. *Camerimage* festival. Torun, Poland. November.
Boje, David M. 2008. *Storytelling Organizations*. Los Angeles, London, New Delhi, Singapore: SAGE.
Clarke, Jamie. 2017. 'Elegies to Cinematography: The Digital Workflow, Digital Naturalism and Recent Best Cinematography Oscars', in *Collaborative Production in the Creative Industries*, James Graham and Alessandro Gandini (eds). London: University of Westminster Press, pp. 105–24.
Csikszentmihalyi, Mihaly. 1996. *Creativity: Flow and the Psychology of Discovery and Invention*. New York: HarperCollins Publishers.
Curtin, Michael and Kevin Sanson. 2016. *Precarious Creativity: Global Media, Local Labor*. Berkeley, CA: University of California Press.
Doyle, Christopher. 1998. *A Cloud in Trousers*. Los Angeles: Los Angeles Center for Photographic Studies and Smart Art Press.
Elliot, David and Marissa Silverman. 2016. *Artistic Citizenship: Artistry, Social Responsibility and Ethical Praxis*. Oxford: Oxford University Press.
Epstein, Edward Jay. 2005. *The Big Picture: The New Logic of Money and Power in Hollywood*. USA: Random House Inc.
Foster Gage, Mark. 2019. *Aesthetics Equals Politics: New Discourses Across Art, Architecture, and Philosophy*. Cambridge, MA: MIT Press.
Gabriel, Yiannis. 2000. *Storytelling in Organizations: Facts, Fictions and Fantasies*. Oxford and New York: Oxford University Press.
Goffman, Erving. 1981. *Forms of Talk*. Philadelphia: University of Pennsylvania Press.
Grasseni, Cristina. 2009. *Skilled Visions: Between Apprenticeship and Standards*. New York: Berghahn.
Greenhalgh, Cathy. 2003. 'Shooting from the Heart: Cinematographers and their Medium', in *Making Pictures: A Century of European Cinematography*, Michael Leitch on behalf of IMAGO (The European Federation of Cinematography Societies) (ed.). London: Aurum Press and Harry N. Abrams, pp. 94–155.
——. 2018. 'Cinematographers' Encounters with Natural Light Colour', in *Rematerializing Colour: From Concept to Substance*, Diana Young (ed.). Canon Pyon: Sean Kingston Publishing.
——. 2020. 'Skin Tone and Faces: Cinematography Pedagogy Which Foregrounds Inclusivity and Diversity in Teaching Lighting'. *Cinematography in Progress*. 2019 conference proceedings published online. Retrieved 28 January 2023 from: https://cinematographyinprogress.com/index.php/cito/article/view/45, pp. 1–23.
Guillet de Monthoux, Pierre, Claes Gustafsson and Sven-Erik Sjöstrand (eds). 2007. *Aesthetic Leadership: Managing Fields of Flows in Art and Business*. Basingstoke and New York: Palgrave Macmillan.
Heidsiek, Birgit (2018), 'Every Story Has Its Own Language: Ed Lachman, ASC', in *British Cinematographer*. Retrieved 30 August 2022 from: https://britishcinematographer.co.uk/every-story-has-its-own-language-ed-lachman-asc/.

John-Steiner, Vera. 2000. *Creative Collaboration*. Oxford: Oxford University Press.
Lachman, Ed. 2018. Press conference and seminar, *Camerimage* festival. Bydgosczcz, Poland. November.
_____. 2002. Press conference, *Camerimage* festival. Lodz, Poland. November.
Leddy, Thomas. 2012. *The Extraordinary in the Ordinary: The Aesthetics of Everyday Life*. New York, Ontario, London: Broadview Press.
Newport-Berra, Adam. 2019. Press conference, *Camerimage* festival. Torun, Poland. November.
Ortner, Sherry B. 2013. *Not Hollywood: Independent Film at the Twilight*. Durham, NC and London: Duke University Press.
Pandian, Anand. 2015. *Reel World: An Anthropology of Creation*. Durham, NC and London: Duke University Press.
Pope, Rob. 2005. *Creativity: Theory, History, Practice*. London and New York: Routledge.
Regev, Ronny. 2018. *Working in Hollywood: How the Studio System Turned Creativity into Labor*. Chapel Hill, NC: University of North Carolina Press.
Thompson, Krista. 2015. *Shine: The Visual Economy of Light in African Diasporic Aesthetic Practice*. Durham, NC and London: Duke University Press.
Trinh T. Minh-ha. 1989. *Woman, Native, Other: Writing, Postcoloniality and Feminism*. Bloomington, IN: Indiana University Press.
Schatzki, Theodor R., Karin Knorr-Cetina and Eike von Savigny (eds). 2001. *The Practice Turn in Contemporary Theory*. London and New York: Routledge.
Strati, Antonio. 1999. *Organizations and Aesthetics*. London, Thousand Oaks and New Delhi: SAGE Publications.
Van Maanen, John. 1988. *Tales of the Field: On Writing Ethnography*. Chicago and London: University of Chicago Press.
Wenger, Etienne. 1998. *Communities of Practice: Learning, Meaning and Identity*. Cambridge and New York: Cambridge University Press.

Filmography

A Summer in La Goulette (1996), directed by Ferid Boughedir, France/Tunisia.
Far from Heaven (2002), directed by Todd Haynes, USA.
Wonderstruck (2017), directed by Todd Haynes, USA.
The Last Black Man in San Francisco (2019), directed by Joe Talbot, USA.

Chapter 10

'Hammered by the Image'
Exceptional Experiences of Art as Aesthetic Impact

Helena Wulff

In her exquisite memoir, *Blue Arabesque: A Search for the Sublime* (2006), the American writer Patricia Hampl describes an exceptional experience released by art: on a spring day in 1972, she was late to a meeting with a friend in the museum cafeteria at the Art Institute of Chicago, where she had never been before. So she finds herself rushing through gallery after gallery to a staircase without looking at the paintings on the walls:

> Then, unexpectedly, several galleries shy of my destination, I came to a halt before a large, rather muddy painting in a heavy gold-coloured frame, a Matisse labeled *Femme et poissons rouges*, rendered in English, *Woman Before an Aquarium*. But that's wrong: I didn't halt, didn't stop. I was stopped. Apprehended, even. That's how it felt. I stood before the painting a long minute. I couldn't move away. I couldn't have said why. I was simply fastened there. (Hampl 2006: 2)

How did this happen? What triggers an exceptional experience, and one of art? Intrigued by the sudden effect of Patricia Hampl's experience, in this chapter I scrutinize transformative exceptional experiences in terms of aesthetic impact. My focal point is this memoir, of which I am doing an anthropological reading. This is in the spirit of an anthropology of texts, as suggested by Karin Barber (2007), where a local text is understood in its social and cultural context. With participant observation's pivotal position in anthropology, texts by interlocutors such as memoirs (published and unpublished) have traditionally been considered only marginally and not at the centre of attention. For some time now, the switch to more eclectic methods and forms of data has opened up new possibilities. This is reflected in the recent proliferation of anthropologies of literature (Narayan 2012; Wulff 2016, 2017, 2021; Hannerz 2021; Wiles 2021) and reading (Boyarin 1993; Reed 2018; Christiansen 2021; Uimonen 2021). While calling for more anthropological studies of memoirs as texts, let us look at the role of the memoir in anthropology. Memoirs have not figured as much as a feature of local life, but predominantly in the form of ethnographic reports by the fieldworker, and then as one writing genre among creative nonfiction, journalism, travel writing, even literary fiction, in addition to conventional academic writing (Wulff 2021). For an understanding of *Blue Arabesque* (2006), though, a textual analysis is not enough. There has to be a visual dimension as well: this is required by the way the writer is gazing at the painting – and the way the woman in the painting is gazing at a fishbowl. I will begin by exploring the memoir as a writing genre in anthropology. It is interesting to note that memoirs by anthropologists, whether about the field or personal circumstances, are driven by exceptional experiences, and that they often take place during travel. And travel is what Hampl's momentous experience takes her on,

Figure 10.1. *Woman Before an Aquarium* by Henri Matisse, 1923. © https://en.wikipedia.org/wiki/File:Woman_Before_an_Aquarium.jpg. Creative Commons.

as she goes on a pilgrimage to France and Morocco in order to find out more about Matisse and his painting *Woman Before an Aquarium*.

Memoirs and Anthropology

Patricia Hampl is not just any writer. She is also a poet, but mainly she is an award-winning memoirist. In addition to *Blue Arabesque* (2006), she has written several memoirs, such as *A Romantic Education* (1981) about her Czech family background, while *Virgin Time: In Search of a Contemplative Life* (1992) depicts her Catholic upbringing, and *The Florist's Daughter: A Memoir* (2007) her mother's death. A recurring insight across this substantial *oeuvre* that also includes journalistic articles and poetry collections, is that memoir writing does not replicate truth but constitutes a fragmented version put together afterwards and formed by long-term concerns:

> Memoir is not what happened (if we're lucky, that's the best journalism). It is what *has happened* over time, in the mind, in the life as it attends to these tantalizing, dismaying, broken bits of life history. Such personal writing is, as the essay is, 'an attempt.' It is a try at the truth.[1]

In anthropology, of course, it was the 'writing culture' debate in the 1980s, and in particular James Clifford (1986) who identified the 'partial truths' of any account. While regarded as sensational at the time, an awareness of writing's partial nature is now taken for granted. A certain selection of what research issues and field experiences are included (and excluded) in writings is simply unavoidable, but should preferably be well argued for. The 1980s was also the time when a demand for details in the research and writing processes emerged, often of a personal nature, and one response was to write in an experimental mode. This was when memoirs by fieldworkers, such as *In Sorcery's Shadow: A Memoir of Apprenticeship among the Songhay of Niger* (1987) by Paul Stoller and Cheryl Olkes, appeared as a genre. Drawing on theory and anthropological methods, this memoir is written in a lucid literary style without academic references. It has been cherished for its engaged narrative of how Stoller became an apprentice sorcerer. At the centre of the story is an exceptional experience, a terrifying one:

> I awoke to the tattoo of steps on the roof of the house ... I did not move, and I heard nothing more. Suddenly I had the strong impression that something had entered the house. I felt its presence and I was frightened. Set to abandon the house to whatever hovered in the darkness, I started to roll off my mat. But my lower body did not budge. I pinched my leaden thighs and felt nothing.

> My heart raced. I couldn't flee. What could I do to save myself? ... I began to recite the *genji how* [protective incantation]. And so I recited and recited and continued to recite it until I began to feel a slight tingling in my hips. ... My voice cracked, but I continued to recite. Slowly, the tingling spread from my legs to my feet. I pinched my thigh – it hurt – and tested my response along the length of my legs. (Stoller and Olkes 1987: 148)

After a while, the tingling sensation stopped and Stoller was able to stand up. The presence had left the room. There is no doubt in Stoller's mind that his temporary paralysis was a test of his aptitude to train as an apprentice sorcerer. The next morning he went to his teacher who said: 'Now I know that you are a man with a pure heart ... You are ready. Come into my house and we shall begin to learn' (Stoller and Olkes 1987: 149, Stoller 1994: 10). Even though Stoller's frightening exceptional experience is very different from Hampl's uplifting revelation, they are equally strong and formative, but most of all they exemplify exceptional experiences as entrances to unexpected opportunities. And they are both totally truthful in the moment, as recalled by Hampl and Stoller respectively.

The growth of memoir as a genre in anthropology has, again, mostly consisted of recollections from the field, but there are also accounts of the personal life of the anthropologist (Jackson 2006; Collins and Gallinat 2010 among others). Even though memoirs would seem to be a genre for older people who have had long and event-filled lives, there are actually quite a few memoirs by younger anthropologists, in their middle age (Wulff 2021). This is the case with Kirin Narayan's *My Family and Other Saints* (2007), where Narayan revisits her childhood and adolescence in India. She grew up during the 1960s in a sprawling family of eccentrics. The memoir circles around her older brother Rahoul, who left school in order to follow a guru, and eventually moved to the US. His spiritual quest was taken up by Narayan's American mother. She welcomes Westerners seeking Eastern enlightenment into their Bombay house by the beach, while her Indian father finds them laughable and retreats into his room with a bottle. Narayan is left to learn about adult life on her own. This is not just a memoir about a bicultural family in India, but on a larger societal level, the story of the prevalence of spiritual quests during this particular period of time.

An early anthropological memoir is Claude Lévi-Strauss's classic *Tristes Tropiques* (1992 [1955]). As it records not only his fieldwork in Brazil but also his travels there, it has been categorized as travel writing, as well. This dual label is how Patricia Hampl's memoir could be identified. Starting out with her jolting experience at the Art Institute of Chicago, it soon turns into travel writing as she goes to France on a pilgrimage in search of Matisse's milieux: to Paris where he worked in his studio, to Nice and Côte D'Azur where he moved, and to Morocco where he found inspiration in the colours, design and the light.

A sister genre to anthropological memoirs is that of autoethnography. Described by Deborah Reed-Danahay (1997: 2; 2019) as 'referring either to the ethnography of one's own group or to autobiographical writing that has ethnographic interest' it is often informed by theoretical perspectives, especially issues of inequality. Incidentally, autoethnographies tend to include exceptional experiences ranging from dramatic to uplifting ones that also happen during travel. Shahram Khosravi's *'Illegal' Traveller* (2010) is a case in point. It starts out with a rendering of how Khosravi in 1987 had to flee Iran, risking his life as he was crossing the border to Afghanistan: 'It was a moonless night. "Good! The darkness shelters us," said my smuggler ... "If I take this step, I will be an 'illegal' person and the world will never be the same again." That night I took that step and my odyssey of "illegality" began' (Khosravi 2010: ix). His long journey via India and London took him to Sweden where he arrived on a plane and:

> tore up the passport, the boarding pass and the ticket and flushed them down the toilet. Needless to say, I did not carry any identification. I had left letters, photos and my Iranian ID-cards behind to be sent to me when I reached Sweden. At Arlanda airport, two policemen waited at the gate and picked out 'asylum-seeker-looking' passengers. (Khosravi 2007: 331)

Khosravi is now a Professor of Social Anthropology at Stockholm University. His journey can, in a sense, be said to have ended. But not quite: his memory of being 'an illegal traveller' stays with him, as does Iran where he is now able to go back when he wants.

A different type of memoir is *My Life as a Spy* (1918) by Katherine Verdery. She had spent long periods of research for several decades focusing on political economy, social inequality and nationalism in communist Romania. In 1989, the secret police files in Eastern Europe became accessible. Verdery had an exceptional experience of terror and betrayal when she found out in her file that she had been surveilled by the secret police, as well as by both friends and lovers, and accused of being a spy. Her memoir was a way to rectify an inaccurate local image of an anthropologist, while revealing the dynamics in Romania during communism.

Art, Aesthetics and the Everyday

For an understanding of how Patricia Hampl's exceptional experience happened, we need to look at aesthetics in anthropology, aesthetics as emotional impact. It was Franz Boas in his *Primitive Art* (1955 [1927]), who first identified aesthetics as a topic for the discipline. Exemplifying with intricate geometrical pattern in art from the North Pacific Coast of North America, Boas argued that an appreciation of beauty in art, and an urge to create such beauty, is universal. Following Kant's (2009 [1790]) ideas on aesthetic appreciation of artistic form as emanating from an appreciation of nature, Boas went on to specify that this appreciation entails an enchantment with form, ranging from rhythm and balance to colour and texture.

Aesthetics has been associated with beauty, taste and value, which in anthropology evoke questions of culture and comparison. In the 'Introduction' to their edited volume *Anthropology, Art and Aesthetics* (1996: 7), Jeremy Coote and Anthony Shelton remind us that the 'universal existence of aesthetic taste and aesthetic impulse' has been acknowledged in anthropology since the discipline's inception, but that it would take until the 1950s and 1960s before a more systematic study of aesthetics in non-Western societies was established. Eventually, the concept of ethnoaesthetics was accentuated in anthropological accounts of art (Myers 2002; Svašek 2007 among others) with proponents such as Nelson Graburn (2005) arguing for an indigenous perspective which would reveal local notions of beauty. In line with a contemporary anthropological perspective, this soon became the dominant approach. Still, there are obviously variations in local notions of beauty, which Howard Becker is concerned with in his *Art Worlds* (2008 [1982]: 131), especially as he discusses the role of experts such as critics. Here aesthetics is 'an activity rather than a body of doctrine'. Aware that most people who engage in art worlds make aesthetic judgements, Becker emphasized the power of critics who 'apply aesthetic systems to specific art works and arrive at judgments of their worth ... Those judgments produce reputations for works and artists.'

Yet, aesthetics does not only concern the arts. As Coote (1996: 246) states 'all human activity has an aesthetic aspect', and continues by qualifying that there is always a concern with 'the aesthetic qualities of aural, haptic, kinetic, and visual sensations'. This resonates with Birgit Meyer's (2009: 6) idea to reconsider aesthetics from being confined to Kant's ideas of 'the beautiful in the sphere of the arts, and its disinterested beholder' by going back to Aristotle's 'much older and more encompassing notion of *aisthesis*'. This notion takes the senses into consideration as it includes 'our corporeal capability on the basis of a power given in our psyche to perceive objects in the world via our five different sensorial modes' (Meyer and Verrips 2008: 21). It is her insights into media and religion that spur Meyer's (2009: 6) view of a 'more encompassing, embodied understanding of aesthetics'. She recognizes that this 'is now beginning to be more widely shared among scholars' as it includes 'the affective power of images, sounds and texts over their beholders'. And this is what happened to Patricia Hampl – the affective power of the painting hit her.

Moshe Shokeid (1992: 234) in his *Cultural Anthropology* article 'Exceptional Experiences in Everyday Life', identifies these experiences as distinguished by 'an arbitrary beginning and ending out of the stream of chronological temporality' and that 'they leave strong marks on the map of our life experiences'. Art is certainly in the realm of the everyday for those who work in it, and the experience of Patricia Hampl at the Art Institute of Chicago also took place in her everyday life. Even though we may associate the notion of the everyday with routine and predictability, it does include serendipitous events. The everyday is sometimes interrupted by the exceptional that might change the course of the everyday.

Peaks, Flows, Epiphanies

A fieldworker's experience of unexpected events can lead serendipitously to crucial understandings of circumstances in the field. Or, like in Paul Stoller's (Stoller and Olkes 1987) case above, such events can push the fieldworker deeper into the field. Then there are the revelatory moments that can spring up during artistic creation. John Blacking (1977: 17), the ethnomusicologist, identified them as 'transcendental states or peak experiences'. In my research on ballet as career and culture in a transnational world (Wulff 2006: 138), dancers sometimes talked with much appreciation about moments of flow (cf. Csikszentmihalyi 1990), when the dancing is effortless and takes them into new zones. This is when they do not have to worry about the technique, which tends to be difficult, even painful – instead they move into artistry. A female dancer depicted such moments as: 'You don't stop where your body ends' and 'You feel like you're completely free ... you feel like flying!' This took place mostly in performance, but now and then in rehearsal. Analytically, those moments are the reward (and the reason) for dancers to keep going in this job, which is exceptionally challenging both physically and mentally. So exceptional experiences can strike during artistic creation and when looking at art: seeing a dance performance or listening to a live concert among specialists such as critics, art collectors and art dealers, as well as members of a general audience, even a first-time visitor to an art event. In his collection of short stories, *Dubliners* (2012 [1914]), the Irish writer James Joyce famously referred to epiphany for a sudden insight of social conditions. A lapsed Catholic, Joyce was most likely still inspired by the religious usage of the concept in Christianity. Incidentally, Patricia Hampl (2006: 3) explains her riveting response to the painting *Woman Before an Aquarium* as having partly been prepared by her traditional Catholic upbringing, where 'the possibility of an ordinary person being visited by apparitions was packed into the dark kit of my mind'.[2]

Exceptional experiences are indeed rare, but memorable, even formative as they often bring life-changing understandings of oneself, other people and social life. They are obviously visual, but can also be aural, sometimes in combination, such as in concerts, installations and performances. In line with Isadora Duncan's legendary statement 'if I could tell you what it meant, there would be no point in dancing it', exceptional experiences of dance, art, images, paintings and so on take place beyond-the-verbal. This insight, which, of course, is well-documented, does raise another critical issue, though: how can we convey a non-verbal exceptional experience in writing? During fieldwork in the Russian tundra, Petra Rethmann (2007: 44) shared many long moments of silence with the people she researched. To her, those moments were 'peaceful and whole, because nothing mattered then except the company of people, motions of the body and hands, tea, or the feel of the weather and the wind'. She goes on to discuss the challenge of translating, as it were, silence into words, as this is something 'which, almost by its very nature, is unspeakable'. Nonetheless, she succeeds in reaching the reader by writing an ethnography of silence by way of the senses accentuating sight and sound, as well as touch.[3] There is no doubt that these moments were turning points in her fieldwork and transformative to her as a person.

When trying to convey an exceptional experience in written words, we strive to find a tone that can capture the magnitude of the feeling, preferably through an unexpected combination of words. Steering clear of clichés is crucial but might require some extra thought. One of the reasons I was caught by *Blue Arabesque* (2006: 5), Hampl's book, was the sentence: 'I was hammered by the image.' It is not only innovative, but it also provides a sense of the weight of the experience. This expression was, incidentally, also picked up in the headline of a *New York Times* review of the book. It read 'Hammered by Art' (Harrison 2006). In the review, the critic Kathryn Harrison observes about Hampl: 'As her subtitle makes clear, she was in pursuit of the sublime, by which she means art with transcendent power, enough that it jolts its audience into exaltation, curiosity and craving. Art as drug, and addiction. Art that can hammer.' As Harrison is a writer in her own right, she makes a point about finding apt wordings that also surprise when she captures Hampl's elevated experience in formulations such as: 'She was arrested – no other word will do – by a painting.'

Recognition and Discovery

Key here is that exceptional experiences spring up when two qualities are at work: *recognition* in the story of the art piece, and *discovery* in its form, such as a new colour or surface. To Patricia Hampl's (2006: 2, 5) strong response to the painting belongs the piece of information that she was not a habitual museum goer or someone who was used to being impressed by art, and not at all dependent on art. In fact, she writes: 'I thought of myself as a person almost uniquely ungifted in the visual arts.' Yet there she was, enthralled by the image. And even though she claims that she is unable to 'explain what the picture expressed', there was a recognition for her in the gaze of the woman in the picture as she was looking at the fishbowl rather than being looked at: 'the clairvoyant image of a future I wanted', Hampl notes. The story of the painting, the one she saw in it, made her even more aware of her unsettled status as a recent college graduate with a degree in English, still navigating grown-up life. She was making a living as a copy-editor at a radio station which was not how she had envisioned her existence. Like the woman in the painting, she desired to spend time contemplating an object. This is commented on in the *New York Times Review*: 'Patricia Hampl's determination to occupy the space between the eye and its object and her success at articulating the mysterious transactions therein grants her authority among writers ... who not only sit and stare but see.' This was the beginning of her feminist stance, an independent woman writer's life.

Incidentally, her epiphanic experience happened, according to Hampl herself, not only because the painting told a story about her present predicament, as it were, but perhaps even more so because of the special blue screen as: 'My eye traced the pattern of the screen that formed the painting's background, a hypnotic blue X/O open-work design that enclosed the woman in the drab solitude of her Western study' (Hampl 2006: 16). And like other revelatory moments of art and performance, this one was suggestive of opening up new possibilities, it released the imagination of the viewer. Hampl imagined what the blue screen concealed: 'a chamber of silks, fantastic patterns in gorgeous disarray, scents of spice and flower' (Hampl 2006: 17). This splendour was a liberation for her, indicating her way forward as a creative writer. She spelled this out in a poem with the title of the painting, which she wrote in 1978. In the poem, Hampl imagines that she is with the fish in the bowl 'glinting inside with the flicker of water, heart ticking with the message of biology to a kindred species'. Daydreaming about the peaceful and happy life inside the fishbowl, she sees herself as 'The mermaid – not the enchantress, but the mermaid of double life.' The idea that she has a double life can be a reference to the mermaid as both woman and fish, and her ability to connect to both species. The mermaid in the poem is 'thinking as always of swimming.' The woman in Matisse's painting is yearning for a carefree life, such as being able to think about nothing else than swimming. The orange fish and the bowl represent the world where the woman wished she lived.[4] And where Patricia Hampl was on her way.

As exceptional experiences are affective, the viewer has to be in an existentially vulnerable or conflictual situation in life, with an openness to this kind of influence. In other words, there is a new colour, surface, rhythm or movement that is striking to the viewer. It is the combination of recognition and discovery that can create an elevated experience of art. At stake is the visual, and John Berger's (1972) classic idea that there are different 'ways of seeing', of looking at the same image: one image or painting or photograph can have many meanings. Berger's point is that we see what we believe: belief and knowledge define ways of seeing. There was a recognition for Hampl in the gaze of the woman in the painting. And as Banks and Zeitlyn (2015: 11) argue, it is useful to consider the concepts of internal and external narratives of an image. The content, or story, of an image is its internal narrative (which may well differ from the intention of the image-maker) while 'the social context that produced the image, and the social relations within which the image is embedded at any moment of viewing' is the external narrative. Writing about the content and form of an image, Banks and Zeitlyn thus point out that the materiality of an image and its contexts can explain the nature of social relations in which it operates.

Hampl did not only bring her memory of being punctured by the painting with her, but a postcard of the painting from the Chicago museum shop. This gave her ample opportunity to ponder over the painting:

> my eye began to move away from the woman's face ... Past the contemplative face, past the bottled world of her gaze, my eye went to the Moroccan screen and stayed there. I suppose it was the first time I saw the *elements* of a painting, took in, without knowing the word, the *composition*, in other words, the *thought*, of a painting. Not simply the thought as of some object, but the *thinking* of the painting, the galvanizing sense of an act of cognition occurring, unfinished but decisive, right there on the canvas. (Hampl. 2006: 15; emphasis in original)

The climax came when Hampl (2006: 4) observed that: 'slightly to the left, a pedestal fishbowl stands, surrounded by pinecones and a few needly branches strewn with artful carelessness. A small white rectangle rests on the table as well – a notepad. Of course: she's a writer.'

Thinking back to her school days, when she was trying to draw, but: 'I couldn't draw, couldn't *see* how to lure images from eye to hand to paper. I could only *get* things by writing them, reading them. In the beginning, truly for me, was the Word.' But standing in front of *Woman Before an Aquarium*, Hampl (2006: 5; emphasis in original) recalled:

> For once I wasn't thinking in words; I was hammered by the image. I couldn't explain what the picture expressed, what I intuited from it. But that it spoke, I had no doubt. I was just starting my life, fresh from university, dumb jobs, no 'skills', outfitted only with a vexed boyfriend life, various predictable dreamy dreams. Plenty of attitude. An English major on the loose at last.

And she goes on:

> I knew that the woman in the painting, whoever, whatever she was, held in the quality of her gaze the clairvoyant image of a future I wanted, a way of being in the world that it would be very good to achieve – if it could be achieved.

This was a liberation for her, indicating her way forward as a distinguished creative writer, personal essayist and poet. She went on to complete an MFA. at the University of Iowa and eventually became a professor of English at the University of Minnesota, teaching on the Creative Writing program for many years.

Towards Building the Blue Screen

By now you may wonder: what about the painting itself and the painter? Who was Henri Matisse and what spurred him to create *Woman Before an Aquarium* in 1921–23? A French artist, who lived between 1869 and 1954, Matisse was primarily a painter but also a draftsman and printmaker as well as a sculptor. Recognized for his use of strong colours and fluid drawing style, his substantial body of work came about during more than fifty years. It made him a forerunner in modern art. But before finding his vocation as an artist, he went to law school and worked as a court administrator. Then an appendicitis forced him to a convalescence, and his mother gave him paints and an easel as an idle pleasure. Fascinated, he discovered that he was able to paint and also enjoyed it immensely. He decided to leave his law studies and instead set out on a career as an artist, to the disappointment of his father.

As Matisse rose to fame, he was inspired by the work of Vincent van Gogh and a range of different art styles and traditions, ranging from Japanese art to Impressionism, Post-Impressionism and Pointillism. It is noteworthy that his work was identified as a part of the *fauve* movement, meaning 'wild' because of the bright colours and unusual bold form. His style evoked severe criticism, which entailed difficulties for him in making a living. And in 1913 his *Blue Nude* painting was burned as an effigy at the 1913 Armory Exhibition in Chicago. But Matisse did not only provoke hatred, he also had enthusiastic followers, not least influential ones such as Gertrude Stein. His friends set up and funded an art school, Académie Matisse, for a few years, where he taught young artists. In old age, Matisse depended to some extent on a wheelchair, but continued his artistic work by making cut paper collages and graphic design. A couple of years before he died, he founded the Matisse Museum in Le Cadeau in France, where his own works were displayed. This contributed to his legacy as a front figure in modern art.

As to *Woman Before an Aquarium*, it is not one of Matisse's most famous paintings, but it was acclaimed. The story of the making of the painting begins as Matisse was captivated by North Africa and the Middle East, their cultures, design and what the light did to colours such as blue, red, green, yellow, black and space there. An Islamic exhibition at the Musée des Arts Décoratifs in Paris in 1903 made an impression on him. He travelled to Munich to learn about Islamic objects that were on display and to Spain for Moorish architecture. Having a faiblesse for brightly coloured and lavishly ornamented textiles, pottery and tiles, he was an avid collector of such objects. But it was the physical visits, the immersion in North Africa, that left the deepest impressions on Matisse's artistry. There he went through a transformation that lasted even a decade afterwards when he had moved to Nice. *Woman before an Aquarium* was especially inspired by his Moroccan journeys in 1912–13 where he saw panelled screens and goldfish like the ones he portrayed in the painting. Matisse's travels opened a new way of seeing, a new rhythm in his work which came to fruition in the special radiance, design and sense of intimacy. So did the golden light of Nice, as it led him towards an impressionistic naturalism which included a 'human element' such as the woman contemplating a fishbowl.[5]

Parting Points

So finally, in this chapter I have discussed the role of exceptional experiences in art as a part of everyday life. The pivotal point has been on how and why Patricia Hampl was mesmerized by the painting *Woman Before an Aquarium*. It was an uplifting once-in-a-lifetime event. We do not have many of them, not even those of us who live for art. For balance, let me, in the very last minute, introduce a case of exceptional experience as dismay.

When I was fourteen years old and very much a moody adolescent, my parents took me to the Edvard Munch museum in Oslo. As we walked around, I found myself bewitched by the painting called *Puberty*. I remember staring at it and feeling utterly horrified: the painting depicts a young girl who is sitting on a bed looking dreadful – thin and depressed, and grey. The whole painting was all grey, I thought. My shock was that the girl looked exactly like I felt. Never had I seen my sordid state expressed like that. But then, slowly, miraculously, the painting made me feel better. I realized that I was not the only one in the pit of puberty. Munch obviously knew something about it, and so did the girl in the painting. I will never forget this painting, and how I felt at first, but how it then transformed me into a happier person. I would be embarrassed to show you a picture of the painting here. One reason is that when I look at it now, it does not seem grey at all to me, but rather warm in its colours. And the girl in the painting, she looks actually quite fine.

I have three parting points: The first one is that an anthropological understanding of exceptional experiences challenges our anthropological writing skills. The trick is to find new combinations of words to convey these beyond-the-verbal events in words. This is thus an occasion to take *The Anthropologist as Writer* (Wulff 2016) seriously and keep developing our writing craft, also into other genres, and to be 'writing otherwise', which is what Hannerz (2016) calls for. My second point is that an investigation into exceptional experiences accentuates a need for methodological eclecticism. And my third point is that as much as we would have liked to, exceptional experiences cannot be ordered or planned. This is the case both in temporary, elusive moments and those that are transformative, changing the direction of your fieldwork or life. Rather than being magical enjoyment only, epiphanies do serious work – often in the form of joy and wonder, but also in the form of dismay like in my last example of *Puberty*. It is thus my contention that exceptional experiences are necessary for an understanding of ourselves and the world we live in.

Helena Wulff is Professor Emerita of Social Anthropology at Stockholm University. Her research interests are in expressive cultural form – dance, art, images, text. Key engagements are now in the anthropologies of literature and writing, with a focus on migrant writing in Sweden. Among her publications are three monographs: *Ballet across Borders: Career and Culture in the World of Dancers* (1998), *Dancing at the Crossroads: Memory and Mobility in Ireland* (2007), and *Rhythms of Writing: An Anthropology of Irish Literature* (2017). Her edited volumes include *The Anthropologist as Writer: Genres and Contexts in the Twenty-First Century*

(2016). There is also the entry 'Writing Anthropology' in the *Cambridge Encyclopedia of Anthropology* (2021) http://doi.org/10.29164/21writing. Drawing on her research, she occasionally writes autofiction and creative nonfiction.

Notes

1. 'On Memoir', Patrica Hampl. Retrieved 15 February 2021 from: http://patriciahampl.com/work/on-memoir/.
2. This refers to 'traditionalist Catholicism', certain religious beliefs and practices that were popular for a couple of decades before the Second Vatican Council (1962–65).
3. In the tundra, the sounds of the silence were 'of the breaking ice, footfalls on the hardened snow, the gush of rivers, the cries of wild swans, the crackling of grass, the puddles of waters that grow into ponds, the yelping dogs, the rustling of feathers in the snow, and so on' (Rethmann 2007: 45).
4. See 'Woman Before an Aquarium'. Retrieved 10 February 2021 from: https://sites.google.com/a/g.clemson.edu/ekphrastic-poetry/-woman-before-an-aquarium.
5. See 'Woman Before an Aquarium', Art Institute Chicago. Retrieved 7 February 2021 from: https://www.artic.edu/artworks/27984/woman-before-an-aquarium.

References

Banks, Marcus and David Zeitlyn. 2015. *Visual Methods in Social Research*. 2nd edition. London: SAGE.

Barber, Karin. 2007. *The Anthropology of Texts, Persons and Publics: Oral and Written Culture in Africa and Beyond*. Cambridge: Cambridge University Press.

Becker, Howard S. 2008 [1982]. *Art Worlds*. Berkeley: University of California Press.

Berger, John. 1972. *Ways of Seeing*. Harmondsworth: Penguin.

Blacking, John. 1977. 'Towards an Anthropology of the Body', in *The Anthropology of the Body*, John Blacking (ed.). London: Academic Press, pp. 1–28.

Boas, Franz. 1955 [1927]. *Primitive Art*. New York: Dover Publications.

Boyarin, Jonathan (ed.). 1993. *The Ethnography of Reading*. Berkeley: University of California Press.

Christiansen, Charlotte Ettrup. 2021. 'Literary Free Spaces: Vulnerability, Shared Reading and Selfhood in Denmark'. PhD thesis. Department of Anthropology, Aarhus University.

Clifford, James. 1986. 'Introduction: Partial Truths', in *Writing Culture: The Poetics and Politics of Ethnography*, James Clifford and George E. Marcus (eds.). Berkeley: University of California Press, pp. 1–26.

Collins, Peter and Anselma Gallinat (eds). 2010. *The Ethnographic Self as Resource: Writing Memory and Experience into Ethnography*. Oxford: Berghahn.

Coote, Jeremy. 1996. '"Marvels of Everyday Vision": The Anthropology of Aesthetics and the Cattle-Keeping Nilotes', in *Anthropology, Art and Aesthetics*, Jeremy Coote and Anthony Shelton (eds). Oxford: Clarendon Press, pp. 245–73.

Coote, Jeremy and Anthony Shelton. 1996. 'Introduction', in *Anthropology, Art and Aesthetics*, Jeremy Coote and Anthony Shelton (eds). Oxford: Clarendon Press, pp. 1–11.

Csikszentmihalyi, Mihaly. 1990. *Flow: The Psychology of Optimal Experience*. New York: Harper Perennial.

Graburn, Nelson. 2005. 'From Aesthetics to Prosthetics and Back: Materials, Performance and Consumers in Canadian Inuit Sculptural Arts; or Alfred Gell in the Canadian Arctic', in *Les Cultures à l'Oeuvre: Rencontres en Art (Cultures at Work: Encounters in Art)*, Michèle Coquet, Brigitte Derlon and Monique Jeudy-Ballini (eds). Paris: Biro Editor, pp. 47–62.

Hampl, Patricia. 1981. *A Romantic Education*. New York: W.W. Norton & Co.

——. 1992. *Virgin Time: In Search of the Contemplative Life*. New York: Farrar, Straus and Giroux.

——. 2006. *Blue Arabesque: A Search for the Sublime*. Orlando: Harcourt, Inc.

——. 2007. *The Florist's Daughter: A Memoir*. Orlando: Harcourt, Inc.

Hannerz, Ulf. 2016. 'Writing Otherwise', in *The Anthropologist as Writer: Genres and Contexts in the Twenty-First Century*, Helena Wulff (ed.). Oxford: Berghahn, pp. 254–70.

——. 2021. *Afropolitan Horizons: Essays Toward a Literary Anthropology of Nigeria*. Oxford: Berghahn.

Harrison, Kathryn. 2006. 'Hammered by Art'. *The New York Times*, 29 October.

Jackson, Michael. 2006. *The Accidental Anthropologist: A Memoir*. Dunedin: Longacre Press.

Joyce, James. 2012 [1914]. *Dubliners*. New York: Harper Press.

Kant, Immanuel. 2009 [1790]. *Critique of Judgment*. Oxford: Oxford University Press.

Khosravi, Shahram. 2007. 'The "Illegal" Traveller: An Auto-Ethnography of Borders', *Social Anthropology/Anthropologie Sociale* 15(3): 321–34.

——. 2010. *'Illegal' Traveller: An Autoethnography of Borders*. New York: Palgrave Macmillan.

Lévi-Strauss, Claude. 1992 [1955]. *Tristes Tropiques*. New York: Penguin Books.

Meyer, Birgit. 2009. 'Introduction: From Imagined Communities to Aesthetic Formations: Religious Mediations, Sensational Forms, and Styles of Binding', in *Aesthetic Formations: Media, Religion, and the Senses*, Birgit Meyer (ed.). New York: Palgrave Macmillan, pp. 1–28.

Meyer, Birigt and Jojada Verrips. 2008. 'Aesthetics', in *Key Words in Religion, Media and Culture*, David Morgan (ed.). New York: Routledge, pp. 20–30.

Myers, Fred R. 2002. *Painting Culture: The Making of an Aboriginal High Art*. Durham, NC: Duke University Press.

Narayan, Kirin. 2007. *My Family and Other Saints*. Chicago: University of Chicago Press.

——. 2012. *Alive in the Writing: Crafting Ethnography in the Company of Chekhov*. Chicago: University of Chicago Press.

Reed, Adam. 2018. 'Literature and Reading', *Annual Review of Anthropology* 47: 33–45.
Reed-Danahay, Deborah. 1997. 'Introduction', in *Auto/Ethnography: Rewriting the Self and the Social*, Deborah Reed-Danahay (ed.). Oxford: Berg, pp. 1–17.
——. 2019. 'Autoethnography', in *SAGE Research Methods Foundations*, Paul Atkinson, Sara Delamont, Alexandru Cernat, Joseph W. Sakshaug and Richard A. Williams (eds). London: SAGE, pp. 1–19.
Rethmann, Petra. 2007. 'On Presence', in *Extraordinary Anthropology: Transformations in the Field*, Jean Guy A. Goulet and Bruce Granville Miller (eds). Lincoln: University of Nebraska Press, pp. 36–52.
Shokeid, Moshe. 1992. 'Exceptional Experiences in Everyday Life', *Cultural Anthropology* 7(2): 232–43.
Stoller, Paul. 1994. 'Embodying Colonial Memories', *American Anthropologist* 96(3): 634–48.
Stoller, Paul and Cheryl Olkes. 1987. *In Sorcery's Shadow: A Memoir of Apprenticeship among the Songhay of Niger*. Chicago: University of Chicago Press.
Svašek, Maruška. 2007. *Anthropology, Art and Cultural Producton*. London: Pluto Press.
——. (ed.). 2012. *Moving Subjects, Moving Objects: Transnationalism, Cultural Production and Emotions*. Oxford: Berghahn Books.
Uimonen, Paula. 2021. 'Anthropological Readings and Literary Gendering in Aesthetic Worldmaking'. Paper presented at *Revolutions in Reading: Literary Practice in Transition*, Stockholm University Zoom, 21–23 June.
Verdery, Katherine. 2018. *My Life as a Spy: Investigations in a Secret Police File*. Durham, NC: Duke University Press.
Wiles, Ellen. 2021. *Live Literature: The Experience and Cultural Value of Literary Performance Events from Salons to Festivals*. New York: Palgrave Macmillan.
Wulff, Helena. 2006. 'Experiencing the Ballet Body: Pleasure, Pain, Power', in *The Musical Human: Rethinking John Blacking's Ethnomusicology in the Twenty-First Century*, Suzel Ana Reily (ed.). Aldershot: Ashgate, pp. 125–42.
——. (ed.). 2016. *The Anthropologist as Writer: Genres and Contexts in the Twenty-First Century*. Oxford: Berghahn.
——. 2017. *Rhythms of Writing: An Anthropology of Irish Literature*. London: Bloomsbury.
——. 2021. 'Writing anthropology', in *Cambridge Encyclopedia of Anthropology*, Felix Stein (ed.). Retrieved 10 February 2021 from: https://www.anthroencyclopedia.com/entry/writing-anthropology

Web Pages

'Hammered by Art', *The New York Times*. Retrieved 20 February 2021 from: https://www.nytimes.com/2006/10/29/books/review/Harrison.t.html.
'Patricia Hampl'. Retrieved 15 February 2021 from: http://patriciahampl.com/.
'Traditionalist Catholicism', Wikipedia. Retrieved 10 February 2021 from: https://en.wikipedia.org/wiki/Traditionalist_Catholicism.

'Woman Before an Aquarium', Art Institute Chicago. Retrieved 7 February 2021 from: https://www.artic.edu/artworks/27984/woman-before-an-aquarium.
'Woman Before an Aquarium'. Retrieved 10 February 2021 from: https://sites.google.com/a/g.clemson.edu/ekphrastic-poetry/-woman-before-an-aquarium.

Chapter 11

Shaking up Worlds, Opening up Horizons
Contemporary Dance Experiences in Ramallah and Beyond

Ana Laura Rodríguez Quiñones

Introduction

Experienced through the imitation of Michael Jackson's steps in front of a TV in a living room in Dakar or Nablus, or discovered in a ballroom during holidays in a faraway country; witnessed during carnival celebrations, or in a great Opera House; learnt from grandmothers and aunts during weddings, or from friends in car parks, or even slowly and painfully acquired during decade-long training – dance is at the crossroad of the ordinary and the extraordinary, the usual and the unusual. It brings together 'that-which-everybody-knows-how-to-do' with 'that-which-makes-you-an-artist'. Dance can be used to distinguish oneself, as well as to claim (and build) a sense of belonging. It involves the whole person, 'body and mind linked', and makes and unmakes social relationships (Neveu Kringelbach 2007). The discovery and embracing of dance often constitutes an important turning point in a person's history, leading to unexpected and passionate life paths (Davis 2015; Menet 2020), or at least changing deeply one's self-representations, relations to others (Aterianus-Owanga 2018), and one's consciousness of one's surroundings (Rodríguez Quiñones 2019). Perhaps because of the physical joy it brings, or because of the indeterminacy and the vagueness of the messages it conveys, which gives space to anyone to fill the blanks with their own expectations (Neveu Kringelbach and Skinner 2012), or because what is at stake in this practice is so difficult to express in words, dance is often experienced as exceptional, even when it has become a routine, a profession, or when it is practiced in mundane contexts.

This chapter explores the exceptionality of dance experiences through three dimensions: the self-challenging opportunities which dance can offer; the new social spaces it may open to dancers; and the transformation of inner worlds that this bodily practice can generate. These three dimensions are of course connected. They are three facets of the same 'self-fashioning' process (Neveu Kringelbach 2013) rendered possible by the interweaving of the intimate, the social and the performative in dance practice. My focus is on a specific dance genre, with its specific history, aesthetic, network of actors and ideals: contemporary dance. I build on results from ethnographic fieldwork conducted in Palestine, Israel and Europe, among Palestinian contemporary dancers and their collaborators.[1] The aim of my research project was to investigate the politics of Palestinian contemporary dance in a globalization context. In this chapter, I focus on individual experiences (mine and others') in order to concentrate on the intimate experience of dance.

Through the example of a dancer's life path, I will first foreground the ways in which dance practice can shuffle the cards of social, class and gender norms, shaking up an individual's world. I will highlight how the valorization of individual talent and personal self-determination in dance practice allows for exceptional social mobility and exceptional life paths. In the second section of this chapter, my analysis is informed by my own practice of dance, and the bodily epiphanies that certain dance experiences have produced. I will attempt to highlight how dance can open new 'imaginative horizons', these imagined, dreamt, projected spaces which are beyond our perception, but yet determine 'what we experience and how we interpret what we experience' (Crapanzano 2004: 2). This focus on my own experience will help me to draw some hypotheses about how dance can bring people out of expected trajectories, and about what, ultimately, makes dance experiences so exceptional.

'What Were the Chances?!' When Dance Radically Changes a Life

My first contact with the fieldwork that this chapter builds on took place in Lausanne, Switzerland, during the summer of 2016. A friend of mine had told me that a dancer, a member of his company, had worked several summers in a dance programme in Palestine. I arranged a meeting with the dancer in a coffee shop. In addition to putting me in touch with various Palestinian artists and programmers, the young Swiss woman told me about her participation in a dance training programme, given over three years to young Palestinians in Ramallah. She remembered with particular emotion the youngest of her students: a fourteen-year-old boy who, she explained, used to tell his parents he was playing football in order to attend the dance class. I met the boy, Kamel, who was not a boy anymore but a nineteen-year-old young man, during my second trip to Ramallah, in April 2017. In the years that followed, we spent a large amount of time dancing, watching dance performances, or just drinking coffee together over a chess game. At some point within these encounters, he told me of the way he came to dance one afternoon, on the rooftop of a hostel in Ramallah.

Challenging Oneself, Getting out of One's Comfort Zone

The *Sareyyet Ramallah*[2] club is a large complex of sports facilities and refreshment stands in al-Tireh neighbourhood, in Ramallah. Kamel told me that, this summer day in 2012, he was supposed to meet with friends in the youth club to play table tennis, but that the youth club was closed. As he wandered through the sports facilities, he heard music coming from one of the dance studios, and stopped by the studio's open door to see what was going on. A young woman, speaking in English, was teaching five or six students some weird dance steps, he told me. After a few minutes, the teacher noticed Kamel's presence and suggested he join them. He laughed at this point of the story, telling me that he answered, 'of course not!' to the teacher. The young woman insisted, asking him if he didn't want to learn something new, and Kamel assured her that he was quite capable of doing what he had observed. She then did a pointe with her feet (holding herself up on the top of her toes) and asked him to do the same. As Kamel was totally unable to do a pointe, the teacher proposed that he attend the dance class until he could do a pointe. Titillated by the challenge, the young man ended up taking all of the programme's courses over several years, even spending three weeks in the dance programme of a northern European university with older Palestinian dancers. When I met him in April 2017, he was auditioning for a project with a European company, for which he would work for the next three years. By the end of the year, he would also have his first solo programmed in a festival and would teach some dance classes in a cultural centre in al-Bireh, Ramallah's twin city. In short, his professional career was starting to take off. 'What were the chances I would run into this dance class?!' Kamel asked me, smiling broadly.

Coming from a conservative Palestinian Muslim family, this career choice was quite unexpected – and, as we will see, socially unacceptable –

for Kamel. First, because, unlike what other studies have shown about contexts that may not have a structured dance field, but where dance can be an economic opportunity in precariousness situations (Neveu Kringelbach 2007; Despres 2016), dance in Palestine is rarely considered a professional option. If there have been various Dabke[3] companies in the region – mostly founded in the 1960s and some of which are still active today – they have mainly been based on the voluntary and unpaid work of dancers, with a few administrative and artistic staff remunerated.[4] Despite a large number of people practicing dance since a young age – Dabke, classical or other – this activity is often seen as a hobby, and I was told by various dancers that families expected their children to quit dance when they grew up.[5] Second, because being raised in a conservative Muslim family meant to have grown up with specific moral values and gendered representations inconsistent with the gender diversity and intimate bodily proximity of contemporary dance practice.

Kamel's first reaction to the dance steps he witnessed was to see them as 'weird' and 'girlish', far from what he imagined a boy like him was supposed to do, and not something he would wish to experiment with. What eventually made this experience desirable was the challenge it represented: the opportunity to excel (physically). This challenge was consistent with a certain form of masculinity he had to perform in his social environment, and it gave rise to an extraordinary self-discipline and determination. Indeed, in a context where there was no professionalizing training, Kamel developed his skills through constant self-training between the courses of the programme and the other workshops he could attend. Along the years, the young boy's interest in contemporary dance was fed not only by the 'fun' he could have while dancing, but also by the expressive opportunities he perceived in the practice. Moreover, he learned to appreciate and value the specific aesthetic of contemporary dance. For example, he trained in stretching a lot and gained an impressive flexibility – a skill that might have first been considered as too feminine – which would help him get hired by foreign companies later on. As it is often the case in dancers' careers, this training brought its share of suffering and injuries, and at the same time contributed to the construction of the young boy's sense of self. This self was nevertheless stepping away from its original social environment.

Kamel was aware from the beginning that his family would hardly accept him taking up an activity such as dance, especially contemporary dance. He therefore lied for years to his parents, telling them he was playing football, when he was actually training in dance. When his family discovered he was not playing football, he still pretended to dance Dabke instead of contemporary dance. Dabke, he told me, was more acceptable as at least it was not something 'new' and 'unknown' but was considered as traditional – and not a Western importation. Moreover, Dabke implied less physical proximity, and kept a certain verticality of the body, unlike floor work in contemporary dance which could be perceived as indecent. When Kamel's parents finally discovered he was not dancing Dabke either, he ran away from home at the age of sixteen, for he wouldn't renounce to practise what had become a passion. In fact, the physical challenge that had been the first driving force of Kamel's commitment to dance had slowly been replaced by the pleasure and the liberty he felt through this practice. Moreover, dance had opened the door of new social worlds to him, social worlds that he was not ready to give up on.

Aiming at Other Social Worlds

Studies on dance in different national contexts have highlighted the way in which embracing this practice may give dancers access to new social worlds. The social mobility offered by dance practice may nevertheless raise some ethical and moral issues among dancers. Neveu Kringelbach (2013), in her study of performers in urban Senegal, shows, for example, how the circulation between diverse dance styles, if it allows social ascension, also includes the circulation between different moral systems. Although dance may be an opportunity for economic success, it can also go hand in hand with moral condemnation from the person's surroundings, especially in the case of female dancers (Neveu Kringelbach 2007). Sorignet, for his part, analyses the ways in which contemporary dancers with working-class or migration backgrounds in France negotiate the divergent values between their original social environment and the contemporary dance world, including sexual and gender norms (2004, 2017). Contemporary dance, and also ballet, come indeed with a range of bodily and social habits, as well as with specific representations of the intimate and the sexual. As Sorignet highlights, dancers' socialization to the 'avant-garde dimension' of their practice participates in the construction of a 'social personality that goes beyond the artistic field' (2017: 381). This social mobility may also generate forms of control over dancers who are not used to a specific context's norms and codes. Wulff (1998), concerning European ballet dancers, and Despres (2016), regarding African contemporary dancers, both show how company directors and administrative staff may try to make some dancers less visible in social events, or at least strictly control their public discourses.

By joining the field of contemporary dance, Kamel also adopted a new lifestyle, with a range of social codes and moral values divergent from those of his original social environment. These social codes and moral values encompassed specific ways of dressing, talking, and getting physically involved with others, as well as leisure activities enjoyed, and expectations about what would be a desirable future. Furthermore, Kamel's dance activity allowed him to travel to different countries in Europe, where he experienced a huge feeling of freedom, far from his family, neighbours and national fellows, and thus far from the social pressure and control he felt in Ramallah. What was morally reprehensible from the perspective of Kamel's family – and valued by Kamel – was thus not only the contemporary dance practice in itself, but also a particular way of life, or at least a certain imagination about it. In Ramallah, this lifestyle has a particular meaning that is not specific to the contemporary dance world but follows the dividing lines between different sections of the population. These dividing lines shed light on the economic, religious, and political diversity of the city.

Indeed, historically designated as a 'liberal, open, and tolerant town' (Taraki 2008: 65), Ramallah embodies nevertheless the great fragmentation, based on social class, and religious and political affiliations, that has been taking place within the occupied Palestinian territories since the Oslo agreements (Aruri 2013). On the one hand, the return of diaspora elites after Oslo (Dana 2019), and the promotion of neoliberal capitalism that followed the agreements (Haddad 2016), gave birth to a mobile middle and upper class, which navigates between the West Bank, bordering or Gulf countries, and Europe. Its members travel abroad, work in international firms or within the numerous governmental and non-governmental aid organizations, and their children study in international private schools and European or North American universities. On the other hand, a large number of people face growing unemployment and precariousness. The populations of refugee camps, for example, are dependent on UNRWA[6] schools for their children's education. Young people without higher education, or still at university, may have two or three jobs in order to live and help their family.

Beyond these economic inequalities, Ramallah comprises groups ranging 'between pure Christianity, conservative Islam, and progressive secularism' (Aruri 2013: 8). Its streets thus represent a melting pot of different lifestyles, with different social groups having their own and differentiated social spaces in the city (ibid.). While some – along with the very large number of tourists and foreigners working in representative offices, bodies for cultural collaboration, or volunteering for non-governmental organizations – meet in clubs and bars where they can drink alcohol and dance to a wide variety of music, practice yoga and pilates in gyms, and eat in European-style restaurants, these places remain inaccessible to others for economic or moral reasons.[7] For some sections of the Ramallawi population, these practices and spaces may also be seen as a sign of the 'Westernization' of Palestinian society and its moral decline, and be thus seen as blameworthy. Navigating between different social worlds is thus not necessarily easy, neither easily accepted by one's surroundings. As Karkabi puts it, Palestinian society knows 'segregation, limitation and supervision ... practiced on the basis of gender, sexuality, class, familial, regional, sectarian and legal-political categories' (2013: 310).

For young people like Kamel, moving away from one's home environment meant stepping out of their network, and not necessarily finding a place in a new social environment. If there is an urban youth, self-named 'alternative' and cosmopolitan network that spreads from Ramallah to Jaffa and Haifa, as studies on alternative music scenes have highlighted (Karkabi 2013; Withers 2021), the Israeli military occupation of the West Bank, and the separation Wall that cuts '48 Palestinians from '67 Palestinians,[8] makes it difficult, however, for the former to circulate as freely as the latter without high risks of being imprisoned, or worse (see Parizot 2018). Moreover, even when accessing a network of individuals sharing the same values and way of life, residing in a confined environment like the city of Ramallah generally means that behaviours socially perceived as blameworthy could hardly go unnoticed, and could lead sometimes to social exclusion from certain spaces, or physical violence from one's family, neighbours or even the police.[9] Ultimately, Kamel managed to migrate to Europe, where he felt he could live more freely, away from the violent structures of the Israeli military occupation and the oppressive social norms, and according to his personal values and expectations.

Exceptional as a Narrative

Kamel's path illustrates the exceptionality that dance can generate in individuals' lives. Of course, this path is exceptional in itself, and owes a lot to chance – but isn't that the case with all life paths? As a practice that valorizes individual talent and personal self-determination, dance allows exceptional social mobility for some people, opening the door to social worlds they would hardly know otherwise. For example, girls from lower social classes in the UK may be acclaimed by the royal family in Opera Houses (Wulff 1998); street children from Mali may perform within renowned festivals in Europe (Despres 2016); and young boys from conservative Muslim families in Palestine may do international tours with contemporary dance companies.

It is certainly necessary to avoid a romanticized vision of this kind of path. As Kamel's example and other studies show, going off the beaten track brings specific social challenges. Moreover, an 'exceptionalism' discourse can render invisible processes of misappropriation or dispossession that dancers might face (Rodriguez Quiñones 2021), such as the control systems pointed out by Wulff or Despres. Finally, if Kamel, as other dancers, speaks about the liberty he found in contemporary dance, the meaning of this liberty is always constructed, built on specific relationships to others, and has to be captured in a situated context (Aterianus-Owanga 2021). This feeling of liberty reflects, for example, a discourse of 'emancipation of the self' that is very common in the world of globalized contemporary dance (Neveu Kringelbach 2013).

Nevertheless, the exceptionality of the experience, the events and the personal talent, is central in many dance narratives. This exceptionality participates in the way people make sense of their practice. If this sense of exceptionality can be analysed as related to the distinction ethos of art fields (Bourdieu 1979, 1992), it may also, as I have proposed in the introduction, be linked to the specificity of dance, and in particular to its bodily experience. The pleasure, the intimacy, or the expressive possibilities opened up by dance practice can participate in the redefinition of gender roles, and in people's self-fashioning processes (Neveu Kringelbach 2013; Aterianus-Owanga 2021). As Kamel's debut in dance shows, the physical and playful challenges of the practice can be a trigger point in itself. Later on, the socialization to a specific aesthetic and the exploration of bodily expression can shake up this person's social worlds, and open up new horizons in their life.

Finally, if the strength of the bodily experiences generated by dance practice is a theme that runs through accounts of different dance genres, contemporary dance has its own specificities. Using dancers' personal experience as the main material for creation, contemporary dance engenders particular moments of vulnerability among artists, moments that might in turn shape dancers' everyday experiences later on. In the next section, I will address this exploration of inner worlds in contemporary dance through an account of a personal bodily epiphany in Ramallah.

An Exceptional Experience in Fieldwork

As part of my research, I have followed the work of Farah Saleh, a renowned Palestinian choreographer and dancer based in Scotland, during creation processes, intensive trainings and performances.[10] Farah Saleh has been working on her project 'The Archive of Gestures' since 2014. Through diverse choreographic creations and video installations, she explores the archiving of 'hidden stories and gestures from the

Palestinian narrative'.[11] During the summer of 2019, the choreographer taught a one-week workshop based on this research. Entitled 'Unfolding your Archives', the workshop was part of a two-week intensive summer school organized by Farah Saleh in cooperation with *les Ballets C de la B* (Belgium), *Sareyyet Ramallah* (Palestine), and the A.M. Qattan Foundation (UK and Palestine). It aimed at building on the body–mind awareness of the participants to understand the meaning of bodily archives. Although having been familiarized with Farah Saleh's research during the previous two years, the experience of her workshop acted as a milestone in my understanding of her work.

Bodily Epiphany in Ramallah

The workshop took place in the newly built centre of the A.M. Qattan Foundation, on the top of a hill in Ramallah. The large windows of the small studio opened onto a spacious terrace, beyond which you could see the rolling hills of the city and the pristine blue of the summer sky. During five days, ten students from Palestine, Italy, France, Switzerland, Norway and Canada warmed up, trained, discussed, stretched and performed in this space. Midday breaks were taken on the terrace with the students and teachers of the other two classes. At the end of the afternoons, some students would propose stretching or massage sessions, and in the evenings, we would have film screenings or presentations of teachers' work.

Farah Saleh's training included Feldenkrais exercises, building connection between different parts of the body while being attentive on how a movement in one part of the body would generate movement in other connected parts of the body. It also included theoretical discussions about the meaning of archives and their political dimension, especially in Palestine, or the process of transformation of gestures into dance movement. We built on our own repertoire of mundane gestures, working on their quality, their speed, their repetition, and transmitting them to our fellow students. We finally discussed the connection between body and memory, the specificity of archives, and how to transform bodily archives into performance.

On the third day of the workshop, after the warm up, Farah Saleh invited us to move simply in one spot, letting movements arise from our bodies. The purpose of the exercise was to pay attention to the images and memories that may surface from the movements of our bodies. I had witnessed Farah Saleh going through a similar process during the creation residencies of her piece 'What my Body Can/t Remember' in Edinburgh.[12] Some days, she would talk to me and the creation's video-artist about the memories that appeared to her while moving in the space: a specific music or noise, a video-clip on MTV, or a dance step she was working on as a teenager. While I could understand the process of remembering the past, the connection between this remembering and Farah Saleh's movements remained obscure to me in Edinburgh. There is a difference between witnessing a process and feeling it in the flesh.

This summer day in Ramallah, a random gesture – a straight arm's swing along the body – brought to the surface a striking memory. The first occurrence of the movement just left me with a vague (but strong) sensation; something similar to these moments when you have some music notes in your mind, but are still unable to find the whole melody or song you know them from; or when you have the feeling of a name or a word in your mouth, but can't formulate it yet. It was the blurry sensation of a particular surface, a strange material, at my fingertips. I repeated the movement. The more I repeated the movement, and made its shape clearer, the clearer the memory got. The sensation at my fingertips was linked to a specific wall, the one running along the alley that led to my grandparents' house in la Havana. With the movement, the setting came back to my memory; the grey and faded blue tiles on the floor, the dusty air, the petrol smell of the street. I felt the air temperature of this long-ago moment, the fresh breeze blowing from the end of the alley. I heard the city noises that were taking place around me, and the voices of the grown-ups who were walking behind me. But most of all, I found the sensations and emotions of this moment; the simple joy of feeling the grainy surface of the wall under my fingers as I swung my arm back and forward; the child's eye view of an alley that I had since visited many times as an adult; but most of all this concentration on the immediate moment and surrounding, and this deep trust in the world, that I could only feel as a very young child.

In the studio, my amazement was so strong that I had to stop moving to process. Sitting on the floor, in the middle of students who were still dancing, I wondered about the meaning of this experience. I knew, from playing piano and taking dance classes, that the body has a memory of its own, a memory which allows your fingers to play a melody in a seemingly independent way, or your feet to re-enact movements you have forgotten about. Nevertheless, this experience was different, as it was not simply my body remembering a movement, but the acting of a movement making memories arise. So, how could I read this experience? What was its meaning? And how could it be related to my anthropological understanding of dance practice?

As a social anthropologist, I rely on a sociological understanding of human feelings, sensations and senses of belonging – I believe that the meaning people give to these feelings, sensations and senses of belonging are the result of an intertwining of their constant interactions with their social surrounding (and its share of power relations) and the choices they make within this frame. Therefore, this experience in a studio in Ramallah can be read as the result of my slow socialization to the contemporary dance world, and more precisely to specific dance techniques, through which I learnt along the years to give particular meanings to my physical sensations. As I said before and as pointed out by other authors (Neveu Kringelbach 2013; Despres 2016), contemporary dance builds on dancers' personal experiences for creation processes. As such, the socialization processes in contemporary dance are very specific, as they not only shape intellectual stances, bodily techniques and moral values, but also inner worlds, a dimension of experience that is more related to sentiments, feelings, and intimate memories, as the one described above. These inner worlds strongly participate in one's senses of self, although being less easily describable. Acknowledging this specificity of contemporary dance, and its consequences, I believe, requires stressing the wide imaginative possibilities opened up by proprioceptive experiences.

The Elusiveness of Proprioceptive Experiences

Proprioception is a strange sense. Although being a primordial canal of our relation to the world – as it concerns the fundamental mediator of this relation: our body – it refers only to, and has for its only reference, one's own sensation. In fact, if seeing, touching, tasting and hearing always imply the confrontation to external objects and stimulus, proprioception only refers to one's sense of position and movement in space. As with the other senses, again, proprioception and the meanings given to it are necessarily social, built in relation to our history and environment. Nevertheless, the indeterminacy and elusiveness of this sense, I believe, can be the subject of specific imagination when it is mobilized in dance practice. Like the 'imaginative horizons' described by Vincent Crapanzano, the spaces created by proprioceptive experiences in dance practice 'extend from the insistent reality of the here and now into that optative space or time – space-time – of the imaginary' (2004: 14). This 'insistent reality' of the here and now reflects a sense of immediacy when dancing, a focus on one's bodily sensations that might, at the same time, generate an impression of accurate perception, while blurring and altering one's perception of surrounding space and time. These paradoxical moments of high concentration and bodily control, and suspension of the instant, are fertile spaces for imagination. In contemporary dance practice, these spaces are the subject of specific socialization as dancers are constantly invited to fill them with their personal memories, thoughts, feelings and imagination.

In fact, while this specificity of proprioceptive experiences concerns all kinds of dance, contemporary dance has some particularities. As highlighted by Neveu Kringelbach (2013), creative processes and forms of transmission in contemporary dance build on personality traits and individuals' histories, and therefore imply a high level of self-consciousness on the part of dancers. Trained to constantly explore their inner worlds through movement, contemporary dancers are thought to connect their proprioceptive experiences to their feelings, sense of self, and ways of experiencing the world. Thus, if contemporary dancers' practice is nourished by their personal life, it can also go the other way. For example, the experience I have described above isn't limited to a physical sensation but brings into light specific feelings and representations linked to a precise moment in my life. This experience consequently questions the feelings and representations of the present moment, by contrasting them. Another specific way to relate to and experience the world is pointed out by Kamel when he tells me that, after years of dance practice, 'dance' was not confined anymore to the studio or the performances, but coloured every movement of his life, as it sublimed even his most mundane gestures: walking across a street was dance, pouring water in a glass was dance. The attention given to physical sensations and the playful relation to these sensations, particularly to the immediacy of dance practice, has seeped into his everyday life.

Conclusion

This chapter explored the exceptionality of contemporary dance experiences through the presentation of a dancer's life path and the narration of a personal epiphany in a dance studio, in order to address the exceptionality of dance experience through its 'external' dimensions (the social and material disruptions dance practice can generate in individuals' lives) as well as through its 'internal' dimensions (how dance practice can shape individuals' inner worlds). Although this distinction between 'external' and 'internal' dimensions may seem artificial, it draws a line between noticeable (and reportable) aspects of an individual's existence and social behaviours, such as moral values or gender norms, and aspects that are less visible (and communicable), such as emotions and proprioceptive experiences. Of course, these latest aspects participate in the former, and vice versa.

Through Kamel's life path, I highlighted the way in which embracing a practice such as dance may bring people to deviate from the path they are socially expected to take. Kamel was born and grew up in a specific context, the occupied West Bank, where going off the beaten track takes a particular signification and brings its share of specific dangers. Nevertheless, the example of his life path echoes other studies on dancers' trajectories and shows how one can be 'absorbed' by the passion for dance. Moreover, this example points at some aspects of dance that can operate as triggers for this passion, such as physical challenge. As I argued, the exceptionality of dance experiences is central in many dance narratives and can be attributed to the distinction ethos of art fields. However, it can also be linked to the specificities of the bodily practice, and the imaginations linked to proprioceptive experiences.

As Motta (2019) points out, others' experience of inner worlds is always an inaccessible field. By delving into my own experience, I tried to shed light on the particular intertwining of proprioceptive experience, memory and emotions that can be accessed through contemporary dance practice. The personal experience I have described is specific to the kind of work developed by Farah Saleh about bodily archives. Not all dance genres deal with such issues. Nevertheless, the questions it raised can shed light on the inner worlds that emerge from, and are shaped by, the particular relation to proprioceptive experiences that is generated by contemporary dance practice. Words do not do justice to these experiences, as they change one's experiential register, engendering a distance that annihilates the immediacy of the experience (Crapanzano 2004: 21). I hope, nevertheless, that this chapter has provided some insights into the social and intimate construction of the exceptionality of dance.

Ana Laura Rodríguez Quiñones is a PhD candidate at the University of Lausanne, Switzerland, with research interests in the politics of performative dance in a globalization context. Her doctoral research investigates the politics of contemporary dance in and about Palestine. Building on a multi-sited and digital ethnography in Palestine, Israel and various European countries, her dissertation addresses the interrelations between bodily and performative practices, national and transnational senses of belonging and claims, and globalization processes. She has published in the Revue Européenne des Migrations Internationales, Multitudes, Tsantsa, and Ethnologie Française and is co-directing a special issue, 'Migrating through the Arts', that will be published in New Diversities.

Notes

I wish to express my deepest gratitude to my colleague Muriel Bruttin for the rich intellectual exchanges, and for her sharp comments on this chapter.

1. Since 2017, I have conducted participant observation during intensive trainings, creation processes, performances and festivals, as well as about forty interviews with artists and programmers.
2. The *Sareyyet Ramallah First Group* is a scout organization established in 1927. In addition to its various sport teams and musical activities, the organization has had a Dabke company since 1967, a contemporary dance company since 2005, and has organized the Ramallah Contemporary Dance Festival since 2006.
3. Dabke is a festive dance practice from the Levant, which was touched by an intense spectacularization during the second part of the twentieth century.
4. With the development of the Ramallah Contemporary Dance Festival since 2006, and the growing number of dancers becoming professional (see Rodríguez Quiñones 2019), this is, of course, changing. Nevertheless, remuneration is still an issue for dancers seeking to earn a living with their dance activity in a context where dance practice is traditionally voluntary.
5. Dance not being considered as 'serious' work is not specific to Palestine. Research on French dancers shows, for example, that dance being considered a professional option depends strongly on familial economic and social background (Sorignet 2010). However, the absence of a structured dance field in Palestine may accentuate this circumstance.
6. United Nations Relief and Works Agency for Palestine Refugees in the Near East.
7. There can also be some kind of interreligious xenophobia, as the case of a swimming pool prohibited to veiled women illustrates.
8. Palestinians, and their descendants, who remained inside the borders of the territory that became the Israeli state in 1948 are called '48 Palestinians. Those who live in territories that the Israeli army occupied in 1967 (Gaza and the West Bank) are called '67 Palestinians.
9. During the years of my fieldwork, there were two reported cases of young women murdered by family members in the West Bank because of behaviour considered immoral. In 2021, violent repression, detention and murder of protestors by the Palestinian Authority's armed forces were also extensively covered by the media. About police and military violence in Palestine, see, for example, Allen 2013.
10. For a more detailed description of my research on Farah Saleh's work, see Rodríguez Quiñones (2021). Farah Saleh has also published on diverse aspects of her research on the archive of gestures (Saleh 2020a; 2020b). This research is addressed in Hochberg (2021); her performance 'Free Advice' has been analysed in Noeth (2019); and her performance 'Parole, Parole, Parole' in Zami (2017).
11. https://www.farahsaleh.com
12. This creation addresses Farah Saleh's experience of Ramallah's lockdown during the second intifada (2000–4). In a space that symbolically reproduces the three rooms she was locked in for weeks (room, kitchen, living room), Farah Saleh explores her bodily archives. During each day of residency, she moves through the rooms, resurfacing memories of these teenage times through body exploration. This process in the studio, but also its continuation during performances, is filmed by a video-artist, and screened during following performances, generating an ever-moving action that reflects Farah Saleh's dynamic understanding of archives. The teaser of the performance can be watched here: https://vimeo.com/306777685 (retrieved 24 January 2019).

References

Allen, Lori. 2013. *The Rise and Fall of Human Rights: Cynicism and Politics in Occupied Palestine*. Stanford, CA: Stanford University Press.
Aruri, Natasha. 2013. 'Ramallah: From "Sumud" [Resilience] to Corporate Identity', *Planum: The Journal of Urbanism* 26(1). Retrieved 14 July 2020 from: https://issuu.com/planumnet/docs/ctbt_planum_n.26-2013_section_2_?mode=embed&layout=http%3A%2F%2Fskin.issuu.com%2Fv%2Flight%2Flayout.xml&showFlipBtn=true.
Aterianus-Owanga, Alice. 2018. 'Le *tànnëbéer* multisitué: Danses et communauté émotionnelle des fêtes sénégalaises en migration', *Socio-anthropologie* 38: 89–108.
———. 2021. 'Libre comme l'autre? Perspective post-exotique sur l'enseignement du sabar en Europe', *Journal des anthropologues* 164–65: 43–66.
Bourdieu, Pierre. 1979. *La Distinction: Critique sociale du jugement*. Paris: Les Éditions de Minuit, Collection Le sens commun.
———. 1992. *Les Règles de l'art: Genèse et structure du champ littéraire*. Paris: Éditions Seuil.
Crapanzano, Vincent. 2004. *Imaginative Horizons: An Essay in Literary-Philosophical Anthropology*. Chicago: University of Chicago Press.
Dana, Tariq. 2019. 'Crony Capitalism in the Palestinian Authority: A Deal Among Friends', *Third World Quarterly* 41(2): 247–63.
Davis, Kathy. 2015. *Dancing Tango: Passionate Encounters in a Globalizing World*. New York: NYU Press.
Despres, Altaïr. 2016. *Se faire contemporain: Les danseurs africains à l'épreuve de la mondialisation culturelle*. Paris: Publications de la Sorbonne.
Haddad, Toufiq. 2016. *Palestine Ltd.: Neoliberalism and Nationalism in the Occupied Territory*. London: IB Tauris.
Hochberg, Gil Z. 2021. *Becoming Palestine: Toward an Archival Imagination of the Future*. Durham, NC: Duke University Press.
Kaddar, Merav and Daniel Monterescu. 2021. 'Dancing with Tears in Our Eyes: Political Hipsters, Alternative Culture and Binational Urbanism in Israel/Palestine', *Ethnic and Racial Studies* 44: 925–45.
Karkabi, Nadeem. 2013. 'Staging Particular Difference: Politics of Space in the Palestinian Alternative Music Scene', *Middle East Journal of Culture and Communication* 6: 308–28.
Menet, Joanna. 2020. *Entangled Mobilities in the Transnational Salsa Circuit: The Esperanto of the Body, Gender and Ethnicity*. London: Routledge.
Motta, Marco. 2019. *Esprits fragiles: Réparer les liens ordinaires à Zanzibar*. Lausanne: A contrario campus.
Neveu Kringelbach, Hélène. 2007. '"Le poids du succès": Construction du corps, danse et carrière à Dakar', *Politique africaine* 3(107): 81–101.
———. 2013. *Dance Circles: Movement, Morality and Self-Fashioning in Urban Senegal*. Oxford and New York: Berghahn Books.
Neveu Kringelbach, Hélène and Skinner, Jonathan. 2012. *Dancing Cultures: Globalization, Tourism and Identity in the Anthropology of Dance*. Oxford and New York: Berghahn Books.

Noeth, Sandra. 2019. *Resilient Bodies, Residual Effects: Artistic Articulations of Borders and Collectivity from Lebanon and Palestine*. Bielefeld: Transcript Verlag.
Parizot, Cédric. 2018. 'Viscous Spatialities: The Spaces of the Israeli Permit Regime of Access and Movement', *The South Atlantic Quarterly* 117(1): 21–42.
Rodríguez Quiñones, Ana Laura. 2019. '"C'était la première fois que j'étais Palestinienne": Appartenances et représentations de la Palestine dans la danse contemporaine', *REMi*, 35(3–4): 85–105.
—. 2021. 'Being a Dancer beyond Being Palestinian: Resisting Identity Assignations through Contemporary Dance', in *Approaches to Migration, Language and Identity*, Jennifer Thorburn and Anita Auer (eds). Berne: Peter Lang Editions, pp. 223–51.
Saleh, Farah. 2020a. 'Defying Distance', *Img Journal* 2(3): 366–79. https://doi.org/10.6092/issn.2724-2463/12264
—. 2020b. '*Gesturing Refugees*: Participation, Affect, then Action?', *H-ART. Revista de historia, teoría y crítica de arte* 8: 63–88.
Sorignet, Pierre-Emmanuel. 2004. 'La construction des identités sexuées et sexuelles au regard de la socialisation professionnelle: Le cas des danseurs contemporains', *Sociologie de l'Art* 5(3): 9–34.
—. 2010. *Danser: Enquête dans les coulisses d'une vocation*. Paris: La Découverte.
—. 2017. '"T'es pas un vrai danseur contemporain": Désajustement et appropriation du statut d'artiste chez les danseurs d'origine populaire', *Revue Suisse de Sociologie* 43(2): 375–400.
Taraki, Lisa. 2008. 'Enclave Micropolis: The Paradoxical Case of Ramallah/Al-Bireh', *Journal of Palestine Studies* 37(4), pp. 6–20.
Taraki, Lisa and Rita Giacaman. 2006. 'Modernity Aborted and Reborn: Ways of being Urban in Palestine', in *Living Palestine: Family Survival, Resistance, and Mobility under Occupation*, Lisa Taraki (ed.). New York: Syracuse University Press, pp. 1–50.
Withers, Polly. 2021. 'Ramallah Ravers and Haifa Hipsters: Gender, Class, and Nation in Palestinian Popular Culture', *British Journal of Middle Eastern Studies* 48(1): 94–113.
Wulff, Helena. 1998. *Ballet Across Borders: Career and Culture in the World of Dancers*. London: Routledge.
Zami, Layla. 2017. *Contemporary Performemory: Moving Through Diasporic Dancescapes in the 21st Century*, Kultur-, Sozial- und Bildungswissenschaftlichen Fakultätder Humboldt-Universität zu Berlin, Dissertation zur Erlangung des akademischen Grades Doctor Philosophiae (Dr. Phil.)im Fach Gender Studies. Retrieved 1 December 2021 from: Online: https://d-nb.info/1185667741/34.

Chapter 12

Participant Growing-Places in and of the World
Rendering the Transformative Atmosphere of a Contemporary Opera in the Making

---

Maxime Le Calvé

Some ethnographic situations teach us so much that the memories of these moments stay forever. They can have a lasting effect on the way we perform anthropology, as we are struck by their atmospheres and transformed by them. This chapter focuses on a series of ethnographic notes from the rehearsal of a contemporary opera, the *Mondparsifal*, staged by the visual artist and performer Jonathan Meese in Vienna in 2017. I present here, in a short series of ethnographic stories, decisive aspects of the collaborative work within the team of this artist. The pervasive qualities which he instilled in creative situations, collectively and individually empowering, have been reported by the singers and by many collaborators as strongly impacting the way they perform their tasks – building up an ephemeral growing-place in which personal growth was made possible within the frame of this theatre production. Coincidentally, my documentation methods also underwent a significant metamorphosis during this period of fieldwork, as I switched to the use of watercolour drawings to put the observed situations to paper on the spot. Reflecting on the process of this change, I use the pragmatist concept of 'growing-place' to reexamine the notion of fieldwork as education, in the light of the concept of atmospheric know-hows. If ethnographic drawings can chronicle what happened on the field, they also bear witness to a transformation of the ethnographers in both their perceptive and expressive capacities: the seismographic trace of a growing activity, threading instantly accountable and shar-able renderings of its atmospheric qualities.

This ethnographic sketching dates back to February 2017. It shows the first piano rehearsal of an opera, the staging of which was the main object

Figure 12.1. First graphic field note, piano rehearsal. Ink and watercolour, Berlin 2017. © Maxime Le Calvé.

of the ethnographic fieldwork. This is the first time we hear, together, the score of the *Parsifal* revisited by a contemporary composer. The piece is long: three hours of music. Apart from the assistant director, none of us can really follow the score. None-the-less, orienting ourselves on the lyrics, we take notes on the music using the partition which arrived in the mail a couple of days ago. I brought my sketchbook and watercolours. It's the first time I dare to produce a drawing in the field – and drawing is a practice that was still quite new to me at the time.

For a period of three years, between 2014 and 2017, I have been witnessing and taking part in the creative process of a leading visual and performance artist, documenting and learning from the senior theatre production team around him. The rehearsal in Vienna of the *Mondparsifal* was among the most prominent moments that I was to experience during this immersion with the artists at work. The analysis of the key characteristics of this constellation of people and institutions consisted above all in discovering how these moments were triggered and sustained – in particular how Meese and his entourage modulated his presence, and the way he let the work unfold around the meeting tables, during the various artistic interventions as well as on the rehearsal stage. Affected by this atmosphere – and by the temporality of the rehearsal process – my ethnographic method underwent a considerable change as I began to introduce drawings and watercolours into my field notes.

These drawings, originally intended to complement writing and photography, have a unique effectiveness in capturing, on the one hand, the fleeting and singular moments that punctuate the creative process, and on the other hand, the more diffuse qualities that touch the participant observer and testify to their emotional involvement in the action. This personal epistemological revelation, and my developing a new set of skills must, I believe, be attributed to the atmosphere that prevailed in the framework of this artistic production. Noticed by the playwright, my ethnographic drawings were published regularly online on the institutional blog during the production, making me explore the genre of the illustrated ethnographic stories as a way of engaging directly with my research partners as a visual chronicler. How can the atmosphere generated by the artist Meese around the production be said to be conducive to this sort of transformative experiences? Was this 'growing' experience only mine or was it actually happening to 'the world', as I was, to quote William James who will help me to find my way through this rather intimate reflection, 'catching fact in the making?' (James 2010 [1907]: 90)

As I review various insights from my fieldwork with Meese and his team, a visual account of the creative process of the opera in Vienna is intertwined with a commentary on the atmosphere of the production, and on the methods of graphic anthropology. I first go through the similarities between the action of drawing and the action of staging, and how a way to stage can become an inspiration for a way to draw and to know. Then I go over the effect of 'patchworking', which is key to contemporary staging and an often hidden dimension to the ethnographic process. In the third section, I describe a type of enrolment which the artist seemed to generate within this project, through which things appeared to be 'falling together' in place. I ponder on my bewilderment and on the ensuing necessary revision of my epistemic practice. In the concluding section, I go back to American pragmatism to articulate my dazzle with an experience of participation which has left a profound mark on my anthropological practice.

Step by Step

My observation of the creative process of the work of Meese began several years before the show in Vienna, as that *Parsifal* was supposed to be staged in another house. My doctoral dissertation deals with the long and turbulent process of the mise-en-scène of the *Parsifal* by Meese, which was originally commissioned by the Bayreuth Festival. I joined the team during that first phase and documented the creation of the sets and

Figure 12.2. Jonathan Meese about to enter the stage during a performance of his *Parsifal* project at Berliner Festspielhaus. Ink and watercolour, Berlin 2017. © Maxime Le Calvé.

costumes for this first work. However, the director Katharina Wagner dismissed the artist and his team after two presentations of the concept (Le Calvé 2018). After a year of ruminations, Meese accepted a proposal to put the *Parsifal* to the stage at another major European performing arts festival, the Wiener Festwochen, in co-production with the Berliner Festspiele. That time, I attended the preliminary meetings and a second design process to its successful conclusion. In parallel, I conducted an ethnography of the activities of the visual artist and performer Meese, in a crossover anthropological approach inspired by the sociology of work, ethnomethodology and theatre studies.

The practice of this artist is an astonishing mixture of provocation and consensus: provocation on stage and in the way of dealing with the most explosive subjects; consensus when it comes to working with his collaborators and with the institutions of the art world. An established visual artist, Meese is also famous for his seemingly always on performance. Each of his public appearances is the opportunity for a speech on art, for the duration of which the rather introvert and sweet Jonathan becomes a full-on propagandist for the 'dictatorship of art', vociferating highly problematic and provoking ideas at a seemingly unstoppable pace, with an ambiguous yet humoristic attitude. Behind the scenes, the artist is supported by a devoted team, which manages his time, his energy and puts him at work. Within the context of his office and studio, I discovered the efficacy of his influence on his team, on his partners and on his publics (Le Calvé 2015), and I attempted to grasp ethnographically the atmospheres that he manages to instil in his works of art (Le Calvé 2018). In particular, I found out that his staging projects for the opera were carried out in a rather strict consistency with his reported experience of the phenomenon of art, of which he gives a lively account in his recurring manifestos, in his discourses and his artistic practice. A theory of arts in practice, inspired largely by Fluxus, into which the artistic action obeys the pragmatic exigencies of the artistic situations, incessantly answering a single question: what does it take to make art today, given the materials, the characters and the public in presence? As 'another mode of knowing', this practice stands as a provocation to the modern definition of knowledge, opposing to it a highly theatrical, participatory, excessive and heterogenous rationality, which can embrace otherness, emotions and embodiment – a practice that bears many comparisons to what John Law defined with the Baroque as a Western alternative to the commonsense scientific model of the neutral and purified knowledge (see Law 2016). Exposure to this 'mode of knowing' isn't innocuous for the ethnographer, especially at a formative stage. Soon enough, I started developing a peculiar mode of epistemological provocation and consensus as I started drawing field notes – receiving the encouragement of Meese.

The practice of ethnographic drawing is multiple, opened to many ways of thinking about the field and about the ethnologist's method. Drawing is both a synthesis and a reconstruction of what is happening before their eyes. The artist is the author, and, at the same time, the line always exceeds what was intended.

> A line, an area of tone, is not really important because it records what you have seen, but because of what it will lead you on to see. Following up its logic in order to check its accuracy, you find confirmation or denial in the object itself or in your memory of it. Each confirmation or denial brings you closer to the object, until finally you are, as it were, inside it: the contours you have drawn no longer marking the edge of what you have seen but the edge of what you have become. (Berger 2013 [1953]: 53)

I still have the feeling that I never really decided to start a drawing practice. Little by little, it brought me 'closer to my object', eventually occupying a generous proportion of my time on the field. This description by John Berger of the artist's gesture, I experienced in two ways: the contours that I have drawn no longer mark only the contours of what

I see, but the contours of what I am becoming, a match, a harmonization ('attunement') with the artistic process in which I am participating, as if I was 'as it were, inside it'. More pragmatically, the sluggish pace of rehearsal in opera allowed me to take the time to draw. As part of the team, I had gained, until that moment, a rather active position in the discussions during the development of the concept and sets. However, when we arrived on the set, my practice of participant observation came up against an enlightening limit: amid the growing pressure and under the hierarchy asserted in the context of the opera rehearsal, my views in the dramaturgical process were no longer desired or considered. In Vienna, I was assigned the position of a personal assistant to the artist. On the plus side, this position came with very little constraint, as Meese isn't the type to order anything from anyone. I sat down and I observed.

In Vienna, during rehearsals in the spring of 2017, Meese doesn't jump on stage at every moment: he respectfully delegates the real work to those who know how to do it and does not stand in their way. Meese is a contemporary artist and is not used to leading teams. The conductor, the assistants, the playwright, and the choreographer hired to direct the movements of the choir, are the repositories of these skills and it is them who lend themselves to structure the collective work. And as one can expect of a production team organized by a world-famous theatre festival such as the Wiener Festwochen, the infrastructure is excellent.

Figure 12.3. 'Kundry macht Kung Fu!' Scene from the rehearsal. Ink and watercolour, Vienna 2017. © Maxime Le Calvé.

While Meese doesn't run the operations in a conventional way, he is none-the-less central in the theatrical work. He comes on stage from time to time to direct the singers and bring in new material. A seasoned performer, he uses his own body to show what he has in mind. In this drawing, we see him on the set working with the singer who incarnates Kundry: he proposes a new gestural element for the character, whose costume for this act is inspired by the heroine of the film *Barbarella*. This proposal is a Kung Fu sequence. He combines gesture with words: 'Not real Kung Fu, but the Kung Fu that children do!' The singer is enchanted, she immediately tries it out, improvising on these new instructions. As the playwright Henning Nass put it in one of his presentation speeches, this staging is populated by a number of Meese's favourite characters, who are challenging the usual reading of the characters of the Wagnerian drama. A weak female character in the original version, who oscillates between the seducer and the mother, Kundry comes out as an independent and strong figure in Meese's staging. Using his visual vocabulary imported from pop culture, fascist visual imagery and children's books, the artist adheres to the most straightforward European Trash tradition: an art of staging opera as a radical reinterpretation, which aims to revisit the work to make it tell stories other than those written in the libretto, by the introduction of utterly foreign material.[1] The actual creation is largely accomplished during the rehearsals, and this quality of spontaneity is meant to be part of the desired aesthetics.[2] The iterations of the scenes, conducted under the combined direction of the conductor and the assistant stage director, allow both for the adjustment of a precise architecture given by the musical text, and for the slackening of the fabric of the gestural performance, giving the performers a freedom they cannot seek to satisfy in the vocal execution. Many props are designed, tried out on the spot, and each iteration must satisfy both aspects, that of the singing and that of the stage performance. With each new image introduced, each decision taken and duly noted, the work progresses step by step, as the elements fall into place. The staging is gradually inscribed, anchored on the rigid skeleton of the libretto, in the bodies, in the props, in the assistants' notes and on my notebook pages. This is a dimension common to the creative process I observe and the one I experience through drawing:

> Another way of putting it would be to say that each mark you make on the paper is a stepping stone from which you proceed to the next, until you have crossed your subject as though it were a river, have put it behind you. (Berger 2013 [1953]: 53)

Making is a 'journey', rather than a project, as the philosopher Etienne Souriau has noted, later quoted by Deleuze and voiced by Ingold

Figure 12.4. Kundry-Barbarella taking over the spear, scene from the rehearsal in Vienna. Ink and watercolours, Vienna 2017. © Maxime Le Calvé.

(Ingold 2013: ch. 3; Souriau 2015 [1943]: 231). In-between, as the river is being crossed, a moment of strong indeterminacy diffracts the existence of the makers: are they going to make it to the other shore? Are they going to sink, pulled to the bottom by the stream? As the mode of existence of the shipwrecked swimmer, there is the experience of an oscillation between success and failure, an experience from which one's existence comes out a bit different each time.

Patch Working

Contemporary opera staging has a patchwork dimension to it,[3] and Meese excels in the art of collage, montage and defacement. The story and elements of the drama have been explored many times before, and crucial dramaturgical decisions are often made in the moment, when all the elements are finally brought together, directly on stage and in complicity with the singers. The final scene of Act II, whose dénouement had been left open, is elucidated in a few instants. In the original libretto, Parsifal leaves the stage with the Grail King's spear in his hand, and Kundry slips away in tears. With Meese's version, the hero escapes from the stage in a canoe with Klingsor, while Kundry-Barbarella, dressed in her faux-leather suit, brandishes the spear like an electric guitar as she is being set on fire in a straw idol. This counter-intuitive interpretation developed during the rehearsal in a few seconds by playwright Henning, brings out new dimensions of Kundry's character and her role in the drama. 'What an image!' 'Incredible.' 'They've done a lot of work', the assistant says to me in a tone that blends humour and respect. With this drawing, I also tried to fix the memory of an ethnographic hunch (Pink 2021). As I already mentioned, as a participant observer during the previous phases of the development of the staging, I sat through the conception meetings in Berlin with a (fragile) right to take the floor and speak my mind. This way, I was able to contribute to an active exploration of the work of Wagner through imagination and modelling. That phase of apprenticeship deeply informed my vision of the artistic process as a practice of taming images, of twisting and repeatedly rendering them in speech, gestures and sketches, and ultimately of giving a space to invite them over, allowing uncertainty to rule up to a certain moment ('we don't have to decide that right away') until they appear on stage as obvious and inevitable. This way of making the images emerge is linked to a specific aesthetic, which shows the seams of creative action, in the 'defamiliarization' style of Brecht, but with a different intention. It is not so much a question of showing that it is not real, as of showing the contingencies in action throughout the creative process, and questioning the all-powerful agency of the artist over the artwork.

Meanwhile, the patchworking applies to my field notes, as I collect pages of notes, photos and one drawing a day. These scenes that I depict are bricks to write a story. They are both field notes and fragments chosen according to a certain angle, to tell what is happening there. I soon discover that each of my drawings also holds that patchwork quality: the draughtsperson also operates a spatio-temporal and idiosyncratic synthesis. I seize an object in the room, and from one thing to the next, I draw the whole situation. Carried away by this activity, by the line that I take 'for a walk' (Ingold 2010) and by the colours that seem to require a touch here and a touch there, I am completely absorbed in expressive observation. I also soon realize that my 'coming out', as a live-drawer and visual anthropologist, is also the resolution of a patchwork of theoretical and existential circumstances, which involve differentiated and exercised regimes of attention. In particular, I notice that my gaze is full of theoretical presuppositions: the legacy of the Chicago School, taking the situation as the basic unit of ethnographic observation; an emphasis given to the narration of singular events, shaped by the ethnography of action and the ethnography of detail learned in Nanterre (Piette 1996): throughout my graphical descriptions 'as close as possible' to the actors, anthropological knowing is at work, without necessarily having to make it apparent (see Houdart 2015). At another level and register of epistemological

Figure 12.5. Side view of the director's table during the rehearsal at Theater an der Wien, with the choreographer, the two assistants and the artist. Ink and watercolours, Vienna 2017. © Maxime Le Calvé.

formation, this practice resonates with the practice of silent meditation, a practice which, applied seriously, considerably rearranges phenomenological capacities[4] (Depraz et al. 2003: 217).

By the gesture of drawing, one can, to borrow the vocabulary popularized by Tim Ingold, enter into correspondence with the object whose shape is being captured. And as the transduction process goes, I also become in touch with myself. I draw what is there, suspending critical judgement on my own creation. I let this image become that of the ethnographic situation. My gesture is set in tune with the gesture of another, and it reverberates the tone of an atmosphere conducive to expression, which suddenly makes this pictorial contribution possible, desirable, even necessary. I let it work for me.

Let It Work

The person in charge of publications is coming to visit us on set. She slips me a little sentence of admiration, after attending part of the rehearsal: 'Everything is so *stimmig* [right and consistently in tune] in this project!' The atmosphere is perceived by and affects all participants. In its coherence and in the impression of an overall harmony of the project, it goes beyond the artwork to embrace all the production activities. Indeed, Meese and his team ensure a presence that brings the whole team and the cast into the creative process with them.

The atmosphere, as conceptualized in the German phenomenological literature, carries within it the future possibilities of actions, through the sensible qualities of the gestures they invite in those who partake in them (Böhme 2016, Thibaud 2002). The first reference in France to the anthropology of atmospheres is the ethnography of an Indian temple in Benares and of the action of its high priest, the *mahatma* (Claveyrolas 2003). The related concept of *Darshan* is a concept used in analogical mode to speak of the effect of immersive artworks provoking a change in the viewer.[5] It is a field of influence generated by a device at the centre of which a figure, often a character represented by an image or a human being, embodies certain qualities of being.

The show behind the curtains revolves around the main artist, as I have already made clear. Jonathan Meese acts with a particular type of 'craft', closer to performance art than to the authoritarian and picky leadership expected of a theatre director. Several of the singers claim to have seen this contract as a chance to work with Meese. 'I didn't want to accept to do another Wagnerian production with a director who climbs up grunting and breathing hard: the Parsifal is often seen as the peak of a career, so directors are often caught in a cloud of ideas. With Meese, I knew it would be different', confides to me, in an informal interview, the bass-voiced singer who has been given the role of Klingsor. That singer turns out to be an outstanding improviser, whose grotesque and obscene inventions often steal the show from the melodrama in the foreground, creating an extra level of contemplation and a comic relief. The casting director managed to provide to Meese a cast of opera performers who are willing to work with movement on the stage – a rare quality in Wagnerian opera singers, we have often been told. The space of rehearsal becomes, according to the methods used in theatre or contemporary dance, a space open to the intervention of singers, but also that of other figures – Parsifal, Richard Wagner, Barbarella, and more than any other, the presence of Meese himself.

The presence of the artist is also managed as a precious resource by the assistants and the director of the festival. As soon as he leaves the rehearsal hall, Meese is propelled through all sorts of appointments and public speaking engagements, press interviews, the opening of his exhibition at his gallery, the opening of a series of his works hanging in the Museum of Fine Arts alongside Velásquez's paintings, VIP events with patrons of the festival. During the rehearsals themselves, he accepts this central position, but rarely takes the floor. With an unusual humility for

Figure 12.6. Jonathan Meese posing with his mother during the press tour at the Kunsthistorisches Museum. Ink and watercolour, Vienna 2017. © Maxime Le Calvé.

the profession of stage director, he leaves it to the assistants to judge when his intervention is necessary, when the singers need it. The artist is using his power in the form of influence rather than coercive assertiveness. He enables his collaborators to intervene on the material on his behalf. Although he rarely intervenes or is asked to take formal decisions, Meese is not inactive at the direction table: he is performing a permanent and thorough 'work' on the score. He cannot read the notes, but he goes through the text none-the-less, writing notes, making drawings in the thick libretto. One could say that the playwright and the assistants are actually developing the staging. However, as they sit next to Meese, one can notice the constant comments, the jokes, the references exchanged on the fly, and sometimes an immediate impulse comes of their little private conference. The playwright jumps out of his chair and goes to speak to the singer or to the prop master. This easy-going partnership produces work which remains within the tried and tested framework of the aesthetics of the artist: the work is created by him, with him and in him.

The stage work that is now emerging is the fruit of a long process of getting to know and trust each other. The skilled team members ask themselves at every moment, just as he does himself: how to make a work by Jonathan Meese, how to make it his work, and what does it stand for?

There are certainly some formal requirements and criteria which I could note over the years and have summarized into an earlier paper (Le Calvé 2015). His aesthetic is rooted in the references of his adolescence in the 1980s, and it is always a little 'off', a little bit of a 'misfit'. Faithful to a trend that already existed in the punk movement, he crosses ambiguous references to Nazi imagery, defaced with an ironic 'framing', which nevertheless has the audience feel the power of the negative, a situational irony.[6] There is also a particular tone to his performances, a singular blend of humour, irreverence and tenderness. This framing is marked, in particular, by the atypical co-presence of his mother Brigitte, 86 years old at the time. And more generally, there is an attitude, a certain aura: a thunderous laughter, a way of greeting every person when he enters a room, his poorly hidden and endearing shyness, and his generosity towards his collaborators. I am well aware that this is a long list of nice things to say, but isn't this also absolutely central in what is happening during the production? Attentive to what is happening, by his presence and his attitude, the artist keeps open a space to associations, to analogies, to play and to joke, a space in which the characters are invited to manifest themselves. The stories they recompose are called upon to evolve. My ethnographic work – also a notable process of getting to know and trust each other – is playing a part in the making of this space. Firstly, as a chronicle published regularly, which is performing it in images and text; but also, as my own presence on the field and my live drawing performance is attuned to this creative action, and therefore modestly contributes to it. These two aspects of this entangled collaboration are sometimes difficult to separate from the very pictures and stories which I produced along with the staging work.

I will conclude this section on the 'things falling together' mode of action of Jonathan Meese with a last field note (and drawing). I'm spending a few moments on the stage right after the curtain falls on the last show. A stage technician is vacuuming up the golden glitter. This image strikes me, so I open my sketchbook and get to work quickly. The man sees me drawing him and he stops for a moment: 'When's the Jonathan Meese comic coming? That would be great!' He looks excited and happy with the results of both the show and my graphic chronicles. Although I don't remember ever speaking to him, he seems well aware of my work, which was posted on the website regularly. I ask him upfront: 'Was it special, compared to the usual stage projects?'

The technician replies: 'Yes, for sure. Jonathan creates an incredibly exciting atmosphere. Everyone is in a good mood, and he communicates that good mood to everyone. All the departments are enthusiastic, everyone has participated. Usually there's stress, people are shouting, they want

Figure 12.7. Technician vacuuming golden glitter on the stage after the curtain has fallen on the last performance of the show at Berliner Festspielhaus. Ink and watercolour, Berlin 2017. © Maxime Le Calvé.

it to be like this or like that. Not at all with him. This is entirely different.' In his entire career, he claims to remember only a single comparable director. 'That's the impression that everyone has made it happen, together.' This ethnographic moment condenses the ethnographic situation and the perspective of an insider. It 'denotes a relation between immersement and movement', as Marylin Strathern has it (Strathern 1999: 6): live-drawing can trigger an ethnographic involvement which, in my experience, also belongs to the order of 'things falling together'.

Complete Experience

When anthropology deals with exceptional experiences, it is particularly interested in those that tear apart the obsolete or constraining illusions of our relationship to the world (see Shokeid 1992, and in this volume). The individualistic perspective constructed in our existential journey becomes, at certain moments, obnoxiously mismatched. A new, often overwhelming reordering can sometimes take place in an instant. Some art forms integrate this dimension of human knowledge and experience.

These artistic movements sometimes directly relate to mystical traditions: this is the case of Fluxus, in particular, which is a major inspiration to Meese. The art historian Pamela Kort – who worked with him on the first *Parsifal* project as consultant – investigated and claimed to have discovered a direct filiation leading to Fluxus (and Meese) that goes back to the barefoot prophets who walked the paths of Europe at the end of the nineteenth century, preaching oriental wisdom (Kort and Hollein 2015). Artists have long been curious and inquisitive on the topic of the transformation of the human beings and their perception of forms.[7] Some of these prophets were also fostering the creation of communities, as did Joseph Beuys later on, and studied and worked on performativity of ritualistic practices. These acts are anchoring personal transformation not in the inner intimacy of the subject but rather in the in-betweenness of a shared, intersubjective world. In particular, the performance arts have flourished as a field of experimentation in and of the world, inviting powerful presence phenomena to reveal themselves in spatio-temporal devices and precise sequences of activities.[8] As such, performance artists have been drawing a field of ethnographic investigation of choice,[9] which in turn demands of the anthropologist new fieldwork experiments to make these insights intelligible to their publics.

Drawing in the field opened up new areas for my practice, and with them, many new research and epistemic questions. The first insights were shaped by the context into which I grew this new skill: the performance of drawing in public, the way that lines always seem to go step by step ahead of my own will or wit, the fashion into which things fall together on paper. That is the core concept of the 'dictatorship of art', which Meese strives to define in every speech and in every manifesto. The artist describes and stages it as an obedience to contingencies – precisely a taste and an ability to let things fall together. The 'dictatorship of art' is a radical concept, disturbing and full of irony, which crystallizes an aesthetic and an atmosphere. It also opens a space for creative action and for those who work together with him. As the participants of the palaver described by Isabelle Stengers, and in opposition with the modern argumentative mode of discussion into which individuals should win and impose truth over their opponents, his way to engage with collaboration is specifically oriented toward an open consensus. Meese is not speaking directly for himself, but for the art, and he respects all inputs as delivered from other perspectives that import as much as his own – once they have made it to come on board. As Stengers notes, this type of collective action is the only one that can achieve 'a very particular and demanding "enrolment"' (Stengers 2016). The devices that invite these voicing phenomena require tireless work to keep them in motion. What kind of anthropology would allow for this kind of voicing, steering clear of the modern logic of expert argumentation, and embracing the co-construction of an ethnographic truth – can we go together beyond the 'ethnographic effect' devised by Marylin Strathern (1999)? This would give us the blueprint of an empirical social science which addresses not the collection of information, but phenomena of growth which happen between the anthropologists and their field, shaping the world and its seekers in non-dual experiences of participation – and a sense of where to look for these 'growing places', where things fall together, instead of focusing only onto the 'misery of the world', where things are falling apart.

The experiences that reshape our lives often gives rise to the sensation of the exceptional: a moment into which everything seems to take its place. Dewey has termed this phenomenon the 'complete experience': it is perceived by the subject 'as a reunification of dissociated elements' (Zask 2007: 144). There are, and Dewey has noted this well in his studies of education and the arts, settings in which these achievements are possible, and others in which they are not. Thus, he proposed in a late book, *Freedom and Culture* (1939), written while teaching the students of Franz Boas in Chicago, to use the term 'culture' exclusively for social frameworks that enable these 'complete experiences' (Zask 2007: 144).[10] These perceptual and spiritual experiences enable their subjects to resolve the dissonances of problematic and questionable situations by establishing what American pragmatists have defined as a temporarily stable framework of 'beliefs' (Peirce 1878). According to William James, these epiphanies must be taken with the utmost seriousness, as a 'workshop of being' which is 'of the world' as much as of our selves:

> Our acts, our turning-places, where we seem to ourselves to make ourselves and grow, are the parts of the world to which we are closest, the parts of which our knowledge is the most intimate and complete. Why should we not take them at their face-value? Why may they not be the actual turning-places and *growing-places* which they seem to be, *of the world* – why not the workshop of being, where we catch fact in the making, so that nowhere may the world grow in any other kind of way than this? (James 2010 [1907]: 90; emphasis is mine)

I draw from these few sentences of James on religion an inspiration, and a way to articulate a feeling which is difficult to put into words. This transformation 'of the world' amounts to a new inscription of the subject in an alternative constellation of existence, which comes with new habits and a new confidence: a new 'faith', in James's religious vocabulary, as the pragmatists defined religion as experience and as a practice of relating to the world and to others.[11] Education is seen here as a transformation of the self and of one's relation with the world: one learns with others, then returns to teach what one has learned, which sets in motion a new learning process. The anthropologist's fieldwork would thus be an education, a way of getting in touch, of sharing the life and concerns of the people with whom one learns a way of doing and being (Ingold 2017).

At its best (and at its worst), fieldwork can be a 'workshop of being', as it is a way to shape and intermingle the world and our acts into knowledge 'most intimate and complete'. No anthropologist has described it better than Evans-Pritchard, who had his own exigencies of what enrolment should entail: 'among the Nuer, I found it absolutely necessary to acquire a small herd of my own. We were then fellow-herdsmen with common interests, common language, common affections, and living the same life in the same conditions; and all this, if it may so be put, imposed on me what "cow" means to a Nuer', wrote Evans-Pritchard (1973: 4). In order to understand what the world is like for a member of a pastoral tribe, adopting a herd of cows was the only way to get closer to the life of these pastoral tribes. I always wondered what Evans-Pritchard had done with his own herd. Did he offer the animals to his closest friends as a thank you present, and perhaps also as compensation for the possible sense of absence that followed his definitive departure? Or did he consider taking them with him to graze them on the lawns of Oxford University, continuing to care for them, watching them give birth and being fed by them? Having adopted a herd of lines, endearing animals that cannot so easily be bequeathed to others, I now find myself obliged to constantly find them new ground to graze on or else see them wither away. Luckily, they are easily satisfied with what I feed them as long as I give them regular exercise, and in turn they continue to nurture my work today. Wittily and alive on their own, they often remind me that they stemmed from Jonathan Meese and his generous atmosphere. The world has changed through them, as they drove me to new places.

Maxime Le Calvé is an anthropologist of art and science, currently postdoctoral research associate at the Cluster of Excellence 'Matters of Activities' (HU Berlin). In his latest ethnographic project, he is exploring haptic creativities and cartographic practices in neurosurgery. Visual ethnographer, he is making use of digital drawing as an investigative device. He is also curating virtual reality experiences, which he frames as collaborative art-science inquiries aiming to stretch the senses of anthropologists and of their publics. He trained in general ethnology in Paris Nanterre and has a PhD in social anthropology and in theatre studies, from EHESS Paris and FU Berlin. He has published on the ethnographic study of atmospheres (co-edited *Exercices d'ambiances*, 2018), on performance art, music, Berlin, people cutting in brains, and ethnographic training. He is also co-curator of the exhibitions 'Field/Works' in Lisbon (2020–21), 'Stretching Materialities' (Berlin, 2021–22) and 'Sketching Brains' (Berlin, 2022–23). See more at maximelecalve.com.

Notes

1. The staging of opera is considered by proponents of contemporary aesthetics to be a re-reading of the works. See on this subject the landmark and often cited debate between Levin (1997) and Treadwell (1998).
2. On the aesthetic of the rehearsal and its practice of 'chaos' in German contemporary theatre, see Hinz and Roselt (2011).
3. See the controversy between Treadwell and Levin on the contemporary practices of 'reading and staging' and the polemics that they trigger (Treadwell 1998; Levin 1998).
4. Given the vast literature on this subject, I would simply refer the reader to a recent anthropological work on the tradition in which I practised at the time, and still practise every day, the art of *vipassana* meditation, which came under the critical scrutiny of Michal Pagis (2019).
5. See, for example, Favero, in his recent work on 'present images' (2018: 53).
6. See on the aesthetics of punk the classic Hebdige (1979); and on the labour of defacement see Taussig (1999).
7. Most of the anthropological literature on this topic builds on Victor and Edith Turner (Turner 1982; 1988) and Richard Schechner (1985). These works challenged the paradigm of 'art for art'. For a historical account from the perspective of theatre studies, see Warstat (2011).
8. Many interesting examples can be found in the seminal book of Erika Fischer-Lichte (2008).
9. Note the article by Fiona Siegenthaler (2013) on the ethnographic method in performance arts, or even more specifically in relation to the case of opera, the work of Paul Atkinson (2010; 2013).
10. In this use of the term 'culture', one can find the German idealism around the notion of *'Bildung'* – the early Dewey was a Hegelian (see Dalton 2002), and the influence of German scholars coming from the tradition of Goethe, Schiller and Herder on the American school of cultural anthropology which was set by Franz Boas (see Vermeulen 2015).
11. See the classics: James (2009 [1909]); Dewey (1962). For a more recent exemplar of a thought on religion inspired by American pragmatism: Latour (2013).

References

Atkinson, Paul. 2010. 'Making Opera Work: Bricolage and the Management of Dramaturgy', *Music and Arts in Action* 3(1): 3–19.
——. 2013. 'Blowing Hot: The Ethnography of Craft and the Craft of Ethnography', *Qualitative Inquiry* 19(5): 397–404.
Berger, John. 2013 [1953]. 'Drawing is Discovery', *The New Statesman*, 29 August 1953. Republished 3–9 May 2013.
Böhme, Gernot. 2016. *The Aesthetics of Atmospheres*. Edited by Jean-Paul Thibaud. London: Routledge.
Claveyrolas, Matthieu. 2003. *Quand le temple prend vie: Atmosphère et dévotion à Bénarès*. Paris: CNRS Editions.
Dalton, Thomas. 2002. *Becoming John Dewey: Dilemmas of a Philosopher and Naturalist*. Bloomington, IN: Indiana University Press.
Depraz, Nathalie, Francisco J. Varela and Pierre Vermersch. 2003. *On Becoming Aware: A Pragmatics of Experiencing*. Philadelphia and Amsterdam: John Benjamins Publishing.
Dewey, John. 1939. *Freedom and Culture*. New York: G.P. Putnam's Sons.
——. 1962. *A Common Faith*. Yale University Press. Retrieved 1 February 2023 from: https://www.jstor.org/stable/j.ctt1npdn9.
Favero, Paolo. 2018. *The Present Image: Visible Stories in a Digital Habitat*. Cham: Palgrave Macmillan.
Fischer-Lichte, Erika. 2008. *The Transformative Power of Performance: A New Aesthetics*. London: Taylor & Francis.
Hebdige, Dick. 1979. *Subculture: The Meaning of Style*. New edition. London and New York: Routledge.
Hinz, Melanie and Jens Roselt. 2011. *Chaos und Konzept: Proben und Probieren im Theater*. Berlin: Alexander Verlag.
Houdart, Sophie. 2015. *Les incommensurables*. Bruxelles: Zones Sensibles Editions.
Ingold, Tim. 2010. 'Ways of Mind-Walking: Reading, Writing, Painting', *Visual Studies* 25(1): 15–23. https://doi.org/10.1080/14725861003606712.
——. 2013. *Making: Anthropology, Archaeology, Art and Architecture*. London and New York: Routledge.
——. 2017. *Anthropology and/as Education*. Abingdon, Oxon and New York: Routledge.
James, William. 2009 [1909]. *The Varieties of Religious Experience: A Study in Human Nature*. Lexington, KY: CreateSpace Independent Publishing Platform.
——. 2010 [1907]. *Pragmatism: A New Name for Some Old Ways of Thinking*. Auckland: The Floating Press.
Kort, Pamela and Max Hollein. 2015. *Artists & Prophets: A Secret History of Modern Art 1872–1972*. Köln: Snoeck.
Latour, Bruno. 2013. *Rejoicing: Or the Torments of Religious Speech*. Trans. Julie Rose. Cambridge: Polity Press.
Law, John. 2016. 'Modes of Knowing: Resources from the Baroque', in *Modes of Knowing: Resources from the Baroque*, John Law and Evelyn Ruppert (eds). Manchester: Mattering Press, pp. 17–56.

Le Calvé, Maxime. 2015. 'Ethnographie dans l'espace de la "Dictature de l'Art" de Jonathan Meese: Comment bien "laisser faire ce qui arrive"'. Edited by Thomas Golsenne and Patricia Ribault. *Techniques & Culture. Revue semestrielle d'anthropologie des techniques*, no. 64 (December). https://doi.org/10.4000/tc.7591.

———. 2018. 'Invocations antagonistes: Les atmosphères condensées de l'artiste Jonathan Meese', *Communications* 102 (May): 153–67. https://doi.org/10.3917/commu.102.0153.

Levin, David J. 1997. 'Reading a Staging/Staging a Reading', *Cambridge Opera Journal* 9(1): 47–71.

———. 1998. 'Response to James Treadwell', *Cambridge Opera Journal* 10(3): 307–11.

Pagis, Michal. 2019. *Inward: Vipassana Meditation and the Embodiment of the Self*. Chicago: University of Chicago Press.

Pink, Sarah. 2021. 'The Ethnographic Hunch'. In *Experimenting with Ethnography*, edited by Andrea Ballestero and Brit Ross Winthereik. Durham, NC: Duke University Press, pp. 30–40.

Peirce, Charles S. 1878. 'How to Make Our Ideas Clear', *Popular Science Monthly* 12 (January): 286–302.

Piette, Albert. 1996. *Ethnographie de l'action: L'observation des détails*. Paris: Métailié.

Schechner, Richard. 1985. *Between Theater and Anthropology*. Philadelphia: University of Pennsylvania Press.

Shokeid, Moshe. 1992. 'Exceptional Experiences in Everyday Life', *Cultural Anthropology* 7(2): 232–43.

Siegenthaler, Fiona. 2013. 'Towards an Ethnographic Turn in Contemporary Art Scholarship', *Critical Arts: South–North Cultural and Media Studies* 27: 737–52.

Souriau, Étienne. 2015 [1943]. *The Different Modes of Existence*. Trans. E. Beranek and T. Howles. Minneapolis: Univocal; University of Minnesota Press.

Stengers, Isabelle. 2016. 'Matters of Concern All the Way Down', in Ctrl-Z. Vol. 7. Perth: Curtin University. Retrieved 1 February 2023 from: https://www.ctrl-z.net.au/articles/issue-7/stengers-matters-of-concern-all-the-way-down/.

Strathern, Marilyn. 1999. *Property, Substance and Effect: Anthropological Essays on Persons and Things*. London: The Athlone Press.

Taussig, Michael. 1999. *Defacement: Public Secrecy and the Labor of the Negative*. Palo Alto: Stanford University Press.

Thibaud, Jean-Paul. 2002. 'L'horizon Des Ambiances Urbaines', *Communications* 73 (1): 185–201. https://doi.org/10.3406/comm.2002.2119.

Treadwell, James. 1998. 'Reading and Staging Again', *Cambridge Opera Journal* 10(2): 205–20.

Turner, Victor Witter. 1982. *From Ritual to Theatre: The Human Seriousness of Play*. New York: PAJ Publications.

———. 1988. *The Anthropology of Performance*. New York: PAJ Publications.

Vermeulen, Han F. 2015. *Before Boas: The Genesis of Ethnography and Ethnology in the German Enlightenment*. Lincoln, Ne: University of Nebraska Press.

Warstat, Matthias. 2011. *Krise und Heilung: Wirkungsästhetiken des Theaters*. Paderborn: Fink.

Zask, Joëlle. 2007. 'Anthropologie de l'expérience', in *Vie et Expérimentation: Peirce, James, Dewey*, Didier Debaise (ed.), pp. 129–46. Annales de l'institut de Philosophie de l'université de Bruxelles. Paris: Vrin.

Afterword

The Sixth Sense

Thomas Hylland Eriksen

I had spent many hours reading about serendipitous coincidences during fieldwork – chance meetings in airplanes, the young Pablo Picasso's artistic epiphany, a river goddess in Igboland, a literary East German refugee in the West, people who had to dance it since they couldn't say it, uncanniness and glimmers of hope, forays into art by anthropologists and into anthropology by artists. At the end of the evening, my mind was positively humming with thoughts about Kant's third critique, Benjamin's *Passagenwerk*, William James and pragmatism, and the implications of the notion of the *Gesamtkunstwerk* for the project unfolding in this book – finally, I had no option but to go to bed. My last fully conscious act that evening consisted in looking up the unfamiliar word *proprioception* on my phone, to be informed promptly by the internet that it amounts to the awareness of one's own body's location and movement. Intriguingly, the same source adds that proprioception is sometimes spoken of as 'the sixth sense'.

In all its apparent sprawl, this book is held together by a thematic unity, which can be described not only as a focus on 'the exceptional' in fieldwork and elsewhere, but which also entails testing the strength of the walls of the ethnographic enterprise: where does ethnography end, and when it does, how can that which begins (whatever it is) be designated? Similar questions were asked earlier: Marcus, Fischer and Clifford are mentioned by the editors, and several of the contributors have previously raised probing questions about the ultimate subject-matter of anthropology. However, the emphasis on the exceptional, as opposed to the everyday and routine, enables the authors to ask questions not just about representation and its ostensible crisis, but also about the significance of affect and the senses for intellectual projects – the ultimate question being not so much what is the nature of the world as how the mind works, to cite the title of a popular book on the subject. It is also worth noting that the authors are determined to approach exceptional beauty, inexplicably moving experiences and the sublime without being animated by an ambition to deconstruct or explain them critically. Readers are allowed to partake in these exceptional experiences on their own terms.

Ethnography is by default and definition 'close up and personal', yet events of existential significance (and thus methodological interest) to the ethnographer are rarely taken up in publications. Yet that is exactly what this book does, thereby probing the limits of ethnography in more than one respect.

It is often during fieldwork that anthropologists have their exceptional experiences, but not invariably. Several of the chapters deal with literary texts, performative arts or paintings, and at least one combines visual art with anthropological reflections on the state of the world. Some write about dance in ways attempting to transcend the boundary between bodily movement and disembodied text. It is not without relevance that one of the editors was a dancer herself, subsequently carrying out research among dancers and embarking on the extraordinarily difficult task of translating the language of dance into that of anthropology.

Occasionally, the life-changing experiences described by the authors are shared by their local interlocutors, but this is not necessarily the case. It is easy to imagine situations which have a strong impact on the ethnographer, but are banal and pedestrian to others, and vice versa. Habit and routine may dampen the experience of the unusual. When I went out fishing at dawn in a dinghy with a couple of Mauritian men, I was awestruck by the serenity, the changing colours of the imposing Morne mountain at sunrise and the salty, tangy smell of the turquoise sea. To my fellows, this was unexceptional. To them, the extraordinary might consist in an unusually large catch (for which they would be inclined to thank God or their ancestors). As ethnographers, we are trained to apply role distance consciously in the field, having learned from Geertz's famous essay 'From The Native's Point of View' that you don't have to be one to know one, self-consciously shifting between deep and shallow play, affect and reflexivity, presumably unlike the people we work with, who are not social scientists studying their own society. In many of the stories narrated in this book, this formula is turned on its head. It is the ethnographer rather than their interlocutors who is taken aback by the sublime or uncanny.

Only with the hindsight of temporal and physical distance is it possible to reflect on the implications of such affective responses, which seep unmarked into ethnographies. Going native, if only for a few fleeting moments, creates a bond between ethnographer and field which opens the possibility, in the words of a chapter author, of 'a transcendence of what is merely traditional by what is true', thereby moving beyond the distortions of culture to a distilled co-presence not only with other people, but with the broader environment. The personal encounter with the Lake Goddess, integrated with a novelist's account, similarly suggests an expansion of the ethnographic field into that which cannot be observed directly or spoken of explicitly, where affect is not merely an object of study, but also a subjective experience.

The very fact that these questions can be raised, signals that ethnographic methods differ from all other research methods. We teach students that in ethnographic fieldwork, the researcher is the main instrument of enquiry, unlike in a laboratory experiment or a quantitative survey. As subjects, we influence the field and our engagement with it; this book reminds us of some of the ways in which the influence goes in both directions.

In the Introduction, the editors describe certain 'exceptional experiences as transformative, as life changing [events] that stay with us forever'. Since anthropologists have long challenged the subject–object boundary, which is so important in the scientific tradition, it is necessary to think systematically through the implications of these experiences. They need not even always be 'exceptional' in the sense of being dramatic or strongly affective. My own early fieldwork in Mauritius, in the mid-1980s, changed my gaze on society permanently, in that the year-long experience of an ethnically diverse plantation society, struggling with the tension between boundaries and creolization, has impregnated my work and life ever since. The mere smell of biryani still triggers memories of an encounter in a cafe at the Rose-Hill bus station in October 1986, when I was given an impromptu lecture, over a plate of fragrant biryani, about the difficulties of entering into a mixed marriage by someone whose experience with the phenomenon was first hand; the mere mention of Queen Victoria still produces a mental image of the statue in front of the Mauritian parliament and some palm trees, signifying an attempt to instil a sense of national identity in a diverse population by drawing on the one past that all the ethnic groups share, namely colonialism.

As the editors and several of the contributors mention, there exists a growing anthropology of the senses, which includes not only vision and hearing, but also smell, touch and taste. Reading the chapters, I was struck time and time again by the visceral landslide of affect and recall that can be triggered by sudden sensory input. During a recent conversation with a drummer who has played on more than a hundred albums, ranging from folk-pop and rock to jazz-rock and acoustic improvisation, we reminisced about our childhood experiences with music. A few years older than me, he mentioned that even today, whenever he listened to The Beatles' 'She Loves You', he could immediately recall the smell and texture of the dinner he had eaten with his family following the exceptional experience of hearing the song and seeing a photo of the band for the first time in the early 1960s.

Returning home, I felt an inexplicable but irresistible urge to listen to a record by the jazz singer Radka Toneff, featuring the guitarist who had played with this drummer on many albums. It had been decades since I last heard the album, and confirming the drummer's observation, Radka's melancholic, vulnerable voice enabled time travel back to 1979, the year in which the album was recorded. Closing my eyes, I was catapulted back to the basement where my friends and I had been horsing around with instruments we were learning to play, wearing flea market clothes and letting our hair grow, smoking rollups and drinking coffee like grown men – we were coming of age, exhilarated by the sheer beauty of jazz and excited to be alive and on the move. Never before had this particular chronotope come alive so vividly to me. Three or four of my friends became professional musicians, while I left for university. The bittersweet memory of a path not taken then led me to dig out Soft Machine's second album, which features Brian Hopper on the saxophone. Unlike his brother Hugh, Brian left the group to study biochemistry at the University of Manchester, soon to be replaced by Elton Dean, a free spirit whose first name was nicked by a certain Reginald Dwight, later to find fame under the sobriquet of Elton John.

This is how memory works in practice. It can be triggered by a smell, a chord, a face; and like *bricolage* in Lévi-Strauss's science of the concrete, it produces new configurations every time. Without affect and the senses, memory dries out. The exceptional experiences described by several chapter authors with reference to the arts challenge the boundaries of ethnographic methodology and writing as usually taught, but may yet bring us close to an essence of being which is always relational, and which is a reminder that nothing is 'not only' this, that or the other. There is a surplus of meaning in human worlds, just as in any great work of art.

Human lives are serendipitous, they share a narrative structure with fiction (and ethnography), and even the most unusual, powerful experience ultimately loses much of its value if it cannot be communicated. This is why it is necessary to pay greater attention to the art of writing. 'Saying something about something', as Geertz sums up his ambition in one of his programmatic articles, is a starting point; but exactly what should be said, and how, requires careful deliberation.

All knowledge is a form of simplification. By communicating their exceptional experiences to an unknown readership, the authors of this book carry out translations which are enlightening and enriching, telling stories that would otherwise not have made it into the purview of anthropology. What makes these often personal and unique stories relevant for social science is their embeddedness in a larger social fabric. One finds it helpful to collaborate with a visual artist; another integrates drawings and watercolours into her field notes; a third discovers potential for conviviality between humans and the environment, while a fourth finds inspiration for a genuinely cosmopolitan anthropology in Kant's admonition 'to study how a human cosmos and an individual polis informed one another'. These intellectual and existential projects do not just challenge subject–object distinctions in a methodological sense but raise questions about the boundaries of the discipline and indeed of language: 'If I could say it, I would not have to dance it.'

As it is described in this book, which foregrounds the senses, affect and moments of existential significance, the human life begins to resemble a *Gesamtkunstwerk*, neither fish nor fowl but with elements of both. Life exudes an *aura* in Walter Benjamin's sense, a radiance which cannot be scaled up, cloned or replicated. The semiosis of life is multipronged, and the intellectual's reliance on language is both a blessing and a curse, a means to achieve order and comprehension but also a recipe for simplification and reductionism. 'The artistic miracle was to see everything and to join with everything', as Rapport sums up Stanley Spencer's artistic vision. Similarly, Uwe Johnson experimented with fictional forms, applying multiple perspectives, dialectical juxtapositions, intertextuality and montage in an attempt to capture as many facets as possible of the world.

Social anthropologists have always opposed reductive generalizations about the human condition, and are acquainted with different ways to make sense of the world. Anthropologists react warily to any statement containing the clause 'nothing but', and are aware that verbal communication between researcher and interlocutor has its limitations since the unsaid is a vital part of the human world of communication. The present endeavour may thus come across as a logical extension of the classic virtues of anthropology, harking back to Boas's historical particularism and Malinowski's emphasis on the small community and its local knowledge. A quotation from the Roman playwright Terence, *Homo sum, humani nihil a me alienum puto* ('I am human, and I think nothing human is alien to me'), has often been invoked by anthropologists. It may well serve as a motto for this volume too.

* * *

One of the most striking contributions of this book is the ambition not only to transcend ethnographic conventions (some would say straitjackets), but also the wish to move beyond critique. Researchers and theorists who study the good life, the good society or the positive effects of mind-altering experiences have rarely made it into the canon. The social scientist who tells his audience that all is fine and that there is really nothing to worry about, seems to belong to a Monty Python skit rather than the academy. Actually, when I was doing research for a book about well-being (not published in English) a decade and a half ago, I soon discovered that anthropologists and other social scientists did not have much to say about the subject. They were obsessed by problems, conflicts and contradictions. It is a brave act, which easily lends itself to unfair criticism, to investigate the wonderful and the sublime without relying on the drama of conflict, contradiction and hidden scripts.

Having looked up the uncommon word proprioception on the internet, I fell into a slumber, and in that liminal state between the conscious and the subconscious, an avalanche of fragmented memories and images meandered across my tired brain, some of them involving all five senses. In quick succession, my mind was host to the image of an old American car adorned with tail fins, a small tin of salty anchovies, a pair of hard-boiled eggs, the main principles of regenerative agriculture, a walk to the local grocery three kilometres away, and an unsuccessful attempt to play 'Giant Steps' on the saxophone. I have played live many times, but lack confidence in my own skills (with good reason); I needed to go to the shop to buy some sugar-free fizzy drinks; I try my hand at regenerative growth whenever in the countryside; I was already looking forward to breakfast and had eggs and anchovies waiting in the fridge; and yes, I was in the market for a small car, having seen a few on the internet; and this particular, fictional seller had no clue as to whether his old Cadillac had a market value of two thousand or forty thousand Euros – was it a rusty wreck or a prized veteran car? Had I ventured to spell out all the connections in detail, the result would have been a poor man's Molly Bloom, eventually – as sleep took command – merging into the first chapter of *Finnegans Wake*. Such are the filigree connections that make up a life. And such are the realities of which we are invited to take part through the unexpected connections and lightning bolts that animate this rich and wondrous book.

Thomas Hylland Eriksen is Professor of Social Anthropology at the University of Oslo. His many publications include *Overheating* (2016), *Boomtown* (2018), *Small Places, Large Issues*, 5th edition (2023) and, in Norwegian, 'Seven Meanings of Life' (2022).

Index

Abrahams, Roger, 27
accusation, 76
aesthetic
  of contemporary dance, 192
  dimension, 140
  impact, 172
aesthetics, 130. *See also* Kant
  and art, 176–77
  spiritual dimensions of art and, 124
affect, 5–6, 132
  of exceptional experiences, 9
  turn to, 2
Alazraki, Robert, 156–58
ambiguity, 111–12
American Anthropological
    Association, 53
Ancient Palace of Justice, 39, 41
art, 4. *See also* Tolstoy
  African, 34–35
  anthropology of, 59, 130
  cinematographic, 166
  cover, 84
  craft and, 164
  and creativity, 130 (*see also*
    creativity)
  denial of, 39
  dictatorship of, 208
  distributive aspect of, 32

interaction with, 32
  as otherness, 101, 102
  perception of, 32
  and reality, 92
  spiritual dimensions of, 124
  as truth, 101 (*see also* truth)
  visionary, 101
Art Institute of Chicago, 172, 175, 178
assumption, 82
atmosphere, 19, 206–7, 215
attention
  regimes of, 213
attraction, 42
authenticity, 44, 79, 150
  of art, 41
Auvergnat
  dialect of, 17
Auvergne, 16, 25

Banks, Marcus, 181
Barber, Karin, 172
  on entextualization, 126–27
beauty, 33, 38, 124, 177
Becker, Howard, 177
Bell, Keith, 97
Berger, John, 34, 181, 209
Biennale of Dakar, 39
Bloch, Ernst, 112, 118

Boas, Franz, 177
Brown, Wendy, 2
Bruner, Edward, 5
Buddhism, 20–22

Camerimage International Festival of the Art of Cinematography, 155
Catholic, 18, 21, 115, 178–79
Cheah, Pheng, 133–34
cinematography, 155
Cliett, John, 3
Clifford, James
  on partial truths, 174
collaboration, 49, 56 –57, 65, 162
collaborative work, 157, 164–65
colour, 113, 159
commitment
  personal and ideological, 74
Coote, Jeremy, 177
Cora, Bruno, 39, 42
cosmopolitan
  anthropology, 103
  network, 195
Crapanzano, Vincent, 199
creative. See also writing
  decisions, 165
  fiction, 128
  process, 200, 206–7
  process of worldmaking, 126
creativity, 129
  collaborative, 155, 160
  social relationality of, 130
critical
  anthropology, 73
  perspective on everyday life, 90
  reflexivity, 51
critique, 1–2, 73, 76
  move beyond, 230
Csikszentmihalyi, Mihaly, 161

Dabke, 192–93
dance, 189
  contemporary, 200
  in Palestine, 192
  Palestinian contemporary, 190
  performance, 191
darkness, 47, 51, 55, 176

dark times, 53
de la Cadena, Marisol, 132–33
De Maria, Walter, 3
description, 141–42
Despres, Altaïr, 193, 196
Dewey, John, 33, 36–37, 43
Doyle, Christopher, 169–69
drawing, 55, 59–60, 206–7, 214
  in the field, 206, 219
  live, 218
  practise of ethnographic, 209
  as a research tool, 54
Dubisch, Jill, 27

Efuru@50, 124
Elliot, David, 168
emotions, 132, 140
  hostile, 40
  unsettling, 27
encounter, 75
  collegial, 78
  disagreeable, 78
  unexpected, 71, 79
  vivid, 27
Epstein, Edward Jay, 165
Evans-Pritchard, Edward E., 132, 221
event
  ethnographies, 142
  miracle, 162
events
  arbitrary, 69
  everyday, 163, 178, 183
  life, 17–20, 35, 90
  literary, 143, 145–46
  live literature, 140–41
  social life, 44
  unexpected, 178
Escobar, Arturo, 132–33
exceptionality, 195–96
experience
  aesthetic, 36
  anthropology of, 5
  arts-based, 140
  collective, 130
  bodily, 196
  dance, 191

embodied, 139
epiphanic, 180
fieldwork, 5
of flight, 109 (*see also* flight)
hostile, 39, 41
in-person, 139
of light, 155
magical and spiritual, 123 (*see also* spiritual)
multisensory, 139
performance, 141
personal, 199
transformative exceptional, 172
uncommon, 35
experiential literary ethnography, 141
experimentation, 58, 219
experiments, 219
fieldwork, 15, 219

Farmer, Paul, 49
Fassin, Didier, 50–51, 71, 79
Favero, Paolo
on immersive images, 33, 42–43
fictional, 113, 149
fieldwork, 5
as education, 205
methods, 72
normative, 71
sideways type of, 23
temporal flow of, 15
flight, 109, 115
Flora Nwapa, 123–28, 134
Foster, Hal, 2
Fox, James, 98
France, 24
rural, 16–17

Gamboni, Dario, 38
Gardner, Peter, 26
gay synagogue
ethnography, 82
in New York, 76, 79, 80
gaze
momentaneous, 33
rapid, 35
GDR, 109, 110, 114, 118

Geertz, Clifford, 6
Gell, Alfred
on magic, 124, 133
on technology of enchantment, 33, 37, 124, 131
gendered, 130, 192
gender norms, 193
Germany
East, 111
East and West, 110
West, 110
Glanville, Jo, 146
Goffman, Erving
on form of talk, 165
Graburn, Nelson, 177
graphic novel, 47
Grasseni, Cristina
on skilled vision, 158
growing-place, 205

Hampl, Patricia, 172, 174–75
Hanging Committee, 96
Hannerz, Ulf, 23, 184
Harrison, Kathryn, 179
Hay Festival, 144–47
Hayot, Eric, 2
Hogan, Erin, 4
hope, 118

Iba Ndiaye Diadji, 39, 41
indeterminacy, 85–86, 189, 199
of belief, 26
Illich, Ivan, 129
imaginative intentionality, 43
Ingold, Tim, 214
on creation, 133–34
on reality, 126
interpretation, 85
Israeli anthropology, 72–73
Israeli-Palestinian conflict, 75–77, 78

James, William, 207, 220
Jell-Bahlsen, Sabine, 129
Johnson, Uwe, 109–19

Kant, Immanuel, 4, 103, 177
on aesthetics, 90

Khosravi, Shahram, 176
knowledge, 51, 209
  humanist forms of, 70
  sociology of, 75
  specific, 35
  specialized, 44
  uncertainty of, 133

Lachman, Ed, 158–60, 162
Lake Goddess, 124–28, 134
Leighten, Patricia, 34
Léopold Sédar Senghor, 35
Lévi-Strauss, Claude, 175
LGBTQ+, 147–50
lightning, 4
literature, 133
  anthropologies of, 173
  modern African, 127
  workers', 117
  world, 124, 126
literary
  ontology, 133
  storytelling, 126
  worldmaking, 124, 128
Luhrmann, Tanya
  on anomalous experiences, 26–27

magic, 131. *See also* Gell
  of one's profession, 163
Manchester School, 72–73
Marienfelde
  Refugee Center Museum, 115
  Refugee transit camp, 110
masks
  African, 34–36
Matisse, Henri, 182–83
Meese, Jonathan, 205, 208–10
memoirs, 173–74
  as genre, 175
memories, 74, 197, 205
  create lasting, 139
Meyer, Birgit, 177–78
miracle
  artistic, 100
misrepresentation, 125, 132
Mitchell, Jon P., 26
Motta, Marco, 201

movement, 198
mundane, 16, 93
  gestures, 197, 200
multimodal
  practices and possibilities, 51, 65
Munoz, Jose, 5
Musée du Trocadéro, 34
Myles, Eileen, 138–39

Narayan, Kirin, 175
narrative
  composition, 143
  ethnographic, 143
  external, 181
  internal, 181
Neveu Kringlebach, Hélène, 193, 200
Newport-Berra, Adam, 167
Nietzsche, Friedrich, 92, 101
Nigerian
  women writers, 125
  women's literature, 129
Nitsch, Hermann, 40
Nordstrom, Carolyn, 58
nostalgia, 114

Ogunyemi, Chikwenye Okonjo
  on chi, 129–30
Oladipo, Olusegun
  on religion in Africa, 132
Olkes, Cheryl, 174
opera, 205
ordinary, 23
  and extraordinary, 6, 189
Ortner, Sherry, 163
Oslo agreements, 194

Palestine, 197
Pandian, Anand, 165
patchwork, 212–13
perception, 43
Picasso, Pablo, 34, 38
Polari Salon, 147–50
practise, 156
  anthropology of, 158
  dance, 195 (*see also* dance)
  ethics of ethnographic, 82

of ethnographic drawing, 209
lighting as, 158
multimodal, 65
religious, 20
of taming images, 213
theory, 160
theory of arts in, 209
present
ethnographic, 71
proprioception, 199–200
public
anthropology, 85
criticism, 97
disengagement from, 50
ethnography, 71, 80, 86
sphere, 49–50

quality
of exception, 90
polyphonic, 143
temporal, 36, 144

Ramallah, 197–99
Rancière, Jacques, 44
on differenciation, 32
reading
close, 110
haunted, 110
reality, 42, 92, 113. *See also* Ingold
distorted perception of, 81
insistent, 199
Reed-Danahay, Deborah
on autoethnography, 176
refusal, 41
rehearsal
temporality of, 206
religion, 131–32, 220
anthropological studies of, 132
religious
colonialism, 127
devoutly, 18
rituals, 40 (*see also* practice)
Rembrandt, 90–91, 101
repulsion, 42–43
Rethmann, Petra, 179
Riordan, Colin, 118
Ruhr Valley, 111, 117

Said, Edward, 78
Samba, Chéri, 34, 36–37
Sareyyet Ramallah, 191
Schatzki, Theodor R., 160
Second World War, 24, 110
post, 50
seeing, 36, 181
cumulative, 43
secret, 81, 86
language, 148
Sedgwick, Eve, 1
Senghor, Léopold Sédar, 35
senses, 6, 140, 177, 199
beholder's, 33, 42
Shelton, Anthony, 177
Shokeid, Moshe, 178
Shusterman, Richard, 33, 36
Simmel, Georg, 90–92, 102
Silva, Paul J., 40
Silverman, Marissa, 168
social
categories, 50
environment, 192
life, 33, 70, 85
mobility, 193, 195
and psychic, 114
relations, 40, 91, 181
and spiritual worlds, 126
transformations, 127
social facts
sacred muses as, 131
Sorignet, Pierre-Emmanuel, 193
Soulages, Pierre, 35
spectator, 35, 37, 44
speculation, 109
Spencer, Stanley, 93–94, 98–100
genres of art, 94–95
spiritual, 22, 93
beliefs, 18
dimension, 127
essence, 134
healer, 19
power, 130
powers, 18, 34, 37, 129
Stanley Spencer Gallery, 97
Stoller, Paul, 141, 174–75, 178
Strang, Veronica, 130–31

Strozzi, Bernardo, 83–84
style, 140, 157
  academic, 58
  life, 194
  lucid literary, 174
subjective, 140
  experience, 142
subjectivity
  individual, 91
suffering, 25, 27, 49, 53, 81, 116–17
supernatural, 16, 27
  powers, 34, 35, 41
symbolic
  forms, 91

Tanzania, 125
Taussig, Michael, 3
Texas, 20
Thompson, Krista, 168
Tinius, Jonas
  on awkward art, 40
Tolstoy, Leo, 89–89
  on art, 89
Trobriand Islands, 131
truth, 74, 92, 113, 174
  ethnographic, 220
  guidelines for, 58
Turner, Edith, 20, 27
Turner, Victor, 5, 70, 85
  on liminality, 144, 146

Ulysse, Gina, 50
uncanny, 16, 18–19, 22–23, 25–27, 70
  Freud on, 16
  Mark Windsor on, 27
  Nicholas Royle on, 16

uncertainty
  epistemic, 133
unfamiliar, 17, 19
University of Toronto Press, 58, 65
unusual, 3, 9, 26, 33, 167, 226. *See also* uncanny
  aesthetic emotions, 33, 40
  encounter, 75 (*see also* encounter)

Van Maanen, John, 156
Verdery, Katherine, 176
victimhood, 116
Vietnamese
  Americal Catholic church, 20, 21
  refugees, 20
visual, 157, 179
  account, 207
  depiction, 63
  vocabulary, 211

Wallman, James, 139
Warren, Kay, 51
water, 129, 131
Wenger, Etienne, 160
Wiener Festwochen, 208, 210
womanist worldmaking, 127
writing
  creative, 144
  culture, 50, 141, 174
  non-verbal exceptional experience in, 179
  otherwise, 58, 184
Wulff, Helena, 14, 193, 196

Zeitlyn, David, 181

www.ingramcontent.com/pod-product-compliance
Lightning Source LLC
Chambersburg PA
CBHW051537020426
42333CB00016B/1975